No Medium

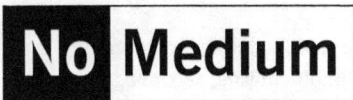

No Medium

Craig Dworkin

THE MIT PRESS
CAMBRIDGE, MASSACHUSETTS
LONDON, ENGLAND

First MIT Press paperback edition, 2015

A Project of Creative Capital | Andy Warhol Foundation Arts' Writers Grant Program
This book was set in News Gothic by the MIT Press.

Library of Congress Cataloging-in-Publication Data
Dworkin, Craig Douglas.
No medium / Craig Dworkin.
    pages   cm
Includes bibliographical references and index.
ISBN 978-0-262-01870-8 (hardcover : alk. paper)
ISBN 978-0-262-52755-2 (paperback)   1. Arts, Modern—20th
century—Themes, motives. 2. Nothing (Philosophy) in art. 3. Arts—Experimental
methods—History—20th century. I. Title.
NX456.D89 2013
701'.8—dc23
                              2012027958

Contents

Acknowledgments

In addition to those whose work I have engaged directly in these pages—Ken Friedman, Aram Saroyan, Nick Thurston, Vladimír Židlický, and others—I have written chapters with admiring gratitude to Andrea Andersson, Jed Birmingham, John Cage, Johanna Drucker, Eric Ellingsen, Barry Esson, Kenny Goldsmith, Branden Joseph, John McDowall, Bryony McIntyre, Simon Morris, Cami Nelson, and Marjorie Perloff. I am also particularly grateful to Darren Wershler, who helped me refine a less parochial sense of media, to Emily McVarish, who taught me to see more clearly the social enmeshment of modes of production, and to Danny Snelson, who has been the most rewarding student and the most challenging teacher—together they made my thinking on these topics possible. A grant from the Andy Warhol Foundation, for which I am exceedingly grateful, allowed me to complete the manuscript. Roger Conover, my editor at the MIT Press, has extended support and encouragement well beyond this particular book; he is a champion, in all senses of the word, and I am proud to have worked with him. Above all, this book is for Anne Jamison, who would rather I had written on some other topic but has, silently, indulged me nonetheless.

An earlier version of chapter 2 served as the editor's introduction to *Reading the Remove of Literature* (York: Information As Material, 2006); chapter 3 was published in *Comparative Literature* 57, no. 1 (Winter 2005): 1–24. An earlier version of chapter 4 was published in *306090* 10 (Winter 2009): 133–143. Earlier, substantially shorter versions of chapter 8 appeared in the *WPRB Program Guide* 10 (September 2003), UbuWeb <www.ubu.com>, *His Voice* 3 (Prague, 2006) (in Czech), *Western Humanities Review* 60, no. 1 (2006), *Making Nothing Happen* (York: Information As Material, 2010), and *Context* 23 (Normal: Dalkey Archive Press, 2011).

1 THE LOGIC OF SUBSTRATE

On ferait mieux, enfin aussi bien, d'effacer les textes que de noircir les marges,

de les boucher jusqu'à ce que tout soit blanc et lisse et que la connerie

prenne son vrai visage, un non-sens cul et sans issue.

[You would do better, at least no worse, to obliterate texts than to blacken margins,

to fill in the holes of words till all is blank and flat and the whole ghastly business

looks like what it is, senseless, speechless, issueless misery.]

—SAMUEL BECKETT

A thing is a hole in a thing it is not.

—CARL ANDRE

In the opening scene of Jean Cocteau's film *Orphée* (1950), amid the bustle of the Café des Poètes, Orpheus is shown a copy of the journal in which the poems of his new rival, the *enfant terrible* Jacques Cégeste, were first published. Orpheus glances at the cover—its spare, thinly bordered design and elegant Didot typeface obviously meant to evoke a volume from Éditions de Minuit—and then flips quickly through, objecting: "Je ne vois que des pages blanches [I see only blank pages]." His companion—an older writer who is respected, not coincidentally, for maintaining decades of principled poetic silence—explains: "Cela s'appelle *Nudisme* [It's titled *Nudism*]." Orpheus tosses the book back with a bitter chuckle and the derisive assessment: "Mais c'est ridicule! [But that's ridiculous!]"

Orpheus's dismissal is the typical response of an establishment put upon by the avant-garde and unwilling to assimilate a gesture (*ce geste*) of radical reduction. As his companion explains: "Moins ridicule que si ces pages étaient couvertes de textes ridicules. Aucun excès n'est ridicule [Less ridiculous than if the pages were covered with stupid texts. No excess is absurd]." Orpheus is too square for the café crowd, and too popularly accessible for a prank at the reader's expense ("Le public m'aime!" he counters). Or perhaps he merely gets the joke—the jest—of its absurd pretensions ("ces gestes," the *Littré* records, also denotes "prétentions ridicules"). *Nudisme* does indeed follow the logic of a gag, moving unexpectedly between the verbal code of its title and the visual code of its interior pages for a cheap one-liner in the style of a *New Yorker* cartoon. At a glance, the whole thing would seem like a hoax. But the specifics are telling, and it is instructive to pause a little longer than Orpheus does before tossing the matter aside; the difference between the sophistication of getting the joke and the greater sophistication of refusing to get the joke depends on how closely one reads a work that seems to ask only that it not be read.

The review's title frames and orients an interpretation of the blank sheets behind it, and since several names might have given rise to the same punch line, one might reflect on what the journal was *not* called. While Cocteau was filming *Orphée*, John Cage delivered his "Lecture on Nothing" at the Artists' Club in New York, where he famously declared: "I have nothing to say and I am saying it" because "what we require is silence; but what silence requires is that I go on talking" (Orpheus's companion, we might recall, has been silent because he has nothing to say ["Je n'apportais rien de neuf"], whereas Cégeste has nothing to say and, in *Nudisme*, has found a way of saying it).[1] Although it would have suited the intellectual moment voiced by Cage, the potential title *Silence* might have come too close to the first book published by Éditions de Minuit, Jean Bruller's *Silence de la mer*. Nor is the journal titled with the Sartrean *Néant* (Sartre's *L'Être et le néant* had been published by Gallimard in 1943), which again might have brought the satirical *mise-en-scène* of the Café des Poètes too close to Cocteau's target: the actual Café de Flore. Nor did he choose *Rien*, which could have signaled either a Dadaist nihilism or rarified aestheticism.[2] The collection is not titled with the psychologized *Manque* (a word that Jacques Lacan would develop as a *terme de métier* in just a few years' time), nor a mystical Buddhist *Vacuité*, nor any number of related words: *vide*, *absence*, *lacune*, *vacance*, et cetera.[3]

Any one of those titles, presumably, would have elicited the same exasperated response from Orpheus. But their differences inflect his impatient dismissal and point beyond it. *Nudisme*, as it happens, already wittily anticipates Orpheus's response. To denounce the publication as a hoax while seated among the believers at the Café des Poètes is to cry, in essence, that the emperor has no clothes (*Le Roi est nu*)—a nakedness that the book itself has already openly confessed.[4] The collection presents itself just as Orpheus accuses it: as the naked truth. But it also presents itself—to borrow Jacques Derrida's phrase—as "vérité comme nudité [truth as nakedness]."[5] Orpheus unclothes a nakedness, but one that has already announced its intention of disclosure even before the book is opened: "nudité à la fois inapparente et exhibée [a simultaneously unapparent and exhibited nakedness]."[6] By doing so, *Nudisme* literalizes the metaphoric: not only "dis-covering" its pages but also enacting, or dumbly presenting, the way that truth is figured. Indeed, as Derrida demonstrates, the figure of nakedness is not just any metaphor, but the very metaphor of metaphoricity itself (what is "déjà une métaphore de la métaphore . . . une métaphore pour dire la métaphoricité [already a metaphor of metaphor . . . a metaphor to render metaphoricity]").[7] In staging its joke,

Nudisme thus offers up the very figuration it would seem to refuse. Even as it eschews verse (the genre that traditionally turns most conspicuously on figural language), the book figures the figure of metaphoric unveiling.

At the same time, the word *nudisme* triggers mechanisms of social and moral reflex. In the best avant-garde tradition of attempting to *épater le bourgeois*, the title performs a quick double punch: first eliciting the shock of the prudish bourgeois reader by announcing a salacious subject and then by denying the prurient (and equally bourgeois) expectation of any titillating material within. Indeed, one should note that the title advertises not merely a classically sanctioned nudity (*nudité*), or a general nakedness, but the specific nudity of a countercultural nudism. By 1950, *nudisme* carried connotations of lubriciousness from which some at the time were attempting to distance the word *naturisme* (naturism). Indeed, "naturist" was gaining ground relative to "nudist" at precisely the same moment of Cocteau's *Orphée*. The French Naturist Association (La Fédération Française de Naturisme) had been founded in 1948, and the attendant lifestyle magazine *La vie au soleil* began publication the following year. The promotion of the term *naturisme*, with its connotations of communal living, environmentalism, and holistic health, etched the pornographic and exhibitionist associations of *nudisme* all the more starkly. While the punning rebus acknowledged by Orpheus works at a level of abstraction, between the sign systems of words and images, any particular sign occurring in that system—"silence," "nothingness," "absence," et cetera—is always historicizable.

Furthermore, in contrast to those other plausible titles, *nudisme* implies an unveiling more than a negation, and the serious reader might consider exactly what has been made naked in (or by) Cégeste's publication. Indeed, part of the work's frisson is the remove at which it pitches the rhetoric of clothing (a rhetoric, that is, of rhetoricity itself).[8] If words, conventionally, are thought to clothe thought, they also—*Nudisme* reveals—cover the page. To conceive of dematerialized ideas clothed by more tangible language elides the degree to which that sense of language is itself dematerialized in relation to the physical materiality of print that would make that language manifest. Print clothes language; which is to say, it clothes a clothing. Given the title, Orpheus might have expected a plainspoken or unartificed poetry, something in the style of an unornamented *genus humile* or *genus tenue*, but Cégeste has stripped away not just the rhetoric of a particular mode but any visible language at all. The work lays bare (*mise à nu*) the page itself: the physical facture of the book as an object; the substrate of print; the typical technological support of poetry at midcentury. If *Nudisme* is provocative (though not quite in the way a licentious reader hopes), it is also—with a similar disappointment and despite its entirely unprinted pages—quite explicit. Throwing off of metaphorical sheets to reveal the tangible sheets of paper beneath its covers, its exhibitionism is, in Jean Baudrillard's deployment of the term, obscene. Obscenity begins, for Baudrillard, "quand tout devient d'une transparence et d'une visibilité immédiate, quand tout est soumis à la lumière crue et inexorable de l'information et de la communication [when all becomes transparence and immediate visibility, when everything is exposed to the harsh and inexorable light of information and communication]."[9] In the process:

> Obscène est ce qui met fin à tout regard, à toute image, à toute représentation. . . . Ce n'est plus l'obscénité de ce qui est caché, refoulé, obscur, c'est celle du visible, du trop visible, du plus que visible que le visible, c'est l'obscénité de ce qui n'a plus de secret, de ce qui est tout entier soluble dans l'information et la communication.[10]

> [The obscene is what puts an end to every look, to every image, to every representation. . . . It is no longer the obscenity of what is hidden, repressed, or obscure; it is the obscenity of the visible, of the too visible, of the more visible than visible; it is the obscenity of that which has no more secrets, of that which is miscible in information and communication.]

Baudrillard's topic, in a prefiguration of the way the Internet would soon be talked about, is a society governed by a network of instantaneous access to uninhibited and promiscuous flows of information: the availability of everything, anywhere, all the time. In this "extase de la communication [ecstasy of communication]," the system of objects he describes is so extensively proliferated that people no longer have agency over them, much less a comprehension of their effects, so that they stand beyond (*ex stasis*) any individual's ability to interpret them.[11] In that respect, Baudrillard's argument runs counter to my own. The works addressed in this book, I will insist, can be both conceptualized and actively read. Moreover, as I will argue, they cannot stand apart from either their audience or each other because there is no outside vantage from which they can be perceived.

Nonetheless, Baudrillard's terms are uncannily resonant with the work at hand. To begin with, the title *Nudisme* suggests not only the confessional cultural moment in which any topic can appear in print, from the most intimate bodily detail to the most mundane domestic event, but it also proposes an ethos opposed to seduction, to the "hidden, repressed, or obscure." At the same time, the literal scene of those exhaustively inclusive statements, the material form of the pages assembled under the sign of nudism, exhibits one aspect of the ecstasy of communication described by Baudrillard. With no representation, nothing to read or see (Cégeste has done away with every look, every image, every representation), the blank unprinted pages of the review reveal the field of poetic communication and textual information, overexposed under "une lumière crue et inexorable [a harsh and inexorable light]."[12] The reader of *Nudisme* has an unobstructed view of the space indifferently ready to take the imprint of any text, treating any topic, with any politics, in any poetic form or style, from the most excessive avant-garde hoax to the most retrograde alexandrines.

The emphasis of Baudrillard's analysis falls on transience and dematerialization, on transparency and disappearance, but one could look as well at the opaque material remainder, at the inescapable residuum of recalcitrant physical matter left behind when certain inscriptions do not occur as expected. In the absence of inscription, the substrate can be seen not as a transparent signifier but as an object in its own right, replete with its own material properties, histories, and signifying potential. The point then is not so much the play of presence and absence that has animated studies of inscription, but rather the recursive realization that every signifier is also itself a sign. Erasures obliterate, but they also reveal; omissions within a system permit other elements to appear all the more clearly. In this case, Cocteau underscores the heft and spatial dimensions of paper, the same statement later made by Heinz Gappmayr with two books of blank pages entitled *Raum* (expanse, room, space).[13] The narratives, with such books, are not about whatever depicted events a text might describe but rather about the activity of the book itself and its readers' actions: the manipulation and handling of the accordion spread, fluttered fan, and flat collapse of spine-hinged strata in papered space. Once such books are shelved, "all that will have taken place"—as Mallarmé writes in *Un coup de dés*—"is the place" (*rien / n'aura eu lieu / que le lieu*). Accordingly, two shots from the café scene show the sewn sheets of trimmed pulp paper making up *Nudisme* being explicitly manipulated—handled and rotated in space, supported and bent, stacked and placed in contrast with other objects (a box of Gitanes Vizir, some books from Éditions Gallimard, a newspaper, a saucer). Far from immaterial, the blank pages vie for space on the café table, and they require two hands, or the support of a forearm, or something larger than a paperback to avoid bending under their own weight. Because of their mass and dimensions, the support of the binding, and the particular ductility of their fibrous composition, the sheets curve and slope with a specific catastrophic coefficient.[14] In marked contrast to Orpheus's careless handling, his companion smoothes the corners of the volume against creasing, further underscoring the specific material properties of the paper, its interaction with other physical bodies, and its susceptibility to marking and imprinting. Moreover, when the older poet first produces a copy of *Nudisme* for Orpheus's inspection, the elevated over-the-shoulder camera angle pointedly includes another set of paper sheets in the center top of the frame: unbound leaves folded to fit on the thigh of someone seated at the neighboring table sketching. In contrast to the unmarked pages of *Nudisme*, the paper on the lap of the café artist is being insistently inscribed with a pencil throughout the shot. Unable to see the drawing or read any words, the viewer of *Orphée* can still quite clearly discern that those same material characteristics of paper that I have just detailed are also those that lend it to inscription: it is light enough to rest on the knee and be taken *en plein air*, thin and supple enough to pass through a press without damaging the type, pliant enough to be sewn.

Moreover, the viewer can perceive those characteristics that lend these particular pieces of paper to certain genres; Cocteau eliminates the trace of the pencil or any inked text, but in doing so he lays bare the substrate as a formal device. In the case of the sketch, for instance, the format suggests that the artist is not undertaking an historical tableau, and in the case of *Nudisme*, the pages have been trimmed to accommodate lyric verse with a sufficiently luxurious and aestheticized margin. At the same time, they are not so unwieldy that even when bound (Cégeste's collection must have about 40 pages) they cannot be tossed lightly aside or slipped discreetly and neatly in a stack of books, as the actors demonstrate. Portable and scaled to an individual reader, the format permits a precise kind of communication. The journal is small enough that it can be carried in public without ostentation, but large enough that it requires a certain care and spread during reading; even though suited to a single private reader and the space of the outdoor table, when opened it announces that it is being read (unlike the sketchbook, say, which is kept easily under the table). It is light enough to be handed easily back and forth without moving more than the arms or upsetting a glass of wine. The publication, in short, is a perfect object for the space in which it is distributed and consumed, and where it plays a defining role in the social network of the café: connecting discrete generations of writers; distinguishing between insiders and outsiders (like Orpheus); reinforcing the homogeneous community of fashionable young habitués; recalling the economic patronage of the princess who funds its publication ("Elle est étrangère et elle ne peut pas se passer de notre milieu [She's not from here and she cannot pass among us]," Orpheus's companion explains); and, above all, advertising the success of Café des Poètes's celebrity patron.

Cégeste's *Nudisme*, of course, is only a prop in a fictional drama. An edition, however, has in fact been realized by designers Jason Fulford and Tamara Shopsin. Their cover sports the title and border in a purplish-blue ink printed offset onto an 80-pound paper stock that has been dandy-rolled for a laid texture on the recto; the cover was then saddle-stapled over sixteen sheets of lighter, 24-pound ivory letter stock. Every page, as Orpheus notes of the first edition, is blank. The second edition, however, is not strictly a facsimile, and the slight differences underscore the significance of the prop's particulars. Unlike the film version, which is noticeably larger and trimmed to a squatter ratio, the new edition trims to a smaller and narrower six by nine inches. The book thus conforms to the standard size of a small-format U.S. trade paperback, making it both more anonymous and more intimate than Cégeste's publication. Lighter, with its pages less prone to curving under their own weight, the new book can be read one-handed (and so perhaps the change of format enacts a kind of physical pun, winking with innuendo in the direction of the prurience promised by its title). Sold in the context of clever note cards and hip museum-shop design novelties (Shopsin's website suggests that *Nudisme* "can be used as notebook or not"), shipped from New York, but retaining its French title, the modern edition does not so much duplicate Cégeste's book, in the sense of restaging its avant-garde gesture of positing poetry of blank pages, as it references Cocteau with a knowing refinement, stylishly tinged with a hint of distanced and ironic nostalgia. However much the two editions of *Nudisme* resemble one another visually, they are conceptually quite different. The New York edition is more likely to provoke a smile than a *succès de scandale*.

In other instances, however, unmarked pages have in fact been put forward as literature, looking very little like *Nudisme* but nonetheless behaving more like the avant-garde challenge proposed in Cocteau's film. In the late 1960s, with New York's Second Avenue coffeehouse Le Metro standing in for the Café des Poètes, Lita Hornick simultaneously played both the princess and Orpheus to Aram Saroyan's Cégeste. Hornick's Kulchur imprint had begun to promote a Lower East Side aesthetic from an Upper East Side address by publishing a series of New American Poetry titles: *Poems Now*, an anthology edited by Hettie Jones; *Screen Tests / A Diary*, a collection of "poems plus film strips" by Gerard Malanga and Andy Warhol; and *Bean Spams*, a collaboration between Ted Berrigan and Ron Padgett. Those publications were followed by a five-hundred-page book bearing only a price ($2.00) and a copyright notice stamped across its cover: "© ARAM SAROYAN 1968 KULCHUR PRESS."[15] Or, to be precise, those stamped lines were the only text added to the factory-supplied wrapper, which also read, on one end: "STATIONERS Seal of Satisfaction / 500 SHEETS / 8 ½ x 11 / SUB. 16 / GR. LONG." Saroyan, already the author of several books, including one from Random House, referred to the Kulchur Press publication as his "first real book of work."[16] Despite that avowal, and the genuinely unconventional list Kulchur had already established, even Hornick remained unconvinced. Like Cégeste's patron, she financed the publication with an extravagant generosity; like Orpheus, she bitterly dismissed the whole enterprise. Years later Hornick recounted her predicament with candid paranoia and still-vivid spite:

> I "published" a ream of blank typing paper by Aram Saroyan, the son of William Saroyan. I didn't really want to do it, but I had a commitment to Aram. . . . I thought he was trying to sabotage my newly successful book publishing venture by forcing me to back out of my commitment and telling everyone I had gone back on my word because I was too bourgeois to understand Dada. Rising to the challenge, I went ahead and "published" the wretched little thing. My distributor wouldn't touch it; so I sold twelve copies myself and, after saving two copies for history, I threw the rest out in the garbage. I didn't even bother to save the paper for typing.[17]

In 1968, a ream of typing paper cost about one dollar. Considering the advance paid to Saroyan, Hornick, accordingly, lost about $1,500 on his book (or around $10,000 today, adjusted for inflation). With a potlatch to trump the Dada gesture she perceived in Saroyan's submission, Hornick ensured that most of the paper from the project would remain, as she was: unimpressed. But with that *dépense* she also acknowledged the force of Saroyan's project, which was not just the idea of a blank book, or of blank paper, but a particular kind of paper that was not to be used as intended. Saroyan's book may be without substance, in the sense of literary "subject matter," but it does indeed have substance in the sense of the stationer's *terme de métier*: the weight measure of the sheets (in this case, as the manufacturer's label states, "sub[stance] 16," indicating a sixteen-pound manufacturer's ream, or four pounds when trimmed to the long-grain business-bond letter-size chosen for the Kulchur Press edition). In fact, although any given sheet from Saroyan's book might look nearly identical to any given page from *Nudisme*, the details, as always, are telling, and they demonstrate how equally unmarked pages can nonetheless enact distinctly different significations. Unlike Cégeste's conventionally bound codex, Saroyan's loose-leaf book takes the form associated with prepublication. With a weight and trim unsuited to commercial printing but optimized for typewriting, the Kulchur Press publication presents paper as if it were coming to the writer, not as it comes from the binder; it is the form of a book *to be*. As William Saroyan, Aram's father, wrote:

> God, how I loved paper and still do. What a delight it is to open a whole big ream of clean white typing paper and to behold the stack. Why, though, why do I love paper? Why is it a delight to open a wrapped ream? Well, seeing all that unused paper permits me to believe I can fill every sheet with writing, and not only with writing but with the kind of writing only I can do.[18]

Written some years after Aram had presented his father with a wrapped ream as a finished literary work, this passage not only speaks to the symbolic status of a ream of paper, but it also betrays the smug tone of counter-oedipal contest, insisting with spirited glee on removing the wrapper—the one thing that could distinguish his son's publication from an ordinary ream of paper—and then reasserting a unique authority by shifting the terms of value firmly back to literary style. "Unlike my son, who cannot fill *any* sheet with writing," the passage seems to imply, "I can fill *every* sheet with writing. And what's more, where anyone might have put their name on a package of paper, my use of that paper would be something that *only I can do*." As I will suggest, Aram Saroyan's work anticipates both charges, displacing the very grounds of a personal style with a work that would not in fact have the same resonance if signed by just anyone. But for the moment it is worth recalling that typewriting, for William Saroyan, had long been both the means and the subject of a story. In "Myself upon the Earth," for example, he writes: "Day after day I had this longing, for my typewriter. That is the whole story."[19] Already by the end of the 1930s the image was a cliché: "William Saroyan sits at his typewriter and writes about sitting at his typewriter without anything to say."[20] Decades later, his son's book, even more resolutely, has nothing to say, but in not saying anything beyond an assertion of copyright it boasts that Aram Saroyan can be an author without even typing. Rendering moot Truman Capote's legendary Parthian shot at Jack Kerouac's *On the Road* ("It isn't writing at all—it's typing"), the Kulchur Press book requires a rejoinder at a further remove: it isn't typing at all—it's publishing.

By invoking the specter of typing, however, the format of Saroyan's book not only underscores its affront to the expressive output of previous modernist generations, but it also firmly places the publication within a series of books in which Saroyan sent up the heroic mythos of those modernist typewriters with a wry understatement, replacing their macho athleticism ("I can fill every sheet") with a stoner minimalism of one-word poems. And yet, for all their whimsical irony, none of Saroyan's minimalist books—including the ultimate *reductio* minimalism of the blank page—quite registers as merely a joke, or as the repudiation Hornick took his Kulchur book to be. Indeed, the critiques they wager are bought at the cost of insisting on literary value, not negating it. Moreover, as scenes in a sorry family drama, each of those early books asserts Aram Saroyan's own right to be identified with the typewriter, however long the shadow cast by his celebrity father's own identification with the machine. While one would expect a mimeographed small-press publication such as his 1967 book *Coffee Coffee* to be printed directly from typed stencils, both of Saroyan's commercially published Random House books also reproduce typewriter typefaces, even though they are printed offset.[21] Moreover, with their otherwise undecorated covers starkly emphasizing the bold exaggeration of the enlarged typewriter typefaces used to set the titles, all three books—published one after the other in close succession—distinctively branded Saroyan's poetry publications. Accordingly, in his correspondence with Hornick about the production of the Kulchur Press book, he wrote: "I'd like to use this typewriter face, in red, on the spine—blown up to about twice its size here."[22] That typewriter face was more than just a signature look, however; Saroyan also claimed it was responsible for the fine points of his signature minimalist style. His statement for the back-cover copy of *Pages* expounds: "I write on a typewriter, almost never in hand. . . . The typeface is a standard pica; if it were another style I'd write (subtly) different poems."[23] An even bigger influence on his poetry, Saroyan claims in the same statement—recalling Henry James's preference for a specific brand of typewriter—was the machine itself: "an obsolete red-top Royal Portable."[24] This seemingly extraneous aside further corroborates the association of the Kulchur Press publication with typewriting and links it more directly to Saroyan's other poetry books. Originally, he recalls, the book would have matched the color of his typewriter, standing in for the inspiring machine itself, which had been rendered unnecessary by the wordless project: "My initial idea for the book was that it should be entirely, wordlessly, red—red cover, back-cover, endpapers, and all pages, with a copyright notation the only printed content."[25] Although it could not have been read in any conventional way, and may never have garnered an enthusiastic audience, the book would have always been literally "red" from cover to cover. As published, his book retains a trace of that red in the manufacturer's label, but the wrapped loose leaves cannot even be examined without destroying the cover. And here we can start to see the logic behind the copyright symbol stamped on the paper wrapper. If it cannot be read in the conventional sense, word by word and page by page, Saroyan's work can still be read as a book, as a cultural object, according to the material specifics of its format. Had Hornick produced this title as a conventional codex, like the other books published by her press, it would have lost its paronomastic countersignature. The standard commercial packaging of the typing paper means that the book is "a ream"—a tidy paragram of "Aram."

The same punning proximity to a proper name recurs in the Charles Eliot Norton Lectures delivered by designer Charles Eames just one year after the publication of Saroyan's book. Unavoidably evoking the name of his wife and collaborator, Ray Eames, he effused about "reams" of paper: commercially packaged paper, he touchingly declared, is "absolutely beautiful stuff. Whatever you do with a ream of paper can never come up to what the paper offers in itself."[26] To do something with the blank paper of Saroyan's ream one would have to remove the wrapper, the one thing that makes it a book rather than merely some packaged office supplies; and so its status *as a book* ensures the nonpareil beauty Eames identified in the sheer material stuff offered by the paper itself. By presenting what the paper offers in itself—a monochrome four-pound block—Saroyan brought his book into dialogue with the design aesthetic and artistic concerns of its time. A prefabricated unit of standardized geometric mass, the uniformly wrapped format of his book situates it further from *Bean Spasms* (or any other work of contemporaneous poetry) and closer to something like the dull white rectangular units of Carl Andre's 1966 series *Equivalent I–VIII*: neat, variously permutated arrangements of unmortared calcium silicate firebricks direct from the construction supply plant. Insisting on its blunt physical presence rather than disappearing as the transparent conveyor of some linguistic message, the ream rhymes with the various modular geometric solids that minimalist sculpture proliferated throughout the 1960s. Furthermore, by using a readymade consumer object, with the label still attached, Saroyan entered his work into a direct dialogue with some of the most instantly recognizable sculpture of the period. In 1964, Andy Warhol had featured rectangular blocks of consumer packaging in his exhibition of Brillo boxes at the Stable Gallery (New York), and by 1968—the time of his first European retrospective—they dominated the entrance to the Moderna Museet (Stockholm) because the simulated grocery boxes had become, in Arthur Danto's assessment, Warhol's most "iconic work."[27] With the colorful swirls of James Harvey's design, the boxes made a campy commentary on all the other, more austere cubes and rectangles that had been stacking up in galleries under the sign of minimalism. If you really want clean surfaces, Warhol's boxes seem to insinuate, here are "24 Giant Size Packages" of scouring soap pads.

"Clean" and "fresh," significantly, are also the terms idiomatically associated with blank typing paper, and although he does not mention the Kulchur Press book in this context, Saroyan's retrospective assessment of the poetry that immediately preceded the ream references precisely the field defined by the twin poles of minimalist sculpture and Warhol's pop art:

> What I was doing in writing a one-word poem during the sixties has long seemed to me to be an equivalent in language to the work of Andy Warhol in painting (his instant, simultaneous, and multiple images of Marilyn Monroe) and Donald Judd in sculpture (his instant, simultaneous, and multiple metal boxes).[28]

Like the move from envisioning a book set in a typewriter typeface to imagining a book the color of the typewriter itself, Saroyan's contextualization corroborates the ream's status as a logical and legitimate extension of his writing practice, rather than the Dadaist break from poetry that Hornick feared. More importantly, Saroyan's historical emphasis—"writing a one-word poem *during the sixties*"—underscores a point, however obvious, that is worth reiterating: the same object signifies differently at different cultural moments. A saddle-stitched booklet orients itself as a cultural object in one way in France in 1950, where its format would have affinities with either nonliterary pamphlets and tracts or publications such as those in the annual series from Éditions Seghers, which were issued in stapled cardboard covers: the blandly politicized postwar surrealism of Paul Éluard's *Corps mémorable*; Léopold Senghor's *Chants pour Naett*; Tristan Tzara's *Phases*; or any number of less well-known names (the most resonant title, no doubt, being Maurice Fombeure's *Poussière du silence* [Dust of silence]). The very same artifact, however, orients itself in another way in New York sixty years later, as the Shopsin/Fulford edition of *Nudisme* attests. There, its business-grade ivory pages suggest the copy-shop vanity press productions of the desktop publishing revolution, while its textured cover nods to the now defunct chapbook ventures of Lyn Hejinian's Tuumba Press, with its wraps of "beautiful paper . . . roughly stapled," and the similarly styled Salt-Works Press, run by Tom Bridwell and Marilyn Kitchell.[29] By the same token, a ream of paper in 1959 or 1979 enters a cultural milieu in which Warhol's boxes have not yet made their statement or have already had their say.

To insist on the sculptural possibilities of paper is to insist on its weight and thickness, however slight and negligible—however "paper thin" it indeed may be. That idiomatic metaphor attests in part to the ideological force of representation, which depends on the illusion of the insubstantiality of the substrate, but it is also an example of the minimal difference identified by Marcel Duchamp as *l'inframince* (the infrathin): that point at which one can just barely begin to perceive a threshold between two states. The concept, Duchamp insisted, could not be directly defined but could be elaborated through examples: the moment between the report of a gun and the appearance of the bullet hole; the temperature change in a seat that has just been vacated; the odor of the smoker's mouth that still lingers in exhaled smoke; the dimensional difference between two mass-produced objects (made from the same mold); the volumetric difference between the air displaced by a clean shirt and the same shirt after it has been worn; and so on.[30] In an interview, Duchamp explained:

> C'est quelque chose qui échappe encore à nos définitions scientifiques. J'ai choisi exprès le mot *mince* qui est un mot humain et affectif et non une mesure précise de laboratoire. Le bruit ou la musique que fait par un pantalon de velours côtelé, comme celui ci, quand on bouge, relève de l'inframince. Le creux dans le papier, entre le recto et le verso d'une feuille mince . . . À étudier![31]

> [It's something that always escapes precise definition. I have consciously chosen the word *thin* because it is a human, emotional word and not a precise laboratory measure. The noise or music made by corduroy pants like these when one moves is tied to the concept of infrathin. The impression formed between two sides of a thin sheet of paper . . . something to be studied!]

Duchamp recognizes that the exemplary *inframince* form of the single leaf of paper, if studied, can be seen as a sculptural, three-dimensional space; in the next breath he continues: "Je pense qu'au travers de l'inframince, il est possible d'aller de la seconde à la troisième dimension [through the infrathin, I believe, it is possible to go from the second to the third dimension]." Tom Friedman makes the same argument in his 1992 sculpture *A Piece of Paper*, in which a sheet of standard letter paper is aligned with perfect congruence on top of a pedestal with a base that also measures 8.5 x 11 inches. As Duchamp noted elsewhere, providing another example of the *inframince*: "*À fleur*. En essayant de mettre une surface plane à fleur d'une autre surface plane, on passe par des *moments inframinces* [*Surface layer*. Attempting to place one planar surface precisely on another planar surface, you pass through some *infrathin moments*]."[32] Michael Asher passed through one such *inframince* moment with another study of paper sheets: his contribution to the first number of Tom Marioni and Kathan Brown's journal *Vision* (September 1975). The table of contents lists Asher's work, indicating that it begins on page 42; pages 42 and 43, however, are joined with an adhesive and so even the absence of any text or image on Asher's page has been obscured.[33] Simultaneously materializing the space between two thin sheets of paper and (like the wrapped sheets of Saroyan's ream) rendering that space inaccessible,

Asher attempts "to place one planar surface precisely on another planar surface." As he wrote in response to Brown's solicitation for work:

> My contribution will be to permanently adhere the two facing pages of my presentation together in order to form one leaf. It is important that the proper adhesive be used so that there is no wrinkle or distortion over the page surface. . . . I am interested in having all three edges line up edge to edge and have them conform to the registration of the other pages in the book.[34]

Asher's focus on the *inframince* space between the slightly oversize pages of *Vision* recalls the two self-indexing pieces published by Robert Barry in *0 to 9*, no. 6 (July 1969): "The Space Between Pages 29 and 30" and "The Space Between Pages 74 and 75." Although their titles make them sound nearly identical, the two works are in fact remarkably different. As the shifting parity of their numerical pagination suggests, the first work indicates a single sheet of paper: presumably the roughly one-tenth of one millimeter of pressed pulp that separates the last page of Bernar Venet's "Proposition for a Play" (page 29) and Dan Graham's "Eisenhower and the Hippies," which begins on the verso (page 30). Barry's second work, however, references two facing pages that form an opening (as it happens, between the last page of a text by Clark Coolidge on page 74 and the first page of one of Bernadette Mayer's contributions to the issue on page 75), so that the space, in this case, denotes either the variable volume of the wedge formed between the angle of the pages when the journal is opened or else the atomic distances that remain along its side-stapled spine and persist across the entire plane of the pages when the issue is closed.

The display of opened journal pages in extended spread is also the subject of Tom Friedman's 1992 work *11 x 22 x 0.005*—a blank sheet of paper partitioned by two symmetrical folds and suspended vertically from a single thumbtack. Like Cocteau's *Nudisme*, Friedman's work both exhibits and withholds a nakedness. The title describes the physical format of the displayed paper sheet, half again as wide as a standard North American magazine opening. Or, in other words, the dimensions of a centerfold. The work, as Friedman explains, is an erased *Playboy* centerfold.[35] The page's orientation and display, extended and tacked vertically to the wall, thus points to both the materiality of the paper and its absent content, to the title and its backstory. Because of its physical properties, if held by a single point the scored sheet must be suspended vertically to keep from folding over on itself under the gravitational pull of its own weight. Hung in that way, however, it also assumes the hands-free position of a masturbatory aid—it is pointedly displayed as a "pin-up," rotated against the textual grain—and so the viewer regards it from the position of the *Playboy* reader interested in more than just the articles. The work inevitably recalls Robert Rauschenberg's 1953 *Erased de Kooning Drawing*, which I discuss in chapter 2, but for the moment I want to note the way in which Friedman's choice of source text implicitly genders his viewer, and in that respect his blank page recalls Laurence Sterne's invitation to his explicitly gendered reader to indulge in sexual fantasy while gazing at a blank page of *The Life and Opinions of Tristram Shandy, Gentleman*.[36] With a latent vocabulary of "conception" and manual activity that establishes the background terms of heterosexual copulation and solitary vice, Chapter XXXVIII of Book 6 opens: "To conceive this right—call for pen and ink—here's paper ready to your hand." The facing page, presumably at that moment already held by the reader's hand, is in fact left blank (save for the header, which only serves to underscore the emptied text block and to frame the space provided for the portrait).[37] Sterne prompts the reader to use that page to sketch an image of one of the novel's characters, the Widow Wadman: "Paint her to your own mind—as like your mistress as you can—as unlike your wife as your conscience will let you."

On the one hand (or with the one hand, as the case may be), the masturbatory *mise-en-scène* of Friedman's work theatricalizes the solitary and presumably private process that resulted in the erased page: an obsessive repetitive manual frottage. By doing so, it literalizes the vernacular phrase "to rub one off" and anticipates the popular criticism that presenting something like a blank piece of paper as art is, *prima facie*, "masturbatory" in the figurative sense of "self-absorbed or self-indulgent."[38] On the other hand, the work performs a sly reversal of cultural clichés. Rather than staining, Friedman's activity in this case cleans up a dirty picture, rendering what he has identified elsewhere as an "obscenely white, empty space."[39] Eliminating rather than producing an image, the work is an austere minimalist counterpart to Marcel Duchamp's biomorphic 1946 *Paysage fautif* (*Defective Landscape* or *Culpable Landscape*): an *informe* particolor stain of ejaculate on thermoplastic (Astralon-brand, to be specific, which is appropriately named and perhaps part of a pun, since the bulbous curvilinear blob of dried and whorled semen looks like nothing so much as an astrophotographic image, a gaseous nebular cloud against the stellar specks of its black satin backing). Although Friedman studiously eliminates the original pornographic image of the magazine spread, he cannot entirely erase the sexual connotation from the imageless page, just as Cégeste's book would have evoked the erotics of nudism even without its title, because the blank page is not a culturally neutral site but one that is already gendered and sexualized. "Malgré la fiction de la page blanche," as Michel de Certeau writes, "nous écrivons toujours sur de l'écrit [in spite of a persistent fiction, we never write on a blank page, but one that has already been written on]."[40] Although it may appear uninked, the blank page is culturally inscribed with an indelible text. Following from the figuration of the blank page as "virgin," writing on or marking the blank page has traditionally been figured as copulation. The "blank page awaiting insemination by the writer's pen," as Teresa de Lauretis observes, is "a notorious cliché of Western literary writing," one that "participates in a long tradition" of figuring imposition on the "virgin page" as a masculine activity, as Susan Gubar puts it.[41] *11 x 22 x 0.005* trades on that cliché, but with a twist: where writing and drawing, figured as copulation, would leave the page sullied and no longer virgin, Friedman's erasure, a kind of subtractive drawing figured as masturbation, restores the page—impossibly—to its virgin state. And with that paradox of an exhaustively violated virgin condition, Friedman's work showcases the extent to which virginity, in both the sexual and paginal senses, is something that cannot be visually verified, but that depends instead on one's faith in the veracity of another's avowal; they both rely on a fact that ultimately only another can know for sure. To believe the page is erased, rather than simply blank, one must trust Friedman's account. Moreover, the viewer's thoughts—whether of the no-longer-present *Playboy* image, or of Friedman's manipulation of that image—are all that is left to arouse interest in the work, which is otherwise an unexceptional sheet of minutely pierced and twice-folded paper. Like the magazine masturbator, the viewer of conceptual art (or at least of this work of conceptual art) falls back on the mental activity of imagination.[42] Friedman augments the work by removing the source text's defining material surface; the conceptual aspect of his page is thus "ce dangereux supplément [that dangerous supplement]"—Jean-Jacques Rousseau's euphemism for masturbation, famously elaborated on by Jacques Derrida—which is discovered to be both essential to the work and also lying, uncontrollably, outside it.[43]

Sterne refrains so that the reader may indulge; Friedman physically removes so that the viewer may mentally impose; their dynamics of withdrawal and completion chart the two apices between which the blank page resonates: the aftermath of a deletion and the origin of inscription; repudiation and invitation; privation and plentitude; the singular result of a specific omission and an opening out onto indeterminate possibility.[44] The potential of both positions is illustrated by one of the most notorious collections of modernist blanks, the poetry section of the September 1916 issue of the *Little Review*.[45] The previous issue (August 1916) had carried the following rebuke from editor Margaret Anderson:

> I loathe compromise, and yet I have been compromising in every issue by putting in things that were "almost good" or "interesting enough" or "important." There will be no more of it. If there is only one beautiful thing for the September number it shall go in and the other pages will be left blank. Come on all of you!

As threatened, the table of contents in the following issue counts seven contributions for which the titles and author names have been replaced with dashes, and the title page reads: *"The Little Review* hopes to become a magazine of Art. The September issue is offered as a Want Ad." The following page carries the reminder *"'The other pages will be left blank',"* and the next eleven pages print only the standard journal header and pagination numerals.[46] Readers answered the want ad by using the blank pages as stationery on which to compose letters to the editor, and one anonymous correspondent, invoking the metaphors of theological mysticism to which blank books seem to lend themselves, replied: "I have never enjoyed any number of *The Little Review* so much as the September. Those blank pages linked with the cosmos: space before creation."[47] When another subscriber writes, "I bless your new enthusiasm and its effects. That half blank number was splendid—what there was of it, but I wanted to see as spirited things on the other pages too," one cannot quite be sure whether she wished the literature section to be filled with writing or the nonfiction section to be erased.[48] The ambiguity of the blank page highlighted by the *Little Review* episode, in which the page is understood as both an ellipsis to be respected and a provocation to incite writing, also animates Saroyan's ream, which achieves some of its frisson by reversing and arresting the expected chronology of writing and reading. Suspended between the origins of composition and the end point of publication, his book ceases to be recognizable at the moment its reader participates by unwrapping the blank pages and using them, as they were originally intended, for typing.

Tom Friedman's *1,000 Hours of Staring* (1992–1997), an unmarked thirty-two-and-one-half-inch-square sheet of paper, offers a slightly differ-ent version of this dynamic. As with the erased centerfold, *1,000 Hours of Staring* both raises its viewers' doubts and asks for their credulity. This blank page functions as a sort of relic; it is the souvenir of an ordeal, imbued with aura, which serves as a prompt for contemplating one's faith in the narratives passed down by the legends that surround it. For all that, the white paper, of course, betrays no visual evidence of the history signaled by its title: the thousand hours during which it supposedly became the object of the art-ist's gaze. With nothing to see save its plain and planar surface, the real interest, again, arises from the audience's cognitive rather than perceptual activity. That mental activity is provoked by what Gérard Genette would term the work's "paratexts"—those documents just across the threshold of the work proper: gallery wall labels, catalogue essays, artist interviews, et cetera. In this case, however, that threshold is more indistinct and permeable than Genette's schema suggests. Given the more dynamic and indeterminate nature of the paratexts for *1,000 Hours*, the relation between those ele-ments and anything that might be isolated as a "main text" accords more to Jacques Derrida's concept of the *parergon*: something that at first glance appears to be an external supplement to the work, but that in fact partici-pates as a necessary and essential part of the work itself. As Derrida explains this dangerously supplemental connection:

> Un parergon vient contre, à côté et en plus de l'ergon, du travail fait, du fait, de l'œuvre mais il ne tombe pas à côté, il touche et coopère, depuis un certain dehors, au-dedans de l'opération. Ni simplement dehors ni simplement dedans.[49]

> [A *parergon* comes up against, alongside, and in addition to the *ergon*—to the work done, to the made thing, to the work itself—but it does not fall away to one side; it touches and cooperates, from a certain vantage, from beyond the operation. It is neither simply exterior nor simply interior.]

Neither incidental nor replaceable, the parergonic title and various descriptions of Friedman's activity possess a certain degree of gravity and validity only because of the existence of the sheet of paper. That sheet of paper, by the same token, is only remarkable because of the paratexts that confer a special status on it, distinguishing it from any other sheet of paper and casting an aura about it. "Ni simplement dehors ni simplement dedans [neither simply outside nor simply inside]," each depends on the other for its definition.

This same logic applies to the tenth number of the journal *Gorgona* (1966). With a purity of execution rare even for the most radical publications, Josip Vaništa refrained from printing so much as the title of the journal on the cover; all of the pages are completely blank. The masthead information was slipped, *hors-texte*, between the journal's unprinted pages on a separate card.[50] In this format, the journal finally lived up to the rhetoric of the eponymous group's neo-Dadaist program, which had been set forth in 1961; Vaništa's founding manifesto proclaimed:

> Gorgona's thinking is serious and spare. Gorgona is for the absolute ephemeral in art. Gorgona does not seek results or work in art. It makes judgment as in the light of the situation. It defines itself as the sum of all possible interpretations. Gorgona does not speak of anything.[51]

Manifesting the terms of the manifesto, the austere pages of *Gorgona* 10 are indeed serious and spare, wide open to a range of interpretive possibilities within which particular definitions and judgments can only be made in the light of its paratextual situation (a situation that includes the manifesto itself). Seen in that light, the pages appear less like an artwork than like tender making good on the manifesto's claim that Gorgona was not seeking works of art; although blank (or rather, only because they are blank), the pages might be taken as consideration for the manifesto's promissory note. To this extent, although *Gorgona* 10 seems, on its face, to speak of nothing, it does not speak of anything *except* its paratexts. The contextual situation that permits it to speak at all is also the subject of its recursive, monotonous discourse. Indeed, the point I want to make about *parerga* is not just that one might expand what can be considered as "the artwork" beyond a single discrete object—a condition that obtains for many works, and for any installation—but that in the case of *Gorgona* or *1,000 Hours* such an expansion reassigns the function normally undertaken by blank paper. Traditionally, a substrate permits inscriptions (ink or paint or charcoal, say) to be legible and to signify as an artwork; here the roles are redistributed so that the *parerga* take on the role of substrate, permitting what might have been a substrate—a sheet of blank paper—to signify. Such works enact a negative semiotics, along the model of a negative dialectics.

In *1,000 Hours of Staring*, the viewer's role is reassigned as well (indeed, "viewer" and "reader" no longer seem like quite the right words for such works). One might say, in brief, that Friedman has looked at the paper for so long that his audience does not have to look at all. And yet, that looking is all to the point. The development of conceptual art that made Friedman's practice possible depended in turn on Duchamp's proposal that art could be antiretinal and still be art; *1,000 Hours* looks back on its own history, transforming its extended stare into a knowing wink by creating a work of antiretinal conceptual art predicated on a sustained, intensive retinal activity. With the same deft twist, Friedman turns the iconic figure for an artist's lack of a concept—staring at a blank page—into the concept itself. From this perspective, his page appears as an extension of Christine Kozlov's *271 Blank Sheets of Paper Corresponding to 271 Days of Concepts Rejected. February-October, 1968.*[52] Or perhaps, emphasizing the performative aspect of the work, it could be seen as a precursor to the thousands of hours of staring undertaken by Ulay (Frank Uwe Laysiepen) and Marina Abramović in the 1980s.[53] Those performances in turn recall Ian Wilson's discussions, in which he made himself present in the gallery to discuss art with visitors. Refusing, on principle, to make or display art objects, Wilson signaled his dematerialized practice with a series of resolutely blank pages presented as his contribution to *Art & Project Bulletin* 30 (1970). Unlike the other blank pages I have been considering, Wilson's were not meant to be iconic or metaphoric, but rather mnemonic: a reminder of his position. The unprinted surfaces of that issue of *Art & Project* served as a sort of proxy for Wilson's practice, insisting on his insistence. Less theatrical still, Tehching Hsieh's thirteen-year plan ("I will make ART during this time. / I will not show it PUBLICLY") employed a similar mnemonic, following his manifesto with thirteen pages bearing only the time stamp of their corresponding years (1986–1999).[54] Despite the fundamental difference between the equally unmarked pages of Wilson and Friedman, the ultimate lesson of those empty sheets, however, is the same: the most conceptual works are always caught up in the most material specifics. They may have been unprinted inside, but the A3 pages of Wilson's number of *Art & Project* were of course still demonstratively substantial enough to require postage, as witnessed by the faded-blue and bruise-purple franking that endures across the surface of the periodical's remaining archived copies. In the end, the haecceity of paper always betrays its symbolism.

With Wilson's few blank pages as a reminder that a specific, inescapable materiality obtains in even the most ideational works, we can look again—really *look*, this time, if only for a thousand seconds or so—at Friedman's *1,000 Hours,* in which the importance of the particulars are underscored by a comparison with Conny Blom's "rationalized re-enactment" of the work. Through a 'pataphysical equation of pages over time, Blom achieved the equivalent of Friedman's thousand hours by staring for one hour at a thousand sheets of paper.[55] With an indolent efficiency, Blom deflates the aura of extended meditative performance and ocular athleticism connoted by Freidman's "thousand hours" (despite the fact that they were accumulated over a five-year period). Blom's impatient version comes off as more of a waggish prank than any sort of serious artistic conversation, but his choice of materials—two reams of wrapped A4 office supply paper—draws attention to the scale and grain of Freidman's sheet. Sourced from the Indonesian April company, Blom's paper, with a density of eighty grams per square meter, is edged and flushed for machine handling and finished with a sizer optimized for heat-fused particle pigments—a "superb capacity high white high performance office paper" for "copy & laser," as the retail wrapper states. The reams are a close cousin of Saroyan's slightly thinner, more pliant, and squatter chlorinated typewriter pages, but they bear little resemblance to Friedman's substantially more textured and structured sheet, a substrate better suited to pencil than toner, which is trimmed to the pattern not of a page but of an easel. It is, perhaps not coincidentally, only marginally larger than Kazimir Malevich's Белое на белом (*White on White*, 1918).[56]

Friedman's page hangs, accordingly, between poetry and the visual arts, between writing and drawing. Given its format and its natural habitat in the Museum of Modern Art (and despite being housed in the Drawing Department, presumably because it is made of paper and not of some other material), *1,000 Hours* seems to aspire to the monochrome canvas of modernist abstraction. But because it is unmarked, any similarity to that white monochrome painting only points one back, in the end, to the paper page. As Thierry de Duve argues: "The painter's virgin canvas shares its whiteness with the writer's blank page more than it does with other artifacts belonging to its own tradition, linen fabric included."[57] That affinity is strengthened by the fact that while the blank, readymade canvas was legitimized by modernism without ever being actualized, the blank, readymade page was in fact actualized in poetry without ever being fully legitimized.[58] To retool one of de Duve's formulations, we might say that the blank page is now a poem, but it never was one.[59] Where modernism adduced the readymade canvas as a picture before any particular canvas was actually produced, thus initiating a set of irrevocable aesthetic judgments and extending the possibility of continued painterly practice—one spurred by the specter of a blank canvas but never foreclosed by the instantiation of any specific canvas—the readymade page was in fact proffered as poetry before a modernist poetics could fully formulate its potential. Today, a blank page put forward as poetry would join a tradition of such works, taking its place in a minor subgenre; moreover, it would come at a moment when the category of "poetry" has been so expanded by other avant-garde incursions and conceptual interventions that the example of a blank page can no longer have the impact on the genre of "poetry" that it once would have wrought. Or, in short: the specific form of the blank page preceded its generic content. Indeed, in addition to the works I have already discussed, as early as 1913 Vasilisk Gnedov published "Поэма конца" (Poem of the end)—a title with no subsequent poetic text—in his collection Смерть Искусству (Death to art), just at the moment when the endgame of monochrome painting was beginning to be strategized.[60] The poem is both literally the end (it is the final poem in Gnedov's booklet) and also figured as the radical conceptual *reductio* of minimalist poetry.[61] But it is also necessarily a beginning. In de Duve's account, the sustenance of modernist painting required that it imagine its future ending in a blank canvas. The continuance of modernist poetry, inversely, seems to have demanded that it forget, or ignore, or never really learn, the lessons of its own history. Painting's prolepsis meets its equivalent in poetry's belatedness.

Read against one another, blank pages tell a story not just about the development of modern art and literature, but about media themselves. In the present collection I consider a number of works that tell the same story: clear film, smooth phonograph discs, erased texts, blank compact discs, white canvases, silent music. Taken together, the chapters collected here argue that contrary to the casual ways in which we use the term, there is no "medium." No single medium can be apprehended in isolation. Moreover, these chapters collectively argue that media (always necessarily multiple) only become legible in social contexts because they are not things, but rather activities: commercial, communicative, and, always, interpretive. This perspective offers a more active version of Lisa Gitelman's important corrective to media history, which understands media as a nexus of "social, economic, and material relationships."[62] Gitelman explains:

> I define media as socially realized structures of communication, where structures include both technological forms and their associated protocols, and where communication is a cultural practice, a ritualized collection of different people on the same mental map, sharing or engaged with popular ontologies of representation.[63]

Although I do not share her presumption of a communicative and technological norm, or the humanist sociology behind "ontologies of representation," our investigations converge—on either side—at the "'threshold' of representation itself" mapped by Mark Hansen, where the irreducibly "robust *materiality* of technology" runs up against practices that need not be discursive, representational, or even communicative at all.[64]

Historically, the word *medium* has denoted a number of related, mutually reinforcing, and by now probably inextricable, ideas. Following its origins in the Latin adjective *medius* ("in the middle"), *medium* takes on the sense of an instrumental intermediary from the late sixteenth century on. One can track the general sense of the word in the *Oxford English Dictionary*, which records its role in designating three kinds of transmitters. First, broad classes or modes: "but yet is not of necessitie, that Cogitations bee expressed by the Medium of Wordes [i.e., as opposed to a gestural sign language]," as one of the earliest examples, from Francis Bacon, attests. Second, conduits: for Thomas Pecke, a reflective looking glass becomes "the Medium to let you see / A wonder," just as the marine seal's sense of touch is gained "through the medium of his whiskers" (the spiritualist sense of *medium* predominated over the nineteenth century). Third, venues: one eighteenth-century reader comments to a journal on the useful information expected from "the medium of your curious Publication"; a late-twentieth-century financial report notes that "foreigners could deal anonymously in British markets via the medium of a Swiss bank." That sense of venue expanded to denote what used to be called "mass communication," whether as a mode (radio, television, magazines) or an institution (often with the definite article: "the media," who are thought variously to distort or report, to inform or dumb down, to influence or ignore their audience). All three senses, furthermore, come together in what might be a synonym for *genre* or *discipline*: "any of the varieties of painting or drawing as determined by the material or technique used."[65] From there, the word came to denote the materials or techniques themselves, eventually moving beyond the bureaucratic departments of the fine arts academy to signify "any physical material (as tape, disk, paper, etc.) used for recording or reproducing data, images, or sound." More recently, of course, the word has come to connote certain kinds of electronics, or "new media."

Intuitively, these definitions all make easy sense, but the evacuated or unmarked works at issue in the present collection put enough pressure on the term to open some fissures in its tidy surface, revealing it to be far less stable than the word's typically unexamined use implies. I am not interested in policing the word's usage in any way, but I do want to call attention to some of the assumptions that attend it. To begin with, one might ask whether media look forward or backward for their definition. That is, does their determining factor reside in their prior inscription or in their inscriptibility? To ask the question concretely: was the paper you are holding already a medium before it was brought together with the ink? Any object, it seems, could conceivably be inscribed in some way, and so the mere potential for inscription expands the notion of "medium" so broadly that it is no longer precise enough to designate or distinguish in a useful way. But for some prior inscription to be the defining factor of media raises other questions. If paper, for instance, is one of the media used for "recording or reproducing" my text here, is it still a medium in Friedman's *1,000 Hours of Staring*, when nothing has been recorded or reproduced? If not, we are left with a situation in which the material specifics of the paper (as I argue above) are integral to the meaning of the work, but where the specific material (the sheet of paper) is not the work's medium. And if, on the contrary, we do recognize that blank sheet of paper as a medium, or if we define media on the basis of inscriptibility, we are faced with the question of how to know when mere materials have become identifiable media. A certain sense of medium is caught between impossible chronologies.

The primary lessons of this predicament are twofold. First, one can never locate a medium in isolation. Media—if there are such things—are only recognizable as collectives. Inscription, obviously, requires material impingement, but the act of reading, despite being so often figured as disembodied, also always involves a material interaction. To know if a compact disc has been used "for recording or reproducing" music, for example, it needs to be played; to actually hear the music, moreover, requires not just a player but speakers. The "medium" of the music, in the sense of its material format, cannot be just the disc alone, but must comprise the networked apparatus of inscriptive relays that also includes a laser and processor, as well as a range of other materials likely including wires and cones, drivers and foam and casings (not to mention an electrical power source). A phonograph disc and a PVC construction pipe, to take another example, are differentiated not by their material, which is molecularly identical, but rather by the various mechanisms with which they can meaningfully connect (the former with a stylus, the latter with a valve). Indeed, the requirement of multiple materials obtains even in the low-tech case of the most conventional poem; to know whether or not a piece of paper has been printed requires sufficient light and enough space to position the sheet in the field of vision. However absurdly obvious these requirements sound when enumerated in this way, they are not trivial for a rigorous definition of media.

The second lesson of the predicament of media is that we are misled when we think of media as objects. Indeed, the closer one looks at the materiality of a work—at the brute fact of its physical composition—the more sharply a social context is brought into focus. To begin with, materials can only be legible as media under certain circumstances; they only make sense in specific contexts. As Herman de Vries, the author of several blank books, put it: "An empty sheet means more than a written one, only meaning is absent."[66] Particular social milieus make that meaning available. We have seen, for example, how a copy of *Nudisme* handed across a table at the Café des Poètes and one ordered on-line from a novelty design store signify differently, and this would be true even if the artifacts were completely identical.[67] Being asked to contemplate an unrecorded compact disc presented by the avant-garde musicologist Jarrod Fowler at a conference on sound art is significantly different than being asked to contemplate the very same disc presented by the sales clerk at an office supply store.[68] Or, a few aisles over, a wrapped ream of blank paper means one thing stacked in that store, but another thing stacked in an art gallery vitrine, and yet another still when shelved in the poetry section of a bookstore. Indeed, as we have seen, Lita Hornick acknowledges the curious, context-dependent economics of the blank page by raising the prospect of recycling the paper from Saroyan's aborted publication ("I didn't even bother to save it for typing"); most of those who would have balked at buying Saroyan's ream of paper would have purchased the same ream from a stationery shop without a second thought.[69] As Robert Morris argues, in support of his claim that "from the subjective point of view there is no such thing as nothing":

> So long as the form (in the broadest possible sense: situation) is not reduced beyond perception, so long as it perpetuates and upholds itself as being an object in the subject's field of perception, the subject reacts to it in many particular ways when I call it art. He reacts in other ways when I do not call it art.[70]

The same logic pertains to how we react to materials when they are presented under the name of one discipline or another. Marcel Broodthaers's 1964 *Pense-bête* (Reminder; literally, "a dumb thought"), for instance, consists of copies of his eponymous book of poetry, held upright in a plaster casing. Under the sign of sculpture, Broodthaers's book is a medium utilized for its uniform strata and lightweight material, which allows the copies to fan slightly at the top without breaking the plaster at their base. To utilize them as a medium for print, however, would destroy the work *as a sculpture*. Under the sign of poetry, the plaster is no longer recognized as a sculptural medium but rather as a poorly chosen and inconvenient binding. Media are aptly named not only because they bear messages between writers and readers, or because they communicate an artist's ideas, but because they negotiate our socially mediated experience of physical objects.

At the same time, the necessity of a particular social context—the exchange by which Morris performs his speech act of artistic nominalism ("I call it art"), for instance—is also why the works under consideration here are in some ways so deeply conservative. For all the extremity of their gestures, and despite the radical *reductiones* instantly recognizable as the defiant dare of the avant-garde, these works reinforce the conventions on which they silently rely. The more they test certain assumptions about their arts, the more they lean uncritically on the other traditions and unchallenged institutions of their disciplines: that poetry is published in periodicals; that visual art hangs on the wall for display; that writers traffic in manuscript paper; et cetera. In his reading of the blank canvas as a readymade, Thierry de Duve articulates this same dynamic; a piece of fabric, presented by the avant-garde as a *picture*, even though it remains unpainted and unprimed, is a technological support that finds its own needed support in an established, establishment convention:

> Even before it is touched by the painter's hand, it already belongs to the tradition of painting, or rather, to a particular tradition—that of Western painting since the Renaissance. While it is prepared to receive the traces of the painter's brush and is thus no more than a support, as part of the artist's materials, it has already incorporated, readymade, the one convention established during the Renaissance—that one is to paint on a stretched canvas. To call it a picture . . . means to acknowledge the presence of that historical convention in an otherwise mundane commodity.[71]

Taken together, in parallax, these two lessons permit us to glimpse the operations that constitute a more robust definition of media. Media, from this perspective, consist of analyses of networked objects in specific social settings. As much acts of interpretation as material things, as much processes as objects, media are not merely storage mechanisms somehow independent of the acts of reading or recognizing the signs they record. Abby Smith, thinking about the archival conservation of digital information, puts the relation boldly: "There is, essentially, no object that exists outside of the act of retrieval. The demand for access creates the 'object.'"[72] In making the same claim for media, my point is not just that media are actively dynamic processes, but that as such they are nested within a recursive structure. Recognizing a compact disc, say, for what it is—acknowledging its medial status—thus comes to be seen as analogous to the CD player's recognition of that disc's digital binary data, which is in turn analogous to a listener's recognition of the playback from the disc as music. Each is an analysis—necessarily material—performed within a specific semantic context. Those objects that are casually referred to as "media," accordingly, are perhaps better considered as nodes of articulation along a signifying chain: the points at which one type of analysis must stop and another can begin; the thresholds between languages; the limns of perception.

The goal of this book, accordingly, has been to linger at those thresholds and to actually read, with patience, what appears at first glance to be illegibly blank. I have tried to attend to such artifacts with what Matthew Kirschenbaum (following Katherine Hayles) characterizes as a media-specific analysis: "a close reading of the text that is also sensitive to the minute particulars of its medium and the idiosyncratic production and reception histories of the work" (though in a persnickety moment I would replace his word "medium" with "materials").[73] Through the specificities of that analysis I sought to understand whether such works can actually say substantively different things, if they can ever speak of more than their blankness. I have tried, as they have, to "farai un vers de dreyt nien [make a poetry of pure nothing]" (as Guillem de Peiteus's Provençal canzon puts it).[74] To that end I tried to refrain from moving too quickly to abstractions and to resist falling back on the sensational metaphysics of either a reified nothingness or the poststructural apotheosis of absence and lack. In the process, I have gazed, all in all—as Blanchot's Orpheus would have demanded, and as Cocteau's Orpheus would have derided—for nearly as long as Friedman at his single sheet. If, in the end, I take ostensibly blank works to be less portentous than Blanchot's Orpheus does, I find them to be far more serious than does Cocteau's. And it is in that middle space—that medium—where alert listeners can hear the echo of all the laughter provoked by the nakedness of media: not just the derisive snicker, but also the chuckle of recognition and the appreciative reaction to a good joke—as well as the Bergsonian laughter of the social, the corporeal laughter of the Medusa, and the convulsive political cachinnations of the surrealists' *l'humor noir*.

2 CENOGRAPHY

When shall that true poet arise who, disdaining the trivialities of text, shall give the world a book of verse consisting entirely of margin?

—KENNETH GRAHAME

In essence whiteness is not so much
a color as the visible absence of color,
and at the same time the concrete
of all colors; is it for these reasons that
there is such a dumb blankness,
full of meaning . . . ?

—HERMAN MELVILLE

In 2006, Nick Thurston published an edition of Maurice Blanchot's *L'Espace littéraire*, although not a word of Blanchot's text remains.[1] Thurston has assiduously erased every page of Blanchot's text. At the same time, Thurston has preserved his own marginalia, reset in a face and font similar to that of the original text.[2] That distance between his reset notes and the original text, in fact, is immediately announced by his title, and part of its play; typographically, a "remove" denotes both the number of point sizes by which a side note is smaller than the main text, as well as the note itself. This book is therefore technically a work of zero remove, in which there are only removes.

Removed, the source is everything, and nothing. *Point de source*, as the French original might prevaricate: point of origin, and—equally—absence of origin. Blanchot himself will ask: "Qu'en est-il de ce point? [What is going on with that point?]"[3] On the one hand, no longer clearly tied to particular passages in *The Space of Literature*, Thurston's glosses and scholia now gesture more toward the space of literature in general, to the page as a substrate of inscription, as one of the media that make up a book. They invoke the long history of reading practices that are inextricably bound to the physical dimensions of writing's material forms. The activity of reading *as* writing—acts of correction, commentary, censorship, contradiction, and all manner of supplementary dangers—is as old as writing itself, but the species of annotation recognizable to us as marginalia only materialized in the middle ages, with the increased sense of the codex page as a space for a visual text rather than a score or cue for vocal performance.[4] The margins of the page have always been a fundamental part of the phenomenology of the codex, since they are the primary site of the reader's physical interaction with the book. Readers typically manipulate a book at the margin, holding it open, adjusting its position, keeping a place with the index finger, turning pages, thumbing through. Reserved for the activities of the reader's body, the frame around the text block further encourages the reader's active participation by providing an uninked space ideal for writing entries keyed to particular printed passages. The margin of the page invites a written record of the ongoing dialogue that constitutes all reading.

The politics of that dialogue are complicated from the beginning. The annotator always has the last word, as it were, but whatever the force of that final say it always remains, quite literally, marginal. Indeed, our sense of the margin in social terms traces directly back to the space of the page, with an etymology originating in the term for the border of a writing tablet or a book. As Michael Camille observes, "The word 'margin'—from the Latin *margo* [/-]*inis*, meaning edge, border, frontier—only became current with the wider availability of writing."[5] Moreover, from the very beginning the margin has always harbored a sense of writing; the word ultimately derives from the same Indo-European base as *mark*, relating the margin not only to boundaries but also to traces, inscriptions, and memorials. All of which, as we will see, are relevant to Thurston's project.

Marginal inscriptions, in every sense of the word, have had a long literary history, and Thurston's book is only one remove from a number of other works in several genres, from the collections of unsynthesized scholarly commentaries known since the Renaissance as *adversaria scripta* to the many modern editions of marginal annotations published as literary collections in their own right, including well known examples by Samuel Taylor Coleridge, Horace Walpole, Hester Lynch (Thrale) Piozzi, Charles Darwin, and E. A. Poe.[6] Transforming manuscript into print, such publications place an emphasis on the distribution of writing, taking advantage of mass print production to disseminate once putatively private and occasional inscriptions as established public texts, ready to receive their own annotations in turn. However, since it is published as an artist's book, *The Remove of Literature* may be closer to more aestheticized versions of the genre, such as William Blake's annotations to Joshua Reynolds's *Discourses* and Emanuel Swedenborg's *Divine Love* and *Divine Providence*; separated from the sources that provoked them and taken on their own, Blake's marginalia read like nothing so much as poems in their own right. One might also recall Susan Howe's poem "Melville's Marginalia," based in part on the marginal notations to her copy of Wilson Walker Cowen's eponymous 1965 Harvard dissertation.[7] For all the affinities, however, Thurston's book is set apart from these works by its distinctive layout. With a spatial design based on the pages of the originally annotated book, Thurston's edition is perhaps more suggestive of Roland McHugh's *Annotations to Finnegans Wake*, in which entries are keyed to passages in Joyce's book by their position on the page (and which reads on its own like a postmodern novel). Moreover, with the notes arrayed around the evacuated text block of Blanchot's book, *The Remove of Literature* takes its place in a small but remarkable group of artists' books that I will discuss in chapter 3: books that purport to present footnotes to absent texts, offering largely blank pages and notes keyed to empty space. But, as we will see, the central texts that those books claim to annotate are almost always fictional; *The Remove of Literature* distinguishes itself—*point de source*—by removing an actual text.

In this respect, the closest analogue to Thurston's book may be Robert Rauschenberg's *Erased de Kooning Drawing*, which was executed in 1953 after Rauschenberg persuaded a reluctant Willem de Kooning to give him a drawing that he could then erase. The work restages an exemplary Dadaist performance in which André Breton erased the lines of a picture as soon as Francis Picabia had drawn them. Following their antics, which emphasized the theatricality of the performance and the absurdity of its negating activity, no visual documentation was retained. In contrast, the product of Rauschenberg's activity has been carefully preserved.[8] To be sure, Rauschenberg's work is also best remembered for its audacious conceptual gesture (although he denied the aggressive negation of the act), but the details of the resulting object are even more instructive.[9] The erased drawing is far from simply a blank sheet of paper, or the more uniform field exhibited by Tom Friedman's *11 x 22 x 0.005*. As Rauschenberg left it, the surface bears traces of ink and crayon, with a shadow of de Kooning's drawing still clearly visible. Indeed, the work insists on the originating conceptual gesture by documenting not its accomplishment, but its incompletion (a more accurate title, following the model of Robert Smithson's *Partially Buried Woodshed*, would be *Partially Erased de Kooning Drawing*).

In one of the vignettes he liked to repeat, Rauschenberg's friend John Cage recalls: "One day when I was studying with Schoenberg, he pointed out the eraser on his pencil and said, 'This end is more important than the other.'"[10] Although the lesson is ostensibly one of aesthetic economy, Cage might also have been thinking of Rauschenberg's work, where the eraser is not only more important than the lead, but also quite similar. Above all, Rauschenberg manifests that erasure is itself a kind of drawing. The sheet is both smoothed and scuffed with the rich facture of the erasers' abrasion across the thin skin of the paper's pored and mole-flecked flesh. As Rauschenberg must have realized, the very act of removing the pigments from de Kooning's sketch resulted in new markings, and so the attempt to eliminate the image creates a bind: further erasing the vestiges of de Kooning's drawing would only result in an increasingly visible surface inscription. Like his 1951 *White Paintings*, which I will consider further in chapter 6, Rauschenberg's *Erased de Kooning* thus reminds the viewer that there are no real absences, only replacements: of one layer by another, *pli selon pli*, precessions of opacities and cancellations of competing materials, each with their own revelations and supersessions in turn.

Cage makes the same point when he formulates one of the fundamental lessons of his infamous composition *4'33"* (a work he claimed was inspired, not coincidentally, by Rauschenberg's *White Paintings*): there is no such thing as silence.[11] Take away one sound, and there are always others—fainter, or more nuanced and neutral, or simply so regular that they have merged into the background. Eliminate those fainter sounds and you only open onto yet others in turn: the barely perceptible shimmer of electrical circuits; the ambient hums that inhabit rooms even before we do; the respiration of space. Continue all the way to the threshold of hearing itself. The tympanic membrane and the organ of Corti resonate with amplitudes approaching the diameter of a hydrogen atom; if the human ear were more sensitive by even a degree we would hear the crash of atoms colliding in their erratic Brownian sweeps, the constant din of fluctuations in molecular density. But even if we could listen in a vacuum, free from the imperceptible white noise of molecular space, we would still be awash in sound. As long as we are alive we never escape the systolic waves of the hematic ocean tiding in the nautilus turns of the ear.[12]

With figural language that evokes both Cage's dictum and Rauschenberg's white canvases, Michel Foucault argues that Blanchot's writing "mettent à nu ce qui est avant toute parole, au-dessous de tout mutisme: le ruissellement ontinu du langage. . . . Langage qui ne se résoud dans aucun silence: tout interruption ne forme qu'une tache blanche sur cette nappe sans couture [lays bare what precedes all speech, what underlies all silence: the continuous streaming of language. . . . A language not resolved by any silence: any interruption is only a white stain on its seamless sheet]."[13] Although Foucault is making a more general point about Blanchot's later philosophy, Blanchot himself suggests a similar regression, "a relation always in displacement," in a striking passage from the final chapter of his 1948 novel *Le Très-Haut*.[14] Casting the possibility of silence into doubt, or at the very least redefining its essence as a series of shunted noises, the passage describes the noises imagined in a silent room, or those that make a truly silent room impossible: "Tout contre moi, un bruit intermittent, de sable coulant et s'écoulant, un halètement ralenti à l'extrême, comme si quelqu'un avait été là, respirant, s'empêchant de respirer, caché juste contre moi [Hard against me, an intermittent noise, of sand shifting and flowing over itself, a panting in extreme slow motion, as if someone had been there, breathing, preventing himself from breathing, hidden right there next to me]."[15] Elsewhere, defending language against the accusation of being "un ressassement interminable de paroles, au lieu du silence qu'il visait à atteindre [an interminable resifting of words, instead of the silence it wanted to achieve]," Blanchot asserts that language's "ressassement sans terme de mots sans contenu . . . est justement la nature profonde du silence qui parle jusque dans le mutisme, qui est parole vide de paroles, écho toujours parlant au milieu du silence [endless resifting of words without content . . . is precisely the profound nature of a silence that talks even in its dumbness, a silence that is speech empty of words, an echo speaking on and on in the midst of silence]."[16]

Shifting and sifting, implied and explicit, the figure of sand underlies Blanchot's sense of silence with a logic that returns us to both the *Erased de Kooning Drawing* and *The Remove of Literature*. *Le sable* (sand), with its abrasive, pumicing ability to sponge, is an instrument of erasure, and the verb s*abler* (to sand) has the same meaning in French as in English: to smooth, to rub out. At the same time, *sable* also denotes the color black, the wraps of mourning, the color of writing ink. Erasing and revealing, *l'écriture sable* and *l'écriture sablée* (a black writing and a sanded writing) each suggest a third term that encompasses both the erasure of writing and its recovery. Like the stifled breath behind the shifting sands in *Le Très-Haut*, both phrases whisper behind *l'écriture s'ablée*: a writing recovered by carefully washing paper or parchment, a palimpsest revealed (or revealing itself). As Émile Littré's *Dictionnaire de la langue française* records:

> **ablué, ée** / a-blu-é ée / *part. passé*. Parchemin ablué.

> **abluer** / a-blu-é ée / *v. a.* Terme technique. Laver, passer légèrement une liqueur préparée avec de la noix de galle sur du parchemin ou du papier, pour faire revivre l'écriture.

A palimpsest always enacts a double play of concealment and revelation, erasing one text to inscribe another and then suppressing the latter to display the first. The palimpsest obstructs to make a view possible. Appropriately, the word means both a document that has been erased as well as one on which writing appears, and it records that doubling etymologically. "Palimpsest," from the classical Latin *palimpsestus* (paper or parchment that has been written on again), derives from the Hellenistic Greek παλίμψηστος (scraped again) and παλίμψηστον (a parchment from which writing has been erased), which in turn ultimately derive from the ancient Greek πάλιν (again) plus ψηστός, from the verb "to sand."[17] Here Blanchot's verbal doubling explains itself. The marked repetition of "sable coulant et s'écoulant" not only mimes the doubled layering of sounds described in the passage, but it also encrypts a palimpsest—literally, "to re-sand," "to sand again"—as the literary analogue of the silence that reveals sound, the breathing that both masks and permits speech. Bringing into view by erasing, the palimpsest is a *parchemin ablué*: writing that has undergone both a cleansing removal and a restoration. Ablution, that restorative cleansing or cleaning of a surface, here attracts its near twin "ablation," another word associated, as it happens, with sand. "Ablation" can of course denote any removal, as in the surgical excision of a body part, but it most commonly refers to removal of the surface layer of an object by sanding, or sometimes, specifically, the removal of sand itself (as by wind).

In English, the route is slightly different, but the destination is the same. "Sand," according to the first listing in the *Oxford English Dictionary*, derives directly from the Old Teutonic *sandjan* (to send) and denotes "the action of sending; that which is sent, a message." Balanced between its verbal and nominative senses—between removing and delivering, erasing and communicating—"sand," like "palimpsest," encompasses both the emission of a message and its omission. Metonymically, "sand" also denotes the bank of a river, or the seashore, the marge or margin, as when Keats writes: "Along the margin-sand large foot-marks went."[18] Recording the footprints of his reading, sand, in the sense of margin, is precisely what Thurston has allowed to remain among his other removes. Which brings us back to Rauschenberg.

As with *The Remove of Literature*, the margins of the *Erased de Kooning Drawing* are far from parerga. To begin with, those margins are the site of inscription: a hand-lettered label (drawn by Jasper Johns, no less) that both mimes and mocks museological conventions: "ERASED DE KOONING DRAWING / ROBERT RAUSCHENBERG / 1953." The label announces that the work appearing above it is not merely a very faint drawing, or a half-erased sketch abandoned by the famous artist and raised to the status of framed display.

More importantly, the label—itself a species of unsigned drawing—also provides the signature and countersignature necessary for the central drawing to have its conceptual force, putting into play the series of reversals that motivates the project. Beyond the label, the picture frame is no less telling. Neither superfluous nor merely decorative, the frame contrasts with the pristine surface of the archival matte and rhymes with the distressed surface of the drawing paper. The frame's delicate overlay of gold leaf (a material with which Rauschenberg was experimenting at the time) has been abraded in places to let a dark dried-blood red show through, and that paint itself in places has been chipped away. Like the erased drawing within, the frame figures a history of application and removal. Nor am I alone in considering the frame an integral part of the work; on the back of the *Erased de Kooning Drawing*, among the collage of institutional accession and loan stickers, a hand-lettered warning, in black marker, reads: "DO NOT REMOVE / DRAWING FROM FRAME. / FRAME IS PART OF DRAWING."

The frame is equally a part of Thurston's book. Although he eliminates all of Blanchot's writing with an "aveugle vigilance [blind vigilance]," he scrupulously retains the frame of Blanchot's *book*, replicating the dimensions of its borders and respecting the running header and pagination.[19] As Blanchot writes, in seeming anticipation of this unforeseen edition of his work: "Écrire se rapporte à l'absence d'œuvre, mais s'investit dans l'Œuvre sous forme de livre. [The act of writing is related to the absence of the work, but is invested in the Work as book]."[20] Similarly, the status of the frame is central, as it were, to Blanchot's understanding of literature itself; in *Literature and the Right to Death* he writes:

> La littérature ne se borne pas à retrouver à l'intérieur ce qu'elle a voulu abandoner sur le seuil. Car ce qu'elle trouve, comme étant l'intérieur, c'est le dehors qui, d'issue qu'il était, s'est changé en impossibilité de sortir—et comme étant l'obscurité de l'existence, c'est l'être du jour qui, de lumière explicatrice et créatrice de sens, est devenu le harcèlement de ce qu'on ne peut s'empêcher de comprendre et la hantise étouffante d'une raison sans principe, sans commencement, dont on ne peut rendre raison.[21]

> [Literature does not confine itself to rediscovering in the interior what it tried to leave behind on the threshold. Because what it finds, as the

interior, is the outside which has been changed from the outlet it once was into the impossibility of going out—and what it finds as the darkness of existence is the being of day which has been changed from explicatory light, creative of meaning, into the aggravation of what one cannot prevent oneself from understanding, and the stifling obsession of a reason without principle, without any beginning, which one cannot account for.]

Margins and centers are a recurrent topic in Blanchot's writing, and one could quote any number of equally evocative passages, but picking up on the word "rediscovering" in the quotation above I want to cite just one other. Describing the "enclosed space" of an infinitely regressive dynamic of reading and writing, Blanchot explains:

> La solitude de l'œuvre—l'œuvre d'art, l'œuvre littéraire—nous découvre une solitude plus essentielle. . . . Celui qui écrit l'œuvre est mis à part, celui qui l'a écrite est congédié.[22]

> [In the solitude of the work—the work of art, the literary work—we discover a more essential solitude. . . . The person who is writing the work is thrust to one side, the person who has written the work is dismissed.]

"Discover," "thrust to one side," "dismissed"—each shares the same definition: *remove*. Reading, for Blanchot, is indeed the remove of literature, and so the thrust of Thurston's title is doubly descriptive, pointing equally to his method and his source.

Absence, silence, blankness, blindness, concealment, displacement, effacement, the outside, the void. . . . *The Remove of Literature* might seem to be an illustrated edition of *L'Espace littéraire*, or a work of concrete poetry visually picturing Blanchot's signature lexicon, or simply his titles: *The Space of Literature*; *The Absence of the Book*; *The Disappearance of Literature*. Replace the indefinite "work" in this passage from Blanchot with the titles of the specific works under consideration here, and the argument proceeds flawlessly, following "a deviation in which the *Remove of Literature* disappears into the absence of *The Space of Literature*, but in which the absence of text always escapes the more it reduces itself to being nothing but the Work that has always disappeared already."[23] Indeed, Thurston's procedure recalls any number of quite specific passages from

Blanchot's writings: "Écrire, c'est produire l'absence d'œuvre (le désœuvre-ment) [To write is to produce the absence of the work (the unworking)]"; "La littérature en se faisant impuissance à révéler, voudrait devenir révéla-tion de ce que la révélation détruit [By turning itself into an inability to reveal anything, literature is attempting to become the revelation of what revelation destroys]"; "Un mot-absence, un mot-trou, creusé en son centre d'un trou, de ce trou où tous les autres mots auraient été enterrés . . . une voix neutre qui dit l'œuvre à partir de ce lieu sans lieu où l'œuvre se tait [A word-absence, a hole-word, hollowed out in its center by a hole, a hole in which all the other words should have been buried . . . a neutral voice that speaks the work from out of this place without a place, where the work is silent]"; and so on.[24] Furthermore, the form of *The Remove of Literature* would seem to describe not only Blanchot's language, but also the language of his critics and explicators: "The description accumulates endless baroque ellipses around whatever it is circling, endlessly expanding upon the eclipse of its center. Its sole excuse for existence is that whatever it revolves around, whatever supports it, is lacking."[25] Again, the examples of such moments are far too numerous to catalogue, but their ubiquity is not enough to justify the relentlessness of Thurston's procedure, which as mere illustration—car-ried on for hundreds of pages—would be excessive, or farcical, or so literal as to constitute a satire of Blanchot's rhetoric, if not itself. "C'est assez dire: abîme et satire de l'abîme [It is enough to say: abyss, and satire of the abyss]," as Derrida begins his meditation around the idea of the frame, going on to explain: "ouverture par le *satis*, *l'assez* (au-dedans et au-dehors, au-dessus et au-dessous, à droite et à gauche), la satire, la farce au bord du trop [opening with the *satis*, the *enough* (inside and outside, above and below, to left and right), satire, farce on the edge of excess]."[26]

The Remove of Literature avoids that farce by actively enacting Blan-chot's text, rather than merely picturing it. That activity is classically decon-structive. On the one hand, the marginalia—the space "above and below, to left and right"—is only marginalia *as such* (rather than merely some writing set in an unusual centrifugal layout) because of its relation to the main text, which in turn is able to be designated as the "main" text (rather than merely one part of a parallel column) only because of the status of the marginalia that gives it precedence. On the other hand, and at the very same time, *with-out* that central text the writing remaining in the margins loses the indexical force that true marginalia (as distinguished from commentary) requires. So even though it has been removed, the abstract force of the central text must still remain in order for us to recognize the peripheral text as marginalia. As "négation qui s'affirme [negation asserting itself]," the body of the text thus takes on an "existence vague, indéterminée, insaisissable, où rien n'apparait, sein de la profondeur sans apparence . . . le sens, détaché de ses conditions, séparé de ses moments, errant comme un pouvoir vide, dont on ne peut rien faire, pouvoir sans pouvoir, simple impuissance à cesser d'être [indeterminate, elusive existence in which nothing appears, the heart of depth without appearance . . . meaning detached from its conditions, separated from its movements, wandering like an empty power, the simple inability to cease to be]."[27] Conversely, although it remains quite visibly and concretely present on the peripheries of the page, the abstract force of the marginal text is nonetheless lost, unable to attain the status of marginalia without the presence of the central text. The text printed in *The Remove of Literature* both is and is not marginalia.

Blanchot repeatedly formulates this kind of contradiction: "rien qui fût visible, rien qui fût invisible . . . cette absence non absente [nothing that was visible, nothing that was invisible . . . that non-absent absence]."[28] For him, such suspensions constitute the "Neuter" (etymologically from the classical Latin *neuter*, composed of *ne* [not] and *uter* [either]: neither of two, not one nor the other). Nongeneric, in the sense of being neither within nor outside of a particular class, the notes in *The Remove of Literature* are Neuter in terms of their genre; they are neither properly marginalia nor entirely freed to be some other genre. But they are Neuter in terms of their activity as well. "Le Neutre," in Blanchot's explication, is "la douce interdiction du mourir, là où, de seuil en seuil, œil sans regard, le silence nous porte dans la proximité du lointain. Parole encore à dire au-delà des vivants et des morts, témoignant pour l'absence d'attestation [the gentle prohibition against dying, there where, from threshold to threshold, eye without gaze, silence carries us into the proximity of the distant. Word still to be spoken beyond the living and the dead, testifying for the absence of attestation]."[29] An activity rather than a category, the Neuter is a "mouvement de 'écriture [movement of writing]," or what Foucault recognizes as "le mouvement de l'attirance, le retrait du compagnon . . . ouvre un espace neutre [the movement of attraction and the withdrawal of the companion . . . opening onto a neutral space]."[30] Attracting and withdrawing from one another, the erased text and the marginal notes describe a neutral space. The essence of the one depends on the disappearance of the other, which cancels the status of the first at the very moment that it has defined the other. Each term is inescapably bound to its relation with the other and yet unable to establish the necessary relation with that other term: neither some genre (marginalia) nor another, neither some thing (text on the page) nor nothing (since it continues to exert its defining force). The two texts, as Blanchot might see it, stand "dans un rapport de non-identification avec eux-mêmes [in a relation of nonidentification with themselves]."[31] Accordingly, *The Remove of Literature* presents its textual elements in "une relation où l'inconnu serait affirmé, manifesté, voire exhibé: découvert—et sous quel aspect? précisément en cela qui le retient inconnu. L'inconnu, dans ce rapport, se découvrirait donc en cela qui le laisse à couvert [a relation in which the unknown would be affirmed, made manifest, even exhibited: disclosed—and under what aspect?—precisely in that which keeps it unknown. In this relation, then, the unknown would be disclosed in that which leaves it under cover]."[32]

For Blanchot, such neutral, recursive, paradoxical movement defines the workings of language in general. Fundamentally an activity of negation, language functions, if it functions at all, only to the degree that it cancels in a series of *mise-en-abîme* reversals. Language takes away in order to give: negating the referent in order to give us the word; erasing the word in order to summon the concept. Language "suppresses," "annihilates," "absents," "distances."[33] Language, in short, *removes.* By removing Blanchot's text, Thurston paradoxically gives us Blanchot's work; he presents rather than absents language—its essence, the defining move of its operation—in Blanchot's understanding. In *The Remove of Literature* "nous voudrions simplement éprouver dans quelle mesure on peut suivre un texte et en même temps le perdre [we would simply feel the extent to which one can follow a text and at the same time lose it]."[34] The book proffers the gift of theft. Which is as much as any work of literature, in Blanchot's definition, can do:

> Qui veut lui faire exprimer davantage, ne trouve rien, trouve qu'elle n'exprime rien. Celui qui vit dans la dépendance de l'œuvre, soit pour l'écrire, soit pour la lire, appartient à la solitude de ce qui n'exprime que le mot être: mot que la langage abrite en le dissimulant ou fait apparaître en disparaissant dans le vide silencieux de l'œuvre.[35]

> [Anyone who tries to make it express more finds nothing, finds that it expresses nothing. Anyone who lives in dependence of the work,

whether because he is writing it or reading it, belongs to the solitude of something that expresses only the word *being*: a word that the language protects by hiding it or that the language causes to appear by disappearing into the silent void of the work.]

Absence, silence, blankness, effacement, the void. . . . Blanchot's signature lexicon is also a kind of signature proper. Foucault, in the passage quoted above, hints at the proper name of his subject with the reference to "une tache *blanche*," and although it seems to have escaped notice, Roland Barthes suggests the same connection in the chapter on writing and silence in *Le Degré zéro de l'écriture*. Following a parenthetical reference to Blanchot and the appropriation of his vocabulary to define a "terme neutre ou terme-zéro [neutral term, or zero element]," Barthes proposes the designation of "une écriture *blanche*" (the play is obscured in the standard English translation, which renders the phrase as "colourless writing").[36] To blanch (*blanchir*), of course, means to whiten, but the word resonates further with Thurston's suppression of Blanchot's text and its replacement by the white space of the page. To blanch is also "to give a fair appearance to by artifice or suppression"; to omit; to turn something aside; to shirk; to withhold what is expected or due. The *Oxford English Dictionary* cites a line from William Warner's *Albion's England* that brings these senses together in bibliographic terms: "but so obscurely hath beene blancht of good workes elsewheare done."[37] *Blancher*, accordingly, designates someone who causes a thing to turn aside, a perverter, an obstructer. Countersigning Blanchot's text, Thurston also forges his name. The proper genre for *The Remove of Literature* may be portraiture.

Indeed, *Blanchot*, in French, is the name for a kind of bird, *une pie-grièche*, an ashen shrike, near anagram of *shirk*, both harassing antagonist and prey to the white owl, which is also its phonic negative (in the photographic sense): *chouette blanche*. The white owl, *chouette blanche*: the owl of Minerva, pale in the sable night. Although he claims to have read him "fort loin [at a great remove]," Blanchot was never far from Hegel.[38] The "shrike" is also the language of the owl, an idiomatic association that stretches back centuries: "shrykyng of these owlys," as Chaucer puts it in his *Troilus and Criseyde*. In Shakespeare, "shriek" is always associated with owls rather than other animals, and in the context of fearful ill omens of death and madness.[39] Death and madness: "la folie d'écrire—*le jeu insensé* [*this insane game of writing*]," as Blanchot quotes Stéphane Mallarmé, reading poetry as philosophy and philosophy as an endless description of literary writing.[40] Taken literally, the cry defined by the shrike is an utterance on the margin of rational language; taken figuratively, we might read it as the speech of the familiar of the goddess of intellect: the most rational of language, a philosophical literature.

Or, on second thought, perhaps the proper genre is a subset of the portrait: *memento mori*. From the Renaissance on, "remove" has meant to assassinate, to author a death—"most violent Author Of his owne iust remoue," as Shakespeare puts it—and death haunts this present deauthored *Remove*.[41] "Margin," recall, has its origin in inscription and memorial, in the "grave," in both senses of the word, and the center contained by that memorial space echoes darkly; in the context of his extended reflections on death, "centre," in Blanchot, always suggests its near homophone: *cendres* (ashes). Moreover, like the English "bleached," *blanchir* is a word idiomatically associated with the skeletal. The Littré illustrates "blanchoyer [to have a white reflection]" with the couplet: "L'on voit avec horreur d'antiques ossements / Blanchoyer à travers de pompeux ornements [One saw with horror the ancient bones / gleaming white through gaudy ornaments]." Which should help illuminate the hypogram undersigning the proper name of the author removed from this book: the phonic skeleton of "Blanchot" disarticulates neatly to "os blanches [bleached bones]."

Point de source: in this evacuated tome, or tomb, the body of the text has been removed. *The Remove of Literature* presents us with "le don d'un poème comme offrande d'un tombeau qui, saura-t-on jamais, pourrait être un cénotaphe [the gift of the poem as the offering from a tomb which could be, for all one will ever know, a cenotaph]."[42] For Blanchot, this is always the case with language: "Quand nous parlons, nous nous appuyons à un tombeau, et ce vide du tombeau est ce qui fait la vérité du langage, mais en même temps le vide est réalité et la mort se fait être [When we speak, we are leaning on a tomb, and the void of that tomb is what makes language true, but at the same time void is reality and death becomes being]."[43] All inscription, for Blanchot, is a "cenographic writing, a writing that nothing fulfills and yet that is the utter fulfillment of writing" (to quote Denis Hollier).[44] But even without such explicit statements, language and literature would be, for Blanchot, fundamentally bound up with death. Every word, following his text, remains. To follow a text, and to lose it: with the marginalia reengraved, the body of the text disinterred, *The Remove of Literature* is a fitting cenotaph, a proper grave, leaving the clear dawn of the mourning of the night—"*l'autre* nuit [the *other* night]," the sable night—to come.[45]

La noche sosegada

En par de los levantes de la aurora,

La música callada, la soledad Sonora

[The pacific night

At the moment of dawn's risings,

The silent music, the sonorous solitude]

—ST. JOHN OF THE CROSS

3 TEXTUAL PROSTHESES

"Prosthesis" belongs to a class of terms denoting arbitrary processes, whose intrusion into the realm of language should be viewed with suspicion.

—THOMAS LE MARCHANT DOUSE

There are books in which the footnotes . . .
are more interesting than the text.

—GEORGE SANTAYANA

Nobody is going to believe that footnotes
changed Writing and Reading. But they did.

—HERIBERTO YÉPEZ

In *Seuils*, Gérard Genette inventories those genres on the threshold of a literary work: dedications and inscriptions, epigraphs and titles, prefaces, notes, and all manner of bibliographic accoutrements—from jacket copy to format. Genette argues that "a text without a paratext does not exist," but he also mentions, in passing, that "paratexts without texts do exist, if only by accident."[1] Paratexts without a text—paratexts *as* texts, one might put it—have also been written quite intentionally, however, and they constitute a remarkable trend in contemporary writing. Drawn from otherwise diverse contexts and written in apparent ignorance of their precedents, these works all stage a related set of tensions: between literal and metaphoric language; between the etymological history of words and the amnesia of their colloquial usage; between the form of a work and its ostensible themes. By attending to the materials and rhetorics of these paratextual works, this chapter hopes to show that those tensions gesture toward the embodiedness of these literary works' bibliographic forms, and to the textual corporeality that all such paratexts sustain as they seek to supplement, support, and displace the body of the text.

On 17 October 1961, at 3:47 p.m., Daniel Spoerri stopped what he was doing and made a map recording the location of all of the objects that happened to be lying on his kitchen table. Each outlined shape was then numbered and described in a corresponding note with the mock precision of one of Robbe-Grillet's *nouveaux romans*. Published as the *Topographie anecdotée du hasard* (Anecdoted topography of chance), subsequent editions included notes to the notes, which infloresce to as many as eight degrees of annotations by as many authors in a self-reflexive discourse network of emendation.[2] In addition to the sober, ostensibly scrupulous, deadpan documentary that records details about the objects on the table—such as the fine print on the labels of packages, the cost of items, and the date they were purchased—the notes include more discursive anecdotes about the circumstances under which objects were acquired and used, reminiscences and arguments among the writers, copies of their correspondence, transcripts of interviews, scholastic disputes, corrections and clarifications, obscure passages from literature and scrapbook clippings from contemporary newspapers, notes on translation, interlingual puns, dirty jokes, and, in some of the later editions, extraordinary, enthused passages from Dieter Roth that abruptly burst the expository tone of the original with hallucinatory extended metaphors and Steinian syntactic permutations.

The *Topographie* thus amplifies a tension between the two competing and contradictory rhetorical traditions that have taken the genre of the note as their vehicle: the personally expressive and the objectively impersonal. On the one hand, the note has always been an anecdotal site that attracts speculative, conjectural, and incidental remarks; it is often the occasion for undocumented testimony or confidential asides—or even, too often, the irrepressible inclusion of material too dear to the writer to part with and yet not, in the honest final accounting, really germane to the topic under consideration. On the other hand, the note, and the footnote in particular, was equally seen to oppose those "particular, anecdotical traditions, whose original authority is unknown, or justly suspicious."[3] Accordingly, notes came to be understood as the proper repository for material beyond the writer's personal authority: recourse to the work of other writers, evidentiary and corroborative bulwarks, the foundation of objective facts, and citations in a standardized—and often imposed—system. From the beginning, that association of the footnote with scientific objectivity was "virulently contested in the early modern period" and the tension could still be felt in the early eighteenth century, when the proper use of the note, as either "a vehicle for displaying the critic's taste and breeding" or "a quasiscientific system for displaying the vicissitudes of textual transmission," was still being opposed.[4] Indeed, "even eighteenth century empiricism was content with weaker positions than those adopted by the triumphant positivists of the following age."[5]

To "note," of course, is to observe closely, and the conceit of the *Topographie* is that it pays meticulous attention to objects that would otherwise go unnoticed: bread crumbs and grains of salt, a stray paperclip or rubber band, an empty bottle, a torn carton, a cracked ashtray, and so on.[6] With its exhaustive and careful analysis of a depopulated *mise-en-scène* in which everyday objects are recorded at a certain moment, frozen wherever they happen to be, the *Topographie* has some kinship with the attention a detective gives to the disposition of clues in a crime novel. Indeed, the structure of the book—with the textual and typographical attention lavished on each individual entry—promises revelations about the significance of the noted objects, which are imbued with an aura of mysterious immanence. In the end, however, the anecdotes fail to divulge any especially interesting secret histories; the banal accounts of quotidian objects ultimately reveal them to be, in fact, rather ordinary. But the book sets in play a dynamic between everyday utility and detached observation that is nevertheless quite interesting. In a sense derived directly from the Old Icelandic *nota*, to "note" also means "to make use of something," so there is some irony in the fact that the cartographic notes of the *Topographie* function only to the extent that they suspend the use of the objects noted. Both the "useless" objects on the tabletop (spilled salt, burnt matches, torn paper bags, et cetera) as well as those utilitarian objects frozen in place and rendered unusable are remotivated by the project of mapping and anecdoting, activities in which they once again serve a definite purpose. The *Topographie* reflects explicitly on this cycle, both with its note that the word "floccinaucinihilipilification" (the estimation of something as worthless) might be used in a way in which it was in fact considered worthless, as well as with Dieter Roth's series of speculations on the contest between "attention" and "use," in which the objects in Spoerri's book oscillate between "artwork" and "commodity," consumption and conservation.[7] More specifically, Roth argues that "one can call symbols discarded commodities, because commodities—so long as you need them—lead an unconscious or unseen life."[8] We will see this dynamic recast in yet another form, as the alternation between the literal and the metaphoric comes to charge the artist's book with its distinctive character, and in which notation itself vacillates between symbolic use and commodified referent; but for now I want to recall the similar logic of an artist's book from precisely the same moment. In Marcel Broodthaers's sculpture *Pense-bête* (1964), as I noted in the previous chapter, books of his early poetry, bound shut by being set in plaster, can either be the subject of *attention*, and contemplated as sculpture, or *use*, and opened and read—but not both.

The *Topographie* is part of what Johanna Drucker has identified as a documentary tradition of artists' books, but it can also be read in a broader literary context.[9] In addition to the ancient trope of the epic catalogue and the more recent lists and inventories of conceptual writing, the *Topographie* takes its place in a tradition of "literary" footnotes. With their origins in Edmund Spenser's self-glossing apparatuses in the *Shepherd's Calendar*, such literary notes stretch from eighteenth-century examples in the works of Pope, Swift, Fielding, and Sterne to the modernist notes of Eliot, Joyce, and Beckett, continuing through the century in books by Vladimir Nabokov, Manuel Puig, Nicholson Baker, and Mark Danielewski among many others.[10] More specifically, the archaeology of the tabletop is itself a recognizable literary motif. In Georges Perec's "Notes concernant des objets qui sont sur ma table de travail" ("Notes Concerning the Objects That Are on My Work-Table"), for instance, Perec describes a table "cluttered almost to excess," which he documents with a combination of anecdote and precision not unlike Spoerri's annotations.[11] Similarly, with a stylistic flair closer to Dieter Roth's annotations, the theme is the occasion for a tour-de-force paragraph early in Thomas Pynchon's *Gravity's Rainbow*. The passage begins with the

> millions of tiny red and brown curls of rubber eraser, pencil shavings, dried tea or coffee stains, traces of sugar and Household Milk, much cigarette ash, very fine black debris picked and flung from typewriter ribbons, decomposing library paste, broken aspirins ground to powder . . .

and surfaces upward and outward to the *News of the World*—an expansive sounding terminus, although its actual presence, Pynchon suggests, is only speculative. And besides, he adds, it too might have "been thrown away."[12]

Discarded refuse, as it happens, is one of several inspirations Spoerri himself has claimed for the *Topographie* project. Fascinated with the idea that one "could retrace the history of every scrap" of garbage in a wastebasket, Spoerri acknowledges the precedent of the *poubelles* (trashcans) of Arman (Armand Fernandez), who created his *sculptures informes* by displaying the contents of various people's garbage cans in museum vitrines.[13] Or worse: for an infamous 1960 exhibit entitled *Le Plein* (Chock full), Arman filled the entire Galerie Iris Clert with trash that he must, with a certain pathos, have been saving himself or begging from others for some time. The *Topographie* similarly salvages what, by 3:48 on that day in October, might well have been detritus. The book displays those disposable items as "the discrete heroes of a modern romance whose destiny leads to the dustbin," so that "amidst this anecdotic mine / Thou labour'st hard to bid thy Hero shine" in this neo-epic catalogue of the transient and banal.[14] At the same time, the compositional procedure of the book is clearly related to Spoerri's contemporaneous *tableaux de piège* (snare paintings): sculptural collages in which the contents of a surface such as a tabletop are affixed with adhesive, so that the support can be rotated ninety degrees and hung on the wall. That rotation both defamiliarizes the generally ordinary objects that now jut outward just above eye level and translates their sculptural forms from the horizontal ground of gravity to the easel painting's vertical plane.[15] A darker version of a carefully arranged tabletop presented as sculpture (although one that still maintains a healthy dash of the absurd), was prepared by Robert Watts at precisely the same time Spoerri was composing his topography. Watts's *Table for Suicide Event* (1961) consisted of a painted wooden folding table supporting a number of objects, from the chilling (assorted metal instruments in a leather case, a single latex glove) to the ominous (a drinking glass and apothecary bottle; note paper, telephone, and some audio tape) to the cruelly campy (a Band-Aid box).

Comparisons with any of these various intertexts might be productively pursued, but one should not lose sight of the way in which the publication of *Topographie*, with its near rhyme of "typography," puts the format of the book into dialogue with its style. With individual items inventoried on separate pages as if they were each worthy of equal attention, the layout of the book emphasizes one of the denotations of "anecdote": a detached narrative of a single incident or event "told as being in itself interesting or striking."[16] At the same time, the *Topographie anecdotée* is a sort of etymological oxymoron; "anecdote," from the privative Greek ἀνέκδοτα, originally meant "secret histories" or "unpublished material" (*OED*). In the end, moreover, a similar historical pun causes the subject and format of the *Topographie* to coincide once more. Despite its record of chance, the tabletop is not a coincidental subject for a keyed reference map; in their bibliographic sense, "index" and "table" were initially "applied somewhat indiscriminately."[17]

With its notes keyed to the tracings of a topographic map, Spoerri's book is structured like Andy Warhol's exactly contemporaneous simulation of a paint-by-numbers kit, *Do It Yourself Landscape* (1962), or Roni Horn's more recent *Still Water (the River Thames for Example)* (1999), a series of offset lithographs in which tiny numerals are overprinted on images of the surface of the water, with corresponding footnotes printed below. But even these image-based systems of annotation have their origins in the history of the book and the development of the footnote as the dominant form of annotation. Although "the practice of linking notes to text had already been employed in glossed books by the late eleventh century," the footnote has its roots in the early modern dawn of printing.[18] As lengthy commentary came to be increasingly incorporated into printed books over the course of the sixteenth century, the unkeyed marginal side notes, set more or less beside their relevant passages, became increasingly crowded, confusing, and in need of differentiation, so "printers employed a series of letters in alphabetical sequence as *signes de renvoi* to link the notes to the text."[19] Although the typical number of glosses actually began to decrease in the late seventeenth century, those keyed passages were also shifting from the sides of the page to the bottom, so that "from a technical point of view, the great [codicological] innovation of about 1700 was the choice of the footnote to the virtual exclusion of other forms of printed annotation."[20]

Initially called "bottom notes" (the first entry in the *Oxford English Dictionary*, from William Savage's 1841 *Dictionary of the Art of Printing*, implies that "Foot Note" was still a secondary term in the middle of the nineteenth century), the sequences of *notae* were repeated anew with each page, in contrast with our current practice of continuous numbering throughout a chapter or book.[21] In either system, the footnote's focus on the page indicates its debt to the history of the book and the shift from scroll to codex. Moreover, the increased use of the footnote "appears to have been part of the printers' efforts to modernize layout as they increasingly distanced themselves from the original manuscript models" in which "comments surrounded the text, top, sides, and bottom, flowing from it like the decorative acanthus that adorned monastery capitals and liturgical mosaics."[22] Such designs carried over into early printed books, in which compositors "contrived to encompass the pages of the text, that they might have the resemblance of a Looking-glas in the frame" (as John Smith put it in his 1755 *Printer's Grammar*). The page, in other words, had come to be glossed to a highly reflective gloss.[23] In contrast, the footnote was seen to "mime contemporary ideals of order, coherence, beauty, and hierarchy" in a neoclassical design aesthetic of restrained elegance and an overall page design based on uniform typefaces, with sections of text distinguished by font rather than face.[24] The footnote as we know it, then, is coeval with the modern principles of book design that emerged with the Enlightenment.

Inextricably bound with this history, the modern typographical conventions of annotation—following a section of text with the callout or indicator of a superscript numeral—are inevitably associated with scholarly publications. Indeed, the extent to which notes form the core of a critical text has recently been put to the test by Simon Morris in his artist's book *Interpretation*, a bibliographic version of site-specific art.[25] Taking essays from two academic writers, Morris erases everything except the footnotes, which remain at the bottom of the page, while the isolated call-out numbers are scattered and suspended in place above, like star charts illustrating Mallarmé's "alphabet des astres [alphabet of stars]": writing's negative image of blackened constellations on the bleached white sky of the page.[26] Morris then gives each writer the other's erased text, from which they attempt to reconstruct the original essay from only the evidence of the notes. Those notes are thus the point of contact between the surfaces of the two essays, and the similarities between the essays indicates the extent to which notes are not merely isolated end points of reference but gesture to the textual spaces between each other, carrying information about their text as a whole.

Notes, moreover, are sufficiently established to carry information even in the absence of any actual annotation. That is, even without a network of notes as such, superscript still operates within its own textual economy. In Walter Abish's short story "Ardor/Awe/Atrocity," for example, the pages bristle as superscript edges its own numerical constellations of spikes and swirls into patterns over the alphabetic grid of the main text's larger lines. Reminiscent of the numbering added to Honoré de Balzac's *Sarrasine* when it was reprinted in *S/Z*, Roland Barthes's limit case of structuralism, the twenty-six sections of Abish's story are each titled with three headwords, grouped in alphabetized sets, and whenever one of those words appears in the story it is marked with a superscript number indicating its place in the sequence of seventy-eight headwords, as in the sentence, "Without Mannix Southern California[7] would be bereft of the distinction between ardor,[1] awe,[2] and atrocity.[3]"[27] The superscript numerals in Abish's story send the reader not to any note, but self-reflexively back to the tagged word in a symmetrical relay. If anything, the numerals merely point to the status of the otherwise fairly conventional story *as text*.[28] Typographically emphasizing the visual text with its series of empty references, the erratic spacing of the superscript punctuates the prose and trips the reader's eye with its "roughened, impeded" surface.[29] An empty formal system disrupting the ostensible "meaning" of the story, these numerals are a perfect example of what Viktor Shklovsky termed "приёмы остранения" (devices of making strange): those techniques by which poetry slows the reader's habitual consumption of the communicative content. In Shklovsky's famous formulation:

> The technique of art is to make objects "unfamiliar," to make forms difficult, to increase the difficulty and length of perception because the process of perception is an aesthetic end in itself and must be prolonged.[30]

Specifically, like Spoerri's patient notice of everyday objects, the superscript numerals in Abish's story focus the reader's attention on generally quotidian vocabulary. "Atrocity," to be sure, is rather charged, but the single most striking headword is "totemic," and in general the noted words are not particularly exceptional: "now," "open," "how," "color," and so on. Where an actual note might have either augmented the story or revealed something about the significance of a particular word, here the system merely prompts the reader to speculate about lexicon: Why, in this idiosyncratic textual system, is any particular word a headword? What might be special about the chosen word? To what extent does vocabulary determine a story? Was this an exercise requiring the writer to use certain words, or were the headwords chosen after the story had been essentially written?[31] Whatever the answers (and none are forthcoming from the text), Abish's story is a good example of the potential of even the quasi-footnote to simultaneously interrupt and structure a text.

Where the text of "Atrocity" establishes a citational system without notes, other books have enumerated notes without a text. The precedent for such works is Gottlieb Wilhelm Rabener's satiric 1743 book *Hinkmars von Repkow Noten ohne Text* (Hinkmar von Repkow's notes without text), which reasoned that since scholars acquire their cultural capital through footnotes that explicate other works rather than through writing "primary" works themselves, a book with only footnotes would be the fastest route to scholarly success.[32] Although the motivations have changed, the idea of a book of "notes without text" continues to be attractive to poets and artists. Like Phillip Gallo's artist's book *Captions from Animals Looking at You*, in which the paratext of captions are reprinted without the illustrations they originally accompanied, books of notes without text isolate one element of the textual apparatus in order to lay bare and better understand the poetics of the note and its functioning as a device.[33] The *note*, as I have indicated, has its etymological origins in denotations of "usefulness," but by obviating the intended communicative value of the notes in their original context and frustrating their functional utility within the system of the book machine, a book can focus attention on what the Russian formalists might have called "the note as such." Or, to put this in the terms of more recent linguistics, these works move the notes away from *use* and toward *mention*.

Indeed, when separated from the body of the text and taken by itself, even the most earnestly objective and utile system of notes can appear as a paratactic prose poem of "new sentences" that invite alogical connections— sometimes surrealist or absurdist, sometimes simply nonsensical.[34] David Antin's "Separation Meditations," which transforms the supplemental clarifications of an editor into evocative and gnomic statements, provides a perfect illustration. Related by compositional practice to Antin's earlier *Novel Poem*, a collage of sentences transcribed from popular novels, as well as to the constraint-based writing of his earlier "Meditations," which were composed from preset lexicons of severely restricted vocabulary, the "Separation Meditations" were taken from some of the endnotes in P. E. Matheson's translation of Epictetus.[35] The opening stanza of the first "Separation Mediation," for example, is drawn from the scholarly notes to chapter XXIV of book III of the *Discourses*.[36] The first five notes in the original volume's appendix read:

1. The places where you now are.

2. Probably refers to the story that Nicocreon ordered Anaxarchus' tongue to be cut out, whereupon he bit it off himself and spat it in Nicocreon's face. Diog. Laert. ix. 59.

3. καρπιστής—*vindex* or *assertor*, the man by the touch of whose wand the slave became free, if his master made no counter claim. The word is used again in iv. 1 and iv. 7. For Epictetus' references to manumission cf ii., 1, note 3.

4. διάχυσις here and later in the chapter, of pleasure as something diffused or expansive (opp. to σνστολή).

5. i.e. 'take my life'.

From which Antin takes:

1. The places where you are now

2. A man who wanted another's tongue cut out

3. By the touch of whose wand the slave became free

4. Here and later of pleasure as something diffused

5. Take my life

Isolating the small six-point type of the original in this way, Antin's poem "is an attempt to render the force of the diminutive."[37] His procedure also illustrates the fact that the codexical articulation of footnotes and endnotes— their separation on the page and within the book—opens them up to reiteration. Ostensibly outside the text that both contains and is framed by it, with a subservient role that nonetheless possesses an authority to trump the text that would seem to master it, the note is a dangerous supplement that establishes "the problematic limit between an inside and an outside that is always threatened by graft and by parasite."[38]

In the new context on Antin's page, for example, the excerpted lines take on a distinctly self-reflexive aspect, gesturing to their new context rather than to the body text of their original volume. Consider a line from the "First Separation," for instance: "The middle finger upraised."[39] The phrase describes a vulgar gesture, of course, but it is also—like Antin's notes themselves—a sort of perverted index: the finger pointing with iconic significance but not, as the forefinger would, to any specific referent. Moreover, the reader of the poem's first line, "The places where you are now," is indeed now in two places: the words of one writer transplanted to a new location. With those glosses cut out of the body of their original text, so that the reader is "reading / omitting," the amputated tongue of the second line is far from gratuitous, as a gloss of the Greek γλῶσσα (tongue) reminds us (an etymology all the more salient in the context of the classical text from which his separations are taken).[40]

After the first two poems in the series, Antin works with much smaller fragments of found text, typically only one or two words, which he repeats and recombines into spare lyrical permutations, so that the entire series is a recognition of poetic "pleasure as something diffused."[41] The formal integrity of those first two poems, however, is revealing and sustained; stanzas almost always correspond to the chapter divisions of the original's notes, and one can follow Antin's reading through the back matter of the original volume. In the first "Separation," for instance, his attention is focused on the spatial logic of the page rather than the linear organization of the notes by chapter; he works from opening to opening, moving backward for three turnings, skip-ping a page, returning to it, jumping back ten pages, and moving forward for another two openings. The second "Separation," in contrast, follows the order of the notes themselves more closely. Beginning with the very first sentence of Matheson's first note to chapter I, it then proceeds sequentially for six pages, tending to move from chapter to chapter as well as from note to note within each chapter. Following the spatializing logic of typography, which separates keyed material, rather than the associative logic of theme or tone, "the point is that the discourses are treated as matters of language without regard to their substance."[42]

Even when he transcribes sentences in their entirety and closely fol-lows the sequence of the notes, Antin's procedure is never mechanical, and the small transformations of his transcriptions are telling. By replacing the original verbal phrase "setting up" with the more prosaic "planting," for instance, Antin alliterates the otherwise verbatim line "planting a palm tree seems to be mentioned as an acrobatic feat," and he syncopates its rhythm accordingly. Moreover, he tends to edit lines so that their references are less specific. As the example above illustrates, Antin typically omits proper names and precise referents, rendering "Caesar" as "the king," for instance, and he thus transforms those original explanatory notes into lines of text that themselves might benefit from a further gloss. At the same time, this prac-tice emphasizes the shifter-like nature of every note's indexical force by sug-gesting a wider range of referents for the reader to imagine ("Nicocreon," that is, indicates a more restricted set than "those who have wanted another's tongue cut out," however small one hopes that latter category might be).

Separating the appropriated notes into small stanzas of two to six lines, Antin exploits what Ron Silliman has called the "parsimony principle": the strong habitual tendency by which readers try to incorporate even the most radically paratactic sentences into a coherent explanatory framework, imagi-natively supplying any necessary logical connections in the process.[43] Given that readers have an instinctual desire for "freedom from logical error or a secure judgment," and suggesting that "no step can be taken without logical process," the Separations' "governing principle / is rational / which makes knowledge articulate," and they suggest that "truth is / of many alternatives / only a corner / where a fact happens to stand."[44] Moreover, Antin typically arranges his notes in numbered tercets to suggest a syllogism. In fact, one of the sections of the poem neatly describes and enacts its syllogistic form:

1. With one another

2. Or any two

3. With a third[45]

With a nice irony, Antin thus gives a scholastic form to material from a work that is explicitly concerned with the seriousness of reasoning and the careful analysis of syllogisms, which—it argues—must not be followed too blindly.[46] His Separations, in brief, underscore the claim that "a convincing impression / is not a criterion of truth."

It is worth remembering that however convincing an impression the letterpress edition of Antin's *Meditations* might make, it is not, following Johanna Drucker's useful delineation, strictly speaking an "artist's book." According to Drucker, "an artist's book is a book created as an original work of art, rather than a reproduction of a pre-existing work."[47] Although the "Separation Meditations" derive from the formal aspects of the book and demonstrate the poetic value of paying attention to the supposedly incidental and secondary bibliographic aspects of books, Antin's work is ultimately published as a reproduction rather than an exploitation of bibliography. True to their name, the "separations" are in fact twice removed: first from the body of the texts to which they refer, and then again from the logic of the page on which they originated. This is certainly not to fault the poems, which gain their syllogistic logic, riddling tone, stanzaic form, and lyric rhythm from that double separation; but the difference between his book and similar works is, as I hope to show next, illuminating.

At the heart of Drucker's definition is the conceptualization of the artist's book as "a book which integrates the formal means of its realization and production with its thematic or aesthetic issues."[48] "Self-conscious about the structure and meaning of the book as a form," the artist's book, in short, "interrogates the conceptual or material form of the book as part of its intention, thematic interests, or production activities."[49] Following this argument, I want to consider several works that might not be readily recognized as "artists' books" (because of their production values, distribution, and the social networks in which they were produced) but that nevertheless conform to Drucker's characterization. In these works, the most metaphoric *and* the most literal understanding of bibliographic apparatuses can be seen to underwrite the logic of their content as well as their form. As with the books by Antin and Spoerri, these books also take their place in a long literary tradition of incorporating paratextual apparatuses. Within poetry, for instance, one might think of the "Explanatory Notes" that appear, without indicators, on the lower half of the pages in Jack Spicer's "Homage to Creeley," or the similar diptych layout of Bruce Andrew's "Getting Ready to Have Been Frightened."[50] Tyrone Williams's "Cold Calls" renders its appropriated, collaged, and recontextualized language *as* a citational system of footnotes hugging the bottom of the page and referencing endnotes; presented directly in this way, without introduction or the advance notice of contextualizing hypotaxis, these poems are indeed cold calls in the marketing sense, but they are also "called out" in the publishing sense of the phrase, and "cold" in the senses of the "detached" and "objective" citation that they echo.[51] For one final example, from a quite different perspective, the beautiful *Cronicas Brazileiras* by Critical Art Ensemble, an intricately structured book that backs its accordion-fold pages with *Annotations to Cronicas Brazileiras* in a play of sheet against page.[52] Unlike any of these works, however, the books I want to examine in this chapter all explicitly thematize their structure.

The first of these books is Jennifer Martenson's *Xq28*[1]. Taking its eponymic title from the chromosomal location of the purported "gay gene," the work addresses the competing implications of developmental models of nature and nurture, or "the ratio of biological to cultural factors," as she puts it. The book balances genetic codes with codes of conduct, the code of the X chromosome with the codex.[53] A 20-page stapled booklet, *Xq28*[1]'s thirteen interior pages are left largely blank, although they are set with headers and footers as if awaiting their contents. At the bottom of those pages a dozen cross-indexed footnotes appear to follow not so much from some erased text as from the superscript "[1]" of the book's title, and to then proceed from numbered note to numbered note as footnotes within footnotes direct the reader forward and backward through the bottom of the chapbook's pages, looping back on themselves with humorous and telling coincidence. Both "probability" and "real," for instance, point to the same explanatory note: "Usually defined as statistically significant obedience to faulty premises . . ."[54] Likewise, following "the long, twisted strands" of Arachne's "spidery . . . threads" through the maze of notes leads readers from both "banned" and "normal development" to the same definition: "this process is known as *indoctrination*"; "women" and "the popular imagination" are similarly both glossed by "a dense, fibrous tissue."[55] Three notes all return to the explanation that "while the spines are relatively durable, the information stored within can be banned at any time": the "destruction of . . . manuscripts"; "perfectly average figures of speech"; and narratives banded "tightly with strands of DNA."[56] As with the genetic code in question, a limited vocabulary of building blocks proliferates into a variety of mutating sequences, folding back on itself in a literal replication. Moreover, the self-sustaining notes continue to function in a book that has, allegorically, questioned reproduction.

Recognizing how "numerous experiments have demonstrated that narratives have the ability to bond tightly," Martenson's sentences graft idiomatic phrases so that different themes and registers are spliced in a sort of intellectual surrealism.[57] Best of all, her ear is attuned to fortuitous found phrases such as "to reside on the very tip of the long arm of the X chromosome," in which the "long arm of the law" and the "tip of the tongue" recombine.[58] In this way, $Xq28^1$ bears a (family) resemblance to Rosmarie Waldrop's deft recasting of Wittgensteinian propositions in books such as *The Reproduction of Profiles* and *Lawn of the Excluded Middle*.[59] Like those works, $Xq28^1$ hinges on its carefully modulated handling of *tone*, a subject wittily and obliquely invoked in the phrase "experts have long advised regular exercise of subtle forms of sexual dimorphism lest the muscle grow flaccid and lose its definition."[60] With such sentences, Martenson reminds the reader of the powerful "side effects of perfectly average figures of speech," and as in the *Topographie anecdotée* her investigation of the metaphoric force of even the most descriptive, objectively nominalist language of science exploits the tension between the footnote's two traditional rhetorical roles.[61]

Moreover, that tension between metaphoric and literal language is replicated by the very form of her artist's book, which plays on the dynamic between the fact of its physical structure and that structure's metaphoric associations. The absent text in the body of Martenson's book recalls the absence of female subjects in the original studies of the so-called gay gene, an omission wryly noted in the very first note: "If, as Wittig says, lesbians are not women, it [*sc.* the failure to seek for a genetic basis for lesbianism] may have as much to do with the fact that no one knows exactly which population to study."[62] Similarly, the typographically marginal position of the notes speaks to what one reviewer has termed "the long-standing argument regarding the marginalization of women in the study of gay culture."[63] Encouraging shifts of style and voice, footnotes further foreground questions of expressive identity as they speak, quite literally, from the margin: always partially excluded from the central text and always subaltern.[64] Indeed, because footnotes establish "a spacing that assigns hierarchical relationships" and "relationships of authority," their hieratic form has proven especially well suited to books that thematize issues of social injustice and psychological trauma.[65] The recurrent motifs of slavery and political agency in Antin's *Meditations*, for example, is not unrelated to the dynamics of his book's form, just as the literal and metaphoric senses of the "repressed" motivates the psychological connotations of the notes in *Xq28*[1]. But there has always been an ambivalence about the role of the footnote and its place below the text, and footnotes can be either subservient or subversive, with "the power to undermine or uphold."[66] At the same time, as we saw with Nick Thurston's *Reading the Remove of Literature*, footnotes are always permitted to speak, to speak back, and to have the last word; even in their traditionally subservient role they can both assert and challenge authority, so that as Toril Moi has argued, we might in fact recognize "the marginal and the heterogeneous as that which can subvert the central structures of traditional linguistics."[67]

With the same dynamic negotiation between the symbolic and the spatial, the layout of Martenson's book, with the blank expanse of its pages emphasized by the division line of the footnotes and the running header, is all to the point in the context of the debate over the relative influence of genetics and environment, gross anatomy and social psychology. In part, those pages are simply mirroring the notes' references to textual lacunae and the destruction of manuscripts, but above the pseudoscientific mockery of claims for innate nature that runs through the notes, they also stand as magisterially silent reminders of both the Enlightenment empiricists' figure for the power of cultural formation and Sigmund Freud's figure for the mechanism of the modern psyche's perceptual apparatus: the *tabula rasa* and the mystic writing pad. We speak to each other through books, but books speak also to, and about, themselves.

When the prefigured "tip of the tongue" returns explicitly in the third note of Martenson's book and is recalled in a later reference to the ancient "oral form" of "female sexuality," its inclusion in a book of glosses enacts the etymological pun we saw in Antin's first "Separation." Nor is such paronomasia limited to the "gloss"; $Xq28^1$ repeatedly conflates the body of the text and the human with precisely such ambivalences.[68] The ninth note, for example, states that "while the spines are relatively durable, the information stored within can be banned at any time," suggesting both the codex and the cortex. Indeed, the meninges, that protective layering of our "relatively durable" spines, is evoked in other notes by the phrases "dense, fibrous tissue" and "spidery mass," which echo the standard anatomical definitions of the "dura mater" and the "arachnoid membrane" respectively.[69] Moreover, in a book directly focused on gender roles and stereotypes of the nuclear family, the translation of the Latin *dura mater* (hard mother) and its meningeal counterpart the *pia mater* (soft mother) fold Martenson's anatomical lexicon back into her discussion of the stakes of science's social construction with a neat and chilling logic.

One precedent for the striking format of $Xq28^1$ can be found in Gérard Wajcman's 1986 novel *L'interdit*, in which the text is quite literally "interdit" (forbidden, suspended, but also spoken between), with only fragmentary notes remaining below the blank pages of what appears to have once been a narrative biography.[70] The unnamed protagonist of that biography suffers from both amnesia and an inexplicable silence so palpable it is taken as an act in itself.[71] The mostly blank pages of the book thus reenact his "trou" (gap in memory), which stares back at the reader like "une orbite vide [a vacant eye socket]."[72] Or perhaps, the notes hint, the erased pages have actually somehow resulted from his mute attempt to "effacer dans une parole, d'effacer cette monstrueuse vacuité dans laquelle il sombrait dès que les regards se détournaient ou que cessaient les mots [rub out speech, to wear down that monstrous emptiness into which he would sink as soon as those around him diverted their gaze or stopped speaking]" because "les mots l'ont déserté [words had deserted him]."[73] Over the course of the book, its blank pages inevitably appear to illustrate a range of themes mentioned in the notes—ruins, withheld secrets, sins of omission, the attentive search for evidence, and so on—and they remind the reader of the supposed illegibilities of their putative source, which the implied editor has catalogued in the notes with a scholarly punctiliousness: "Tout un passage qui s'intercalait ici a été rayé et demeure illisible. *En marge*: 'Contradictoire' [An entire passage which is inserted here has been struck out and remains illegible. *In the margin*: 'contradictory']"; "Il avait d'abord écrit: 'fugitive,' puis l'a rayé [He had first written 'fugitive,' then crossed it out]."[74]

L'interdit could well be read as a graphic attempt to present the sense of any "vie, avec ses ombres, ses dessous, ses jardins secrets, ses énigmes [life, with all its shadows, its hidden faces, its secret gardens, its mysteries]," but its increasingly theological narrative focuses more narrowly on the difficulty of narrating an event so traumatic that one must say "J'ai perdu la possibilité d'habiter dans un monde de paroles [I have lost the possibility of living in a world of spoken language]."[75] Specifically, the novel suggests one solution to the problem of representing the Shoah; this book of blank pages proposes a book of blank pages as a nonrepresentative monument in which, paradoxically, the "rôle des morts [catalogue of the dead]" would be written invisibly and read off in silence, so that "la page elle-même [the page itself]" would be not so much "derrière ces noms [behind the names]" as the "fond blanc de la page que chaque nom qui s'inscrit montre en silence [white substrate of the page, which each name written upon it indicates in silence]."[76]

Intervening in the poststructural debate on presence and absence in language, the blank pages of *L'interdit* negotiate between the spoken and the written until the transience of speech comes to be confused with the blank page from which its record seems to have evaporated, at the same time that the physicality of writing comes to be aligned with the bodily presence associated with the breath of speech. Like the narrator's strange silence, the pages of *L'interdit* appear as willful acts, and part of the import of its footnoted format is to frame the blank of the page as a space not merely with the *potential* to bear writing but as a place still numinously immanent with the writing it had once borne and seems to carry, ghostly, still. The protagonist contrasts writing with "la parole elle-même qu'il regarde comme un mensonge qui vient brouiller son absence véritable [speech itself, which he understands as a lie that comes to be confused with its sheer absence]."[77] In contrast with writing, he

> oppose continuellement à la parole qui ne ferait que rappeler le souvenir des mots, tendre leur image, leur apparence dans un souffle. Parler lui semble une affaire de mémoire, on se souvient des mots, tandis qu'écrire, au contraire, ce serait prendre leur chair à bras-le-corps, une chair silencieuse, morte, une matière.[78]

> [continually opposes the spoken word, which can only recall the memory of words, can only hold out their image, their semblance in a sigh.

Speaking seemed to him to be a matter of memory: we remember words, while with writing, in contrast, we grapple bodily with their flesh: their silent, dead, matter.]

That mingling of our bodies with the body of the text is further figured by Wajcman as the form of the book itself, which rethinks the grounding of corporeal identity in terms of a negative ontology. At various points, *L'interdit* equates the codex with the biographical narrative of a life, and with memory in general:

Les archives de la mémoire ressemblent à ces livres de l'Extrême-Orient qu'on lit à rebours et dont les feuillets peu à peu s'oblitèrent et se décolorent à mesure qu'on s'enfonce à travers les niveaux multipliés jusqu'au titre à jamais illisible.[79]

[The archives of memory are like those Asian books which one reads backwards, and in which the pages are canceled bit by bit and faded to the extent that one penetrates through the multiple levels all the way to the forever unreadable title.]

Moreover, the conflation of the codexical and biological body is made explicit in *L'interdit*, which grounds that metaphor in both the theological mysticism of its narration and the literal structure of its pages. The key to the logic of its form is the concept of a textual prosthesis; the novel pivots on a note near the middle of the book: "Sans doute involontairement (mais pas tout à fait par hasard) on retrouve ici la pensée kabbaliste d'un corps dont la chair même serait faite de lettres [No doubt involuntarily (but not quite entirely by chance) one finds here the kabbalistic concept of a body, the very flesh of which would be made of letters]."[80] By the end of *L'interdit* this conflation is so complete that an allusion to Shakespeare's "livre de chair" hangs indeterminately between its two possible denotations: both a pound of flesh, but also, always equally, a book of flesh.[81]

Ranged at the bottom of otherwise blank pages, the amputated references in these books line the back wall of the page like stacks of artificial limbs: legs with feet that note (in the archaic sense of the contraction "I know not") and arms with fingers pointing stiffly into space. Even without the kabbalistic concept of a body made of letters, footnotes are the prostheses of the textual argument, and in the case of $Xq28^1$ and *L'interdit* the absent textual body comes to be defined and structured by its appendages and supports so that the core of these books is like the body of Edgar Allan Poe's Brevet Brigadier General John A. B. C. Smith. The corporealization of the text precedes these books, of course, as the lexicon of paratexts suggests: the *foot*note and the index (with its etymological origins in the forefinger). However, even without that anatomical terminology, the footnote would be related to the body by its deictic, indexical nature. Like the set of nondescriptive signs that defines the grammatical index, the functioning of the paratextual indices—including not only notes but also the table of contents, the index, and the bibliography—requires a spatial and physical context. For the writer, that context is what relates the footnote to the spatial and material logic of collage; the footnote, as Hugh Kenner suggests, "is a step in the direction of discontinuity: of organizing blocks of discourse simultaneously in space rather than consecutively in time."[82] But the same is true for readers as well. In the acts of reading provoked by the paratextual index, not only are the spatial coordinates of the page and the volume of the volume evoked, but the reader's body is put into motion: the eye moves, the head tilts, the hands and fingers work the pages, the arms and torso shift as the book is handled and manipulated. Drawing on Maurice Merleau-Ponty's dynamic *schéma corporeal* (bodily field), William F. Hanks has made a similar point in grammatical terms:

> In acts of deictic reference, speakers integrate schematic with local knowledge. It is critical to an understanding of deixis to recall that even very "local" elements of context, such as a speaker's own corporeal experience and perceptual field, are susceptible of schematization.[83]

Or, in short: a relational predicate is necessary for a full analysis of the indexical phrase.

Jenny Boully's *The Body*, another book with the layout of $Xq28^1$ and *L'interdit*, itself figures its formal structure of notes without referents in the terms of an explicitly linguistic context. Not only does the book mask the identity of its characters with the pseudonymic conventions of a *roman à clef*, but dramatic irony is one of its recurrent themes, with examples, explicit mentions, and the incorporation of what appears to be a definition from a handbook of literary terms.[84] But the reader soon realizes that irony would have been a theme regardless of these passages; the notes refer to a context that the reader cannot know, and material is quoted without citation so that "we are unable to determine whether the exact wording has a source."[85] Moreover, the ironic nature of the notes in this text are *mise en abîme*: footnotes speak in a dramatic aside, commenting knowingly beyond the purview of the body text. As its title underscores, *The Body* once again literalizes the metaphoric printing term of the "body" of the text, but whereas Martenson's pamphlet eliminates that body in order to sharply question the physiological grounding of social categories and Wajcman's solemn philosophical novel displays its pages in an act of mourning, Boully's *Body* more casually figures the eroticized human body of an absent lover.

Understanding that the withheld referent can be an adventure as well as a frustration, and picking up on the idiomatic sense in which information is "buried" in footnotes, Boully further narrativizes this structure of knowing and unknowing with a thematic thread of hidden treasure. Commingling with scenes of questing and seeking, the buried treasure metamorphoses from a bodily scene of two sisters who "became brave and decided to look for our holes" to a cartographic scene in which the mapmaker "purposely placed the 'X' in an obvious, yet incorrect location"—perhaps at 62° 17' 20", 19° 2' 40", an angle that cryptically appears, with the addition "37.29 N, 79.52 W" in one of the later notes.[86] Following a good enough hunch, the reader may recognize the first point not as "a mere entry of latitude and longitude" but as the location of the buried treasure in Robert Louis Stevenson's *Treasure Island*, and with a sufficiently detailed map the reader can discover that the second set indicates a location just outside of Roanoke, Virginia—Hollins College, to be precise, where Boully happened to be an undergraduate. But which set is the "obvious, yet incorrect location" and which is the treasure?[87] Is the first merely another clue to the fact that the unattributed quotation in the subsequent note is itself in fact from the fourth chapter of Stevenson's novel?

> I felt in his pockets, one after another. A few small coins, a thimble, and some thread and big needles, a piece of pigtail tobacco bitten away at the end, his gully with the cracked handle, a pocket compass, and a tinder box, were all that they contained, and I began to despair.[88]

The passage colors the following note, a nostalgic vignette about a girl and her father, but it may well also prompt the reader to recall a similar catalogue from one of Boully's much earlier notes:

In the prop room, she found the collection of butterflies, fossilized bones, her mother's hairbrush, bedsheets, belonging to a past love, an earring she lost when she was ten, and a box containing letters which X would compose to her until her death.[89]

Is the return of that pseudonymous "X" marking the spot of discovered treasure—a treasure that in this case might in fact be the hidden associative logic of the book's cryptic notes (as when the inclusion of quotations from Stevenson in footnotes recalls the title of his 1892 book *A Footnote to History*)—or is it merely another purposely misplaced lead? In the end, the answers to such questions remain indeterminate, but provoking and permitting their asking may be the ultimate point; Boully confesses in her notes that she desires "someone who would pay close attention to details."[90] Someone, in other words, who *notes*.

With its story of buried treasure and its reverse references to an absent origin, *The Body* reenacts the paleographic history of the footnote's evolution. Not only is the original first footnote lost to us, but the ancestor of the footnote itself was used to indicate an absence; the asterisk, one of the critical marks that survived the translation from manuscript to print, appears in early printed books "with its original function, to mark omissions."[91] And I can note, without giving anything away, that at the root of the index is a mystery as well.

As with works comprised solely of footnotes to absent texts, indices have been written to nonexistent books, as if taking the notorious late-sixteenth-century Catholic indices—the *Index librorum prohibitorum* (List of banned books) and the *Index expurgatorius* (List of expurgated books)—to literal extremes. James Ballard's "The Index," for instance, purports to be "the index to the unpublished and perhaps suppressed autobiography" of one Henry Rhodes Hamilton.[92] Part science fiction, part picaresque, and part burlesque, its alphabetized entries gesture provocatively, giving glimpses of their source's unattainable body. Hamilton seems to have been a cross between Forrest Gump, Albert Schweitzer, and Don Juan. Working backward from the index, one can infer the range of his midcentury exploits;

he is on the beach on D-Day and then with Churchill at Yalta, pilots Chiang Kai-shek, is invited to Dallas by Lee Harvey Oswald, warns John F. Kennedy of danger, receives the confidences of Einstein, Fermi, Gandhi, and so on. At the same time, the index is incongruously filled with the names of modernist writers and entertainment celebrities, suggestions of sexual escapades and messianic religious cults, the recurrence of psychiatric illness, and a single hilarious reference to Burl Ives. Part of the fun of such a work—and this is true of all the other works under consideration here—comes from trying, like one of the participants in Simon Morris's *Interpretation* project, to imaginatively reconstruct the single coherent narrative to which the fragmented references might possibly obtain. The success of such works depends, accordingly, on their ability to both invite and ultimately resist integration, as individual entries gesture toward a text into which they cannot be entirely absorbed. Ballard's "Index" trades on such incongruity, but it also betrays a linear narrative that emerges from the list of headwords despite their alphabetization, which would lead one to expect a random distribution of references. As the entries progress alphabetically, they also tend to reference sequentially higher page numbers in the missing autobiography, which in turn appears to be organized chronologically; a more or less linear narrative thus develops in "The Index," with its denouement following the takeover of the United Nations by Hamilton's cult and his call for world war against both the United States and the USSR (all revealed in section "U"). The final sections record his arrest by Special Branch and incarceration on the Isle of Wight (section "W") and the government's denial of a Star Chamber trial or any knowledge of Hamilton's whereabouts (section "Y"). The final entry suggests the ominous finale from which the document itself was born:

> Zielinski, Bronislaw, suggests autobiography to HRH, 742; commissioned to prepare index, 748; warns of suppression threats, 751; disappears, 761.

This narrative of threatened indictment, betrayal, and discovery, aligns the form and content of Ballard's "Index," returning the work to the etymology of its title, which derives directly from *indicare* (to disclose, divulge, betray, give away, inform on).

With its simultaneously ominous and comic narrative, science-fiction-tinged surrealism, and alphabetic structure, "The Index" anticipates both

Peter Greenaway's novel *The Falls* and Charles Finlay's short story "Footnotes."[93] The former, based on the author's eponymous film, purports to be one of the volumes in a biographical dictionary, recording the victims of a "violent unknown event." The volume at hand contains those victims whose last names begin with the letters "Fall—" and Greenaway slyly works in the meanings of all of the English words beginning with "fall—," as well as thematizing questions of probability and chance so that the story and its structure coincide with the German *Fallen*. With a bewildering multiplication of possibilities that loop reflexively from entry to entry with a nested structure of films within films, Greenaway constructs a mirrored hallway of fictions and conspiracies engulfing one another so that every ground is at risk of being found to be illusory, and every apparent illusion is documented in detached, objective, scientific reports.

Finlay's work, which takes the form of bibliographic citations presented as footnotes, is set about fifteen years in the future and is also the fragment of an account of some lethal unknown event. As in *The Falls*, victim lists are compiled, concerns over fictitious symptoms surface, and "anecdotal" evidence suggests that the event has linguistic consequences.[94] From the notes one can adduce that the disaster was some sort of biological epidemic, apparently with neurological symptoms and perhaps with evolutionary consequences. However, even after a congressional "Investigating Committee" was convened, private emails requisitioned, and "special reports" issued, details about the event "remain difficult to explain," debates continue about "what really happened," and key witnesses disappear without being questioned.[95] As with Ballard's "Index," the genre of suspense and the form of the index coincide in these works, with their references to undivulged stories of indictment and disclosure.

Footnotes, indices, and bibliographies are not the only paratextual conventions of the book, and all such devices can be exploited for conceptual ends. The traces of social and institutional contexts in details of bibliography, for example, is the subject of Terrence Gower and Mónica de la Torre's wickedly parodic artist's book *Appendices, Illustrations & Notes*, which recreates ephemera to nonexistent books and exhibitions.[96] Their book teases out the cynical social networks and intellectual laziness disguised by the clichés and formulae of genres such as the review, the jacket blurb, and the author bio. Paul Fournel's novel *Banlieue* (Suburbia) gives a similar treatment to a single book. Although once again the body of the text is entirely absent, leaving the centers of the book's small pages blank, *Banlieue* is replete with a sur-plus of bibliographic accoutrements: those elements that entail what Hugh Kenner has called "the book as book" and the mechanization of its codexi-cal discourse.[97] The book includes legal disclaimers and a copyright notice, epigraphs, margins, headers and numbered footers, a dedication, table of contents, index, errata, title page, allographic foreword and afterword, intro-ductory notes from both the publisher and the author, a pedagogic supple-ment, back-cover blurbs, a bio-line—even a suggested price and universal product code. And, of course, footnotes. The edition advertises that it has been specially annotated by the Inspector of the Ministry of Education "for use in schools." Once again, the metaphoric valence of a hieratic biblio-graphic structure suggests a context for the content of the book. The cartog-raphy of *Banlieue* maps the suburbs of the book: those outlying regions of the page (the footer and header) and the neighboring sprawl of commercial puff and commentary that crop up around the supposedly central text like bed-room communities of the mind—*arrondissements* just beyond the *terrain vague* at the edges of the book's recognizable sections.

Part of *Banlieue*'s conceit, moreover, is that its form withholds a tit-illating content, hints of which the reader can only deduce. Suggesting a tale of class violence somewhere between Alan Sillitoe's "The Loneliness of the Long-Distance Runner" and Anthony Burgess's *A Clockwork Orange*, the supplementary texts imply that the "provocation" of the "incendiary" main story—a narrative containing prurient scenes of "violent eroticism"—was originally a "scandal" that led to legal action.[98] The reader's imagination, of course, creates more lurid scenes than even the most explicit prose Fournel could have furnished, and this fiction of a scandalous story contrasts, or perhaps ironically underscores, the metaphoric implications of the book's form. At the same time, the pages of the chapbook are to some extent simply the punch line to a conceptual one-liner. Despite the hints of racy content, and the book's opening disclaimer that "ce texte est une pure fiction. Toute ressemblance avec des personnages existant ou ayant existé serait fortuite et indépendante de la volonté de l'auteur [this is a work of pure fiction. Any resemblance to persons living or dead is coincidental and unintentional on the part of the author]," the vacant pages of the fictional (fiction) *Subur-bia* are indeed an accurate account of one of the stereotypical accounts of postwar "suburbia": a social space that is vacuous, uniform, and devoid of narrative interest.

Despite its publication under the imprint of the OuLiPo, *Banlieue* is not a procedural text, and its constraints, such as they are, do not present much of a hindrance. Indeed, one should keep in mind that the formal conceit of all of these works permits the comfort of the *impression* of a system, while freeing the author from the demands of actually having to adhere to a rigorous formal structure. This dynamic explains, in part, why most of the works considered here tend toward a rather sloppy, indulgent eclecticism; without the constraints of a genuinely fixed form, these works clothe what is at heart freely composed expressive writing in the guise of disjunction and artifice, or the post-Cagean procedures of ready-made found material sifted together by the rule of happy chance. These works, in short, are the disorderly simulation of an ordered form of disorder. From this perspective, one might compare the visual poetics of these books to structurally similar but conceptually very different works such as Vito Acconci's "Drop (on the side, over the side)" or Alastair Johnston's *Heath's German Dictionary*, both of which present much more austere versions of the evacuated page by appropriating and erasing reference books, leaving only the framing elements of typographic layout.[99] In contrast, the annotating impulse evident in Spoerri's *Topographie* and mimed by the other works I have considered illustrates the way in which *gloss* is suspended, depending: in its excess, threatening glossolalia, and always, with an omission, the threat of loss. That loss is the exclusionary rule proven by these works, and which this chapter has tried, futilely, to avoid for itself: "Any interpretation," as Ludwig Wittgenstein enumerated this first law of the paratext, "still hangs in the air along with what it interprets, and cannot give it any support."[100]

4 HARD CORE / SOFT FOCUS ███████████████

model n[1]. A structural design. . . . Something which resembles something else. . . . *Euphem.*: a person employed to pose nude.

o tijolo chegando . . . é o projeto da casa,
é o corpo na cama.

[a brick arriving . . . it's the plan of a house;
it's a body in bed.]

—ANTONIO CARLOS JOBIM

Hard-core: dedicated; determined; devoted; die-hard; faithful; fundamental; intractable; intransigent; loyal; obstinate; resolute; resolved; rigid; serious; single-minded; staunch; steadfast; stubborn; uncompromising; unmeasured; unwavering; unyielding.

In its earliest uses, "hard-core" is linked to poverty. The *Oxford English Dictionary* disperses its archaeology of "hard core" between two volumes, depending on whether the phrase coalesced around one or the other of its constituent terms. The dictionary records the first two print occurrences of the phrase associated with the word "hard":

1936. *Nature* 12 Sept. 441/2 Possibly 200,000 would be practically unemployable on any ordinary basis—the 'hard core' as it is called.

1940. *Economist* 3 Feb. 193/2 One of the more encouraging developments of the last few months is a substantial loosening of what has hitherto been regarded as the 'hard core' of unemployment.

The connection survives in contemporary dictionary definitions: "*hard-core* poverty" and "the *hard-core* unemployed," as *Webster's* illustrates the usage of the word.

A poverty of discrimination conflates the unemployed and the over-employed, those subject to hard labor, with too much ease. That idiomatic association of "hard core" with both unemployment and unskilled labor may have originated in the use of the phrase to refer to material that circulated between those on the narrow threshold of employment and destitution. At the very least, the idiomatic usage would have been strengthened by the phrase's even earlier appearance in passages describing the *mise-en-scène* of the most abject labor. The *Oxford English Dictionary* records the first occurrences of the phrase as it appears associated with the word "core":

1851. MAYHEW *Lond. Labour* II. 281/1 'Hard-dirt', or 'hard-core', consisting of the refuse bricks, chimney-pots . . . broken bottles . . . oyster-shells, &c., which form part of the contents of the dustman's cart.

1851. MAYHEW *Lond. Labour* II. 317 (Hoppe). The phrase 'hard-core' seems strictly to mean all such refuse matter as will admit of being used as the foundation of roads, buildings, etc.

1880. S. M. PALMER in *Macm. Mag.* XLI. 252 Rough bits of all kinds of material, which goes by the name of 'Hard Core'.

"Hard core," it turns out, was originally an architectural term, a way of designating the minute material particulars of construction.

Noise into information, incidental detritus repurposed as the fundamental building blocks of construction, the cast-off or eccentric reimagined as foundational—the "hard core," in this sense, was understood to be both essential and foreign, both heterogeneous and constitutive, extraneous and incorporated.

"Hard core," in fact, also carried a hint of incorporation in the sense of embodiment. As a conglomerate of partially absorbed material too tough to be entirely pulverized or completely assimilated, "hard core" emphasizes the toughness of the core. But there is some redundancy in that emphasis because "core" already connotes hardness and resistance: "an irreducible nucleus or residuum" as the *OED* puts it; a kernel of indigestible or impervious matter; an allergen paradoxically lodged at the defining heart of some thing's essence. Among its metaphorical usages, that recalcitrance already associated with "core" refigured the corporeal body in terms of toleration. Later in the *OED* definition for the word "core" we find:

fig. Something that sticks in one's throat, that one cannot swallow or get over; also, in allusion to ADAM'S APPLE (sense 2), said of part of the original corrupt nature still remaining. *Obs.*

c1460 *Play Sacram.* 757 Lord I haue offendyd the in many a sundry vyse That styckyth at my hart as hard as a core.

Despite the serious (hard-core) and faithful (hard-core) source, the punning play is explicit in the text of the medieval mystery drama: "heart" = *cor* (Latin).

The play, moreover, enacts the very logic of the hard core that it mentions in its *mea culpa* of sundry vice. In its moment of summation, at the very core of the drama, the non-cycle spectacle *The Coxton Play of the Sacrament*—the most crudely sensational, offensively anti-Semitic, and bluntly literal specimen of the genre to survive—momentarily falters, an error or illegibility sticking in its throat. Early editions of the manuscript corrupt the opening line of an antiphon for the Office of Corpus Christi, reading: "Now folow me, all and summe, / And all tho that bene here, both more and lesse, / Thys holy song, *O Sacrum Dominum*, / Lett us syng all with grett swetnesse." The slip, simultaneously, is both theologically more correct and liturgically less correct. Rather than "to the Lord" (*Dominum*), the call should instead be "to the meal" (*conuiuium*). The intended call is to the *sacrum conuiuium* (holy feast).

Lat. acc. *sacer* (sacred): *sacrum, sacram, sacrum.*

The "sacrum," in medical terms, is the heart of the pelvis, the solid core supporting and protecting the genitals. The origins of the word are a mystery. Some have conjectured an association with resurrection (either because it was believed that the bone had to be intact for the body to rise or because it was an attribute of Osiris); others have speculated that the bone was offered in animal sacrifices.[1] More likely, the Latin name too literally mistranslates the Greek term for the same anatomical structure: *hieron osteon*. Although the phrase does indeed mean "holy" or "sacred bone" in Greek, it equally denotes a "strong bone." In the ancient world, the *hieron* was thought to be the one part of the body that was indestructible, because it was so exceedingly hard.

"Corrupt," "offendyd," "vyse"—"hard-core" also connotes, of course, the most explicit and graphic pornography, a kind of sexual literalism, the opposite of both mystery and play.

Pornography, however hard, is a category of aesthetics. Not surprisingly, "hard-core," in that sense—as a rhetoric, or style—also bears traces of the asymmetrical social relations of labor and poverty. Class is clearly legible in the genre's history, from its stock of narrative fantasies to the demographics of both its workers and viewers. More recently, the history of hard-core pornography has merged with the history of the Internet and associated technologies for recording, distributing, and storing data—all of which may be blurring some of the class-based demarcations of its genres. The exact statistics for online pornography are hard to come by, and have been fiercely contested, but one effect of the Internet has been to redistribute the architecture of hard-core, dispersing it from the easily identifiable and containable brick and cinderblock (hardcore) buildings relegated to economically marked social spaces: town peripheries, not yet gentrified transitional zones, and impoverished urban neighborhoods. The attempts to regulate Internet pornography might be seen as an extension of zoning laws, as municipal planning pursued by other means.

The legal term for hard-core is "obscenity." The word *obscene* is also of uncertain origin, with folk etymologies suggesting mysteries played out behind the curtained stage (*ob scena*) of an exhibitionist erotic drama. Less glamorously, the word most likely comes from the Latin *cænum*, meaning "mud," "filth," "detritus"—the very world, that is, of the Victorian dustmen, rag and bone shop keepers, and bricoleur construction workers documented by Mayhew among the "hungry and naked . . . poorest of the poor; after they have had one meal, they do not know how to get another." "Very hungry," their fare at best is often only a "meal composed of nothing else" but "bread and grease."

Latin *cæna*: common late empire corruption of *cena* (meal).

Meal, n.[2] Forms: OE-eME *mæl*, OE (Anglian)-ME *mel*, eME *mæle*, ME *mal, malle*.[2]

What constitutes the obscene, in legal terms, is as uncertain and obscure as the word's curtained etymology. After screening Louis Malle's 1958 film *Les Amants*, in which the attentive viewer can catch a quick glimpse of one of Jeanne Moreau's breasts, United States Supreme Court Justice Potter Stewart famously averred:

> I have reached the conclusion, which I think is confirmed at least by negative implication in the Court's decisions since Roth and Alberts, that under the First and Fourteenth Amendments criminal laws in this area are constitutionally limited to hard-core pornography. I shall not

today attempt further to define the kinds of material I understand to be embraced within that shorthand description; and perhaps I could never succeed in intelligibly doing so. But I know it when I see it, and the motion picture involved in this case is not that.[3]

But what if, instead, we saw it only when we knew it?

Blur is one of the unrealized projects proposed by John McDowall as part of his "Traces and Translations" collaborative series of book works. The book would present a sequence of rectangular monochromes—chromatic bricks assembled in a series of muted and autumnal fields of ochers and rusts, unexceptional browns and greys.

As the afterword reveals, each swatch is in fact the average pixel color of a source image; or, to be precise, of two different source images, both of which happen to blur to the same mathematical mean. For every set of matches, one of those paired images was drawn from a work of high art, the other from online pornography. In each monochrome, the building blocks of the image are indistinguishable within the image itself; each block of color is an extrapolation of its constituent pixels, a projection of its miniature parts. Similarly, in the single uniform color of each page the two very different source images of the monochrome are indistinguishable. With its origin thus undecidable, each brick is a perfectly ambivalent index, pointing with equal insistence to each of the abstracted sources. Looking at the reconstituted model of a rendered hue, the reader, in some sense, is always looking at both.

Moreover, beyond the chance match of their digital averages, the final set of image pairs was arrived at by a further aleatory filter. An Internet search engine was used to find the pornographic images, following the rule that the webpage containing the image must match at least two of the descriptive terms from the page that contained the art image. So, for example, a search for "El Lissitzky" and "constructivism" returned a page featuring the video *El Paso Wrecking Corp*, which was listed under the distributor's category "Construction Men." The image of the VHS box, as it happened, had precisely the same average pixel color as the Lissitzky painting that had initiated the search. The chance of such a match is exceedingly low, since it requires that both images average to exactly corresponding values in all three of the separated color channels (red, green, and blue), each of which is set to a tonal value between 0 and 255. There are, accordingly, over 16 million possible combinations.

These chromatic bricks thus propose a set of formal equivalents, putting pressure on the prepositional terms in our grammatical models for visual experience. How do we understand the genitive preposition to function when we say we are looking at a picture *of* something? That it belongs to that thing, or that it is a logical consequence of its nature (a projection, or model)? When we look at one of the blurred images, can we still say that we are looking at a picture *of* a VHS box? (The question is only postponed, but not answered, by specifying that we are looking at a picture of a picture of a picture of construction workers printed on a VHS box.) Were it partially blurred, in the intentional soft focus of glamour photos and sentimental erotica or simply by the chance spherical aberrations of a defective lens, we would surely still say so. But when distortion achieves a total obfuscation? Do we see it only when we know it? Only when it is recognizable?

For that matter, what are we looking *at* when we view any work, distorted or not, and whether we think of it as art or pornography? Which facets do we privilege and which do we suppress? And when we compare or equate images, what is their relation? Can we see the connections and dissimilarities among ink and paper and chemical sizers, pigments and oils and stretched canvas, light polarized between layers of liquid crystal and plastic—or do we only see it when we know it?

Blur is not, of course, the only work to ask these questions in this way, and if each of its pages points to two sources, it also points to a number of procedurally equivalent works as well. In a 1989 series, for instance, Sherrie Levine took copies of four masterpieces of modern art, sectored the images into large blocks, and averaged the colors of each sector, reproducing the results in a series of prints. Her colophon description of the portfolio reads:

> The twelve-color woodblock prints in the portfolio *Meltdown* have been created by Sherrie Levine by entering images, after Duchamp, Monet, Kirchner, and Mondrian into a computer scanner that spatially quantizes and transforms these images into the minimum number of pixels, thus determining each of the colors in the four prints.[4]

As woodblocks, Levine's prints gesture back to the craft prehistory of her modernist sources; at the same time, they push those sources proleptically forward to the postwar monochromes of Yves Klein, Olivier Mosset, and Brice Marden.

More recently, the Belgian artist Pieter Vermeersch has also worked with the average colors of other artists' paintings, entering into dialogue with particular collections (such as that of the Museum Dhondt-Dhaenens in 2004) or intervening in the category of painting itself (as at the Prague Biennial in 2005). Like Levine's series, his color fields of averaged values gesture ironically and nostalgically to the long history of modernism: the grid; abstraction; monochromaticism; readymade appropriation; institutional critique. Working in a smaller rectangular format than Levine's squares, however, he also plays with the porous border between art and decoration that so troubled modernism. Vermeersch's 2004 installation *Average Colors III*, for example, is something like a domesticated version of Gerhard Richter's mock-monumental *Achtzehn Farben* (1966/1992): an 8-by-15-foot arrangement of eighteen large monochrome plates painted according to industrial paint sample cards. Where Richter magnifies the paint sample, projecting it to the scale of the modern art museum wall, Vermeersch reduces museum holdings to a series of small uniform swatches that look like nothing so much as paint samples from an interior decorating store.

The same impulse to statistically analyze and average can also be seen in recent video. Cory Arcangel's 2005 edition of Dennis Hopper's film *Colors*, for instance, plays single lines of resolution from the film one at a time, with each individual pixel extended vertically to fill the screen. The soundtrack continues to play, but the image now appears like a thin and agitated version of the old broadcast test pattern sent scrolling in a scanning curtain of pulsating colors. Distended at this level of resolve, the film's new running time is over a month.

Like a rotated still from Arcangel's *Colors*, Jason Salavon's 2000 digital print *The Top Grossing Film of All Time 1 x 1* displays James Cameron's film *Titanic*, frame by frame, with each frame blurred to its averaged pixel color. Salavon has restaged that work with different sources (parsing *MTV's 10 Greatest Music Videos of All Time*, for example), but he has also accumulated rather than dilated found photographs, layering them in transparent tiers of statistical blur.

Averaging and amalgamating images, these projects accrue and compile generic poses into ghostly demographic blurs: one hundred family photos of *Special Moments* (2004), arranged by subject—newlyweds, graduates, kids with Santa, et cetera; *Every Playboy Centerfold* (2002), by decade; school pictures for *The Class of 1988* and *The Class of 1967* (both 1998) culled from Fort Worth yearbooks; and listings of *Homes for Sale* (2002), a spectral send-up of the architectural unconscious in conceptual art (from Dan Graham's 1967 *Homes for America* to Hans Haacke's *Shapolsky et al. Manhattan Real Estate Holdings, A Real-Time Social System, as of May 1, 1971* (1971) and the ongoing industrial taxonomies of Bernd and Hilla Becher). Not incidental to these real estate investigations, Samuel Yates's quest to determine the average color of the city of Palo Alto provides one final example of chromogrammatic aggregation. In 2001, Yates set out to photograph each municipally partitioned lot and assess the average chromatic values. Furthermore, like Richter and Vermeersch, Yates summons the quotidian commercial material of paint in an art context; he has promised that the result will be marketed as a shade of exterior latex house paint. It turns out to be an unappetizing shade of green: the color of day-old split-pea soup.

The interface of software such as Adobe Photoshop permitted (and no doubt suggested) all of these works, but they evince the more general logic of the digital world. The formal equivalents of digital media—in which all content in any genre is translated into binary code—opens the way to the logic of the blur: the chance equations of dissimilar works and the unexpected 'pataphysical swerve between different semiotic systems that happen to share certain signifiers even if they organize them with entirely different semantic codes. One of the long-standing problems with thinking of visual works in structural terms has been that they seemed to lack discrete units of double articulation; the formal structure of a painting, for instance, had nothing neatly analogous to Western writing's system of alphabetic letters and words. Digital imaging and analysis, however, provide the necessary unit of articulation: the pixel.

> *Pixel* (etymologically from *pictures element*): the smallest discrete sample of an image; a unit of measuring resolution (the hard core, recall, is both unmeasured and resolved).

Craze: (aphetic from *acrase*, from French *écraser* [to break] or Old Norse *krasa* [to shiver, to crash]): "to break (a thing) so that the parts still remain contiguous," as in a pixelated screen or image.[5]

Pixilated (etymologically from *pixie*): "crazed," in the sense of losing one's mind, of being led irrationally astray.[6]

Every tactic is another tactic's strategy.

5 THE DATIVE OF FORM

There will be time, there will be time

To prepare a face to meet the faces that you meet

—T. S. ELIOT

Out of the portfolio, off of the wall, printed in the bound format of the book—a method of storing and displaying photographs since the days of the daguerreotype—the photograph enters into a series and a dialectic, a dialogue. The two facing pages of the "opening" (the term for the double page spread of an open codex) pair each photograph with text, or another image, or simply the blankness that is their back, their opposite, and the history of their origin—the sheets from which their ghostly materializations first took form. The page here is always *against* the image (in both senses of the word). The codex also establishes a fixed series—a precession of images in orbit around the spine—a sequence of phases as the pages are turned. "Phase," from φάσις (appearance, specifically the successive phases of the moon), is not only a stage of development (in which "developing" is a key phrase from photography), but it is also always related, via φάιυω (to show, to make appear), to the phantasm, the apparition, a spectral shine.

That shine has illuminated photography from its earliest days in the mid-nineteenth century, when the *medium* of the process was taken literally. Manipulated, the auras and ectoplasmic emanations of spirits were coded and recorded as blurred apparitions, bodies floating free in ambiguous space, facial emanations. As Tom Gunning has emphasized with respect to those spirit photographs:

> *Phantasmatic* denotes images that oscillate between visibility and invisibility, presence and absence, materiality and immateriality, often using transparency or some other manipulation of visual appearance to express this paradoxical ontological status.[1]

Vladimír Židlický's "manipulation of visual appearance"—his insistence on the medium of photography, with its range of technical effects, its mechanisms of illusions, and its uncanny registration of multiple phases (the moment of the shutter, the moment of development, of the fix and then the print: "There will be time, there will be time," as Eliot reminds)—registers the same paradoxes. Moreover, they are often haunted by the buried history of photography's otherworldly imaginings: faces obscured by the shine of fluid and billowing white emanations; bodies transfixed by what seem to be electrical currents in spark across the ether; the blur of aura. The spirit photograph is an allegory of photography itself, of the fantasies of embodiment that would make the body both ghostly and material, transparent and palpable, light and matter both transient and fixed. One might productively read Židlický's fantasies in the same light.

facere: Latin: to make, to do

The two stages of Židlický's practice—the camerawork and then the subsequent encounter with the surfaces of the negative—emphasize the photograph as a made thing, an artifact or artifice, rather than a merely found or recorded scene (the long debate over whether a photograph could be copyrighted hinged on precisely this distinction).[2] Moreover, the facture of these works, in the sense of both their process and their distinctive surface textures, facilitates a qualified effect. Exploiting an essential facet of photography, necessarily inherent in the medium and yet seeming to erase or violate the very ground of the photographic image, Židlický's additions or modifications constitute a kind of dangerous supplement, a surfeit of signs (where "surfeit" [sur + facere] is not just the overdone, or a transgression, but what is done or made on the surface of something). And here is where his photographs of faceless models allegorize an important lesson about media. The etymology of the word "substrate" (sub [underneath] + stratum [something spread]) suggests a certain orientation, and a phenomenological presumption, as well as a hierarchy of parts and a metaphysics of surface and depth. But surfaces are not necessarily exteriors. Modes of representation tend to call on illusions of depth, figuring surfaces as facades or screens for projection, but from the perspective of media, surfaces are not coverings; they are simply thresholds at which materials abut. Moreover, as we have seen in the previous chapter, the apparent hierarchies of substrate and inscription inevitably deconstruct: substrates permit inscription, to be sure, but inscription—by the very same token—is what permits materials to become substrates.

This dynamic manifests itself in the ambivalence with which the materialities of media both obviate and motivate representational narratives in Židlický's photographs. On the one hand, the disfiguring violence of his obscuring manipulations disrupts their illusionistic scenes and hence any absorptive, untroubled, voyeuristic contemplation of the bodies imaged in the prints, even as those remaining fragments of pictured images are what permit us to see the postproduction manipulations of the photograph as non-representational in the first place. On the other hand, in the context of those represented figures, the irruptions of nonfigural inscriptions are opened to their own narrativation. Only in the context of the naked bodies do the marks signify as a certain kind of defacement, with all the social and psychological resonance of misogynist sexual violence. The nonfigural disruptions of the represented scene, unexpectedly, produce a narrative in which they are them-selves thematized. Furthermore, that context of nude, exposed bodies evokes and colors the technical photographic process of "exposure"—a machinic, chemical, material event allegorized by the images of naked bodies. The blinding white of overexposure and the blinded black of underexposure char-acterize Židlický's interventions into the space of the photographed scene. On the other hand, and at the very same time, the irruptions of figural images opens those nonfigural inscriptions to their own narrative diegesis. The areas of erasure—blackened out or blenched—are also recollections of the scene of photographic processing: the requisite blackness of the darkroom and the white of the undeveloped paper. For all that they disrupt representation, the erasures in Židlický's photographs figure an originary, and necessary, moment *of* figuration. They are both prior to the developed image that they create and also figural representations in their own right, evoking glimpses of the scene of development witnessed by the photographer.[3]

The thin material stratum of the page thus opens onto a scenic depth even as its disruption of the figured three-dimensionality of the image reveals, beneath its apparent depth, only a relation between unranked materials, each equally necessary to the final form of the whole: salts and cellulose and halides and molecules of water with a number of other chemicals in precise and bonded proportions. By aligning the substrate with the surface, contradicting its ostensible placement below (*sub*) the image and combining the gestural marking of erasure with the representational marking of the image, Židlický's photographs both enact and figure the depthlessness of a figure without a face, without any primary or outward aspect, and they illustrate the false faciality of depth. These photographs, in short, collapse the logic of their substrate with the thematics of their disfigurations. As Susan Stewart argues:

> If the face reveals a depth and profundity which the body itself is not capable of, it is because the eyes and to some degree the mouth are openings onto fathomlessness. Behind the appearance of eyes and mouth lies the interior stripped of appearances.[4]

Surfaces open onto surfaces; what seems to be an interior reveals only a radicalized exteriority, no longer tenable without the appearance—the apparition, the shading—that seemed to lend it depth. Lying behind the face that used to be represented by the photograph, the interior here spreads out (*sternere*, the origin of *stratum*), but it also dissembles, as the prevaricating word in Stewart's sentence unintentionally divulges: the interior lies. At first glance, the postproduction gestures of Židlický's light-writing (photo-graphy), manipulation (work with the hands) and effacement (*ex* + *facies*) would, *prima facie*, seem to obviate the "first face" of the camera's mechanical registration. But those erasures, so often obscuring or obliterating the face of a female model, also serve to return a face to that work. *To face* denotes "to trim, adorn, deck, furnish . . . to cover the surface either wholly or partially"[5]—precisely what Židlický's obliterating markings achieve. Reading further in the dictionary reveals that "to face," moreover, is both to lie and to meet openly. A "visage," similarly, denotes both an authentic face and a dissemblance, a portrait or reproduction. Faced defacements, many of these photographs are thus visages without visages. Simultaneously shown and veiled, manifest and occult, accurate records and optical illusions, these traces return us to the figure of photography itself. They embody the fundamental paradox of the ghost, which must be both palpably formed in order for us to register its existence and yet must also, by definition, remain—if it is to persist as a specter—immaterial.[6] The *Random House Unabridged Dictionary*, not coincidentally, illustrates the word "faceless" with the phrase "a faceless apparition."

Without features (from Anglo-Fr. *feture,* from O.Fr. *faiture* "fashion, shape, form," from L. *facura* "a formation," from *facere*), the ghostly, ghastly effaced figures in these photographs are depersonalized: prosopopoeia of the disenfranchised and anonymous; individual persons objectified as their bodies are fetishized (Port. *feitiço*, "charm, sorcery" from *feitiço* "made by art, artificial, skillfully contrived," from O.Fr. *faitis*, L. *facticius*, from *facere*).[7] In the bookselling trade, *facetiae* is a synonym for pornography. But viewers, while they ought rightly to be fazed by the sexual politics of the recurrent defacements in Židlický's oeuvre, should not be too quick to make facile judgments about ethics.

<h2>visage</h2>

The second volume of Gilles Deleuze and Félix Guattari's *Capitalisme et schizophrénie* offers an account of faciality (*visagéité*), which a full analysis of Židlický's portraits cannot avoid confronting. The face, in their account, is not simply a body part (not all particular human faces are "facial," in their sense of the word); rather, the face is their term for a schema, a kind of chanceled histogram, that both describes and constrains the relationships it diagrams.[8] "Le visage est une organisation spatiale structurée [The face is a structured spatial organization]"[9] that operates like an imperial landscape—a territory that has been surveyed and gridded for a particular purpose—so that when any individual human face becomes facial it wraps the head in the way a cartographic projection covers the spherical surface of a globe, with all its homogenizing distortions and perspectival prejudices and ulterior political designs on experience ("Le visage est une carte, même s'il s'applique et s'enroule sur un volume [The face is a map, even when it applies itself to, and wraps itself around, a volume]").[10] Faciality, accordingly, is the process of taxonomizing otherwise discrete terms into immobile stratifications; it arranges binary pairs into hierarchies of surface and depth. It operates as an interface, structuring data.[11] In a more specific instance, the face, for Deleuze and Guattari, is the authoritarian system of convention by which an inscription can function as a signifier. Or, to phrase it in the terms of my concerns here: the face is the system by which sheer materials are legible as media. Consequently, a head without a face comes to be aligned with the "corps sans organes [body without organs]," taking part in Deleuze and Guattari's critiques of interiority and communicative models of representation.[12] Their goal is "d'échapper au visage, défaire le visage [to escape the face, to dismantle the face]," because "le visage a un grand avenir, à condition d'être détruit, défait. En route vers l'asignifiant, vers l'asubjectif [the face has a great future, but only if it is destroyed, dismantled. On the road to the asignifying and asubjective]."[13] Facelessness is a situation where it becomes possible "to bring out the presences beneath representation, beyond representation" and where form no longer lords over matter.[14]

Some of the metaphors used by Deleuze and Guattari—light and shadows, film and camera—point to photography, and in a related set of essays Deleuze describes the painting of Francis Bacon in terms that could equally describe Židlický's practice. Opposing figuration, which is bound with narrative, scenes of depth, and perspectival landscape (faces, in other words), Deleuze privileges correlations and cohabitations: "la corrélation de deux secteurs sur un même plan également proche [the correlation of two sectors on a single plane, equally close]."[15] From his position, "la peinture . . . a comme deux voies possibles pour échapper au figuratif: vers la forme pure, par abstraction; ou bien vers le pur figural, par extraction ou isolation [painting has two possible paths for escaping the figurative: toward pure form, through abstraction, or toward the pure figural, through extraction or isolation]."[16] Deleuze clearly favors the latter, exemplified by Bacon's paintings, which triangulate abstraction and figuration: removing figures from narrative spaces, disrupting illusion, thwarting representation, and yet retaining enough of the figure that the intensity and force of all the nonrepresentational markings can be read. Through this figural strategy, "nettoyage et traits comme procédés [techniques of local scrubbing and asignifying traits]," "de produire des opérations de brouillage, des phénomènes de flou, des effets d'éloignement ou d'évanouissement [operations of brushing, the phenomena of blurriness, the effects of elongation and fading are produced]," until "le visage a perdu sa forme en subissant les opérations de nettoyage et de brossage qui le désorganisent et font surgir à sa place une tête [the face has lost its form by being subjected to the techniques of rubbing and brushing that disorganize it and make a head emerge in its place]."[17]

Where Deleuze and Guattari saw the face as an all-encompassing conceptual map, a comprehensive system that permits the compass of binary terms, Emmanuel Levinas saw the face as offering an irreducible other that cannot be comfortably mapped onto any totalizing, comprehensive system capable of fathoming both the self and the other. Thus, to be required to envisage a face, according to Levinas, is a question of ethics (indeed, it is a question of the ethics *of* ethics).[18] To face the other in Levinas's terms is to recognize the infinity of the other's alterity—a recognition that can only be made in generosity:

Car la présence en face d'un visage, mon orientation vers Autrui ne peut perdre l'avidité du regard qu'en se muant en générosité, incapable d'aborder l'autre les mains vides. Cette relation par dessus les choses désormais possiblement communes, c'est-à-dire susceptibles d'être dites—est la relation du discours. La manière dont se présente l'Autre, dépassant *l'idée de l'Autre en moi*, nous l'appelons, en effet, Visage. Cette *façon* ne consiste pas à figurer comme thème sous mon regard; à s'étaler comme un ensemble de qualités formant une image. Le Visage d' Autrui détruit à tout moment, et déborde l'image plastique qu'il me laisse.[19]

[For the presence before the face, my orientation toward the Other can lose the avidity of the gaze only by turning into generosity, incapable of approaching the other with empty hands. This relationship, established over the things hereafter possibly common, that is, susceptible of being said, is the relationship of discourse. The way in which the other presents himself, exceeding the idea of the other in me, we here name *face*. This mode does not consist in figuring as a theme under my gaze, in spreading itself forth as a set of qualities forming an image. The face of the Other at each moment destroys and overflows the plastic image it leaves me.]

Vision, for Levinas—even the sympathetic vision of recognition or identification—is a violent mode of relating to the other, because it "immobilizes its object as its theme."[20] Moreover, the ethics of the face is predicated on an unethical, primal urge:

L'épiphanie du visage suscite cette possibilité de mesurer l'infini de la tentation du meurtre, non pas seulement comme une tentation de destruction totale, mais comme impossibilité—purement éthique—de cette tentation et tentative.[21]

[The epiphany of the face brings forth the possibility of gauging the infinity of the temptation to murder, not only as a temptation to total destruction, but also as the purely ethical impossibility of this temptation and attempt.]

The place of the visage in Židlický's photographs—suspended by gestures that destroy and overflow the face—holds open the possibility of invoking the radical alterity of the other: of what must be answered *to*, and in front of which one must answer *for*, as an interlocutor. The case of the effaced, here, is the ethics of the encounter; "pour le dire en termes de grammaire, autrui n'apparaît pas au nominatif, mais au vocatif [to put it in grammatical terms, the other does not appear in the nominative, but in the vocative]" or "in the dative."[22] To answer *to*, to answer *for*—that is to say, to face (up to).

These works are thus duplicitous, though not insincere. Like the optical illusion of the reversible two-faced figure famously demonstrating the constructive aspects of perception—either a beautiful young woman or an ugly old woman, depending on whether you can see her face (and depending on your stock of cultural stereotypes)—these photographs are a litmus test for the viewer: do you see a psychological symptom or a philosophical allegory? Sexual politics or ethical propositions? A freedom from the responsibility of confrontation or a confrontation with the responsibility of envisioning? Recognition or the unrecognizable? The answers are what each of us must face, must stand up to without shrinking from recognizing some unwelcome fact, before images that constitute both the interpellating vocative—the judicial, juridical voice that calls on us to "appear at a summons" (*apparere*), like an apparition—and the generous, sacrificing dative of form.

6 TANGENT

Wovon man nicht sprechen kann, darüber muß man schweigen.

[Whereof one cannot speak, thereof one must keep silent.]

—LUDWIG WITTGENSTEIN

Salut . . . à n'importe ce qui valut

Le blanc souci de notre toile.

[A toast . . . to whatever was worthy

of the white attention of our canvas.]

—STÉPHANE MALLARMÉ

The genre of translation—regardless of the tone of what is being translated—has long been understood to be elegy. Compared to the original, any translation, or so the assumption goes, is never as good; it doesn't live up; it serves, abjectly, as a regrettably necessary crutch; it merely substitutes for the real thing—paling, predictably, in comparison. Doomed from the start, translations are thought to fail, by definition, to achieve the status of art. The "poetry," as Robert Frost famously defined it, is "what gets lost in translation."[1] Untrustworthy (it always loses the poetry), translation's fidelity is suspect from the beginning; a good translation is said to be "faithful"— faint praise for an exception that throws the basic character of all the other translations into doubt. Though just how faithful even the best translation can be is called into question by conventional wisdom: *traduttore, tradittore*, as the appositive Italian adage goes ("a translator," to translate, "is a traitor"). Translation, from these perspectives, is an event of inevitable loss and betrayal.

Even theoretically, the task of translation, traditionally understood, runs up against the limits of its paradoxical demands. On the one hand, the best translation is thought to be the one that most closely approaches the original; but that original is precisely what needs to be replaced by something different, something "other," since its own difference—its foreignness—is what called for translation to begin with. And so it cannot, on the other hand, ever be approached too closely. This paradox explains, perhaps, part of why failure seems to define translation from the start; translation must avoid the perfection that would cause it to cease to be recognizable *as* a translation. In this way, the problem of translation thus replicates the problem of mimesis: the most realistic artwork would not be identifiable as an artwork. Some inframince difference must assert itself, even as that difference is what translation seeks to eliminate.

But what if the fundamental assumptions behind these received ideas were wrong, or could at least be imagined otherwise? What if the foreignness of another language—the inescapable material particularities and unavoidable formal peculiarities of its systems and signifiers—instead permitted and encouraged translation? Those estrangements and reconciliations, the inassimilabilities and accommodations of translation, would also be one way to understand the networked materials we recognize as media, both old and new. And finally, what if those translations were recognized as equals to, or even improvements over, the original—precisely to the extent that they departed from it?

Take, for example, the triptych of 72-by-36-inch abutted canvases that form part of Robert Rauschenberg's 1951 series *White Paintings*, each with an application of commercial white house paint laid in smoothly unexpressive and uninflected roller strokes. The material specifics of that deskilled production are significant; in comparison with an artist's brush, the roller produces a more uniform surface, spreading the viscous liquid in even swaths and evoking the mechanized production of industrial or nonartistic practice: more hardware store than atelier, more impersonal servomechanism than signature painterly craft (anyone, Rauschenberg insisted, could apply the paint, and the work's conservation instructions include directives for repainting as the luster dulls). Those associations orient the canvases toward the future, aligning them with the techniques of minimalism and conceptual art as they would develop over the 1960s. But from another perspective, the *White Paintings* also seem to look back; within a narrative history of painting they appear as variations on the monochrome, taking their place as one manifestation or instantiation of an idea that a number of artists translated into material form throughout the twentieth century.[2] In particular, Rauschenberg's paintings add a hue to Aleksandr Rodchenko's 1921 trio of *Pure Colors: Red, Yellow, Blue*. Rodchenko's monochromes were themselves a despiritualized, desemanticized, and distilled response to Kazimir Malevich's starkly reduced palette of geometric forms from the teens, most notably his signature *Black Quadrilateral*, the beautiful *Red Quadrilateral*, and the iconic *White on White*. Replaying Rodchenko's conceptual endgame gambit, Rauschenberg's paintings seem to offer a comparable rebuke to his own contemporaries, casting a quiet cold stare at the psychologized gestures and overwrought facture of abstract expressionism and offering an unheeded warning to the imminent egomaniacal spiritualism of Yves Klein's self-branded blue.

From a slightly different perspective, however, the *White Paintings* can be seen less in terms of the monochrome tradition of twentieth-century painting and more as an attempt to translate part of the essential logic of another medium into the realm of painting. John Cage had seen the *White Paintings* early on, incorporating some of them into his legendary *Theater Piece No. 1* at Black Mountain College in 1952, and he astutely proclaimed them to be "airports for shadows and dust." The metaphor seems at first to be whimsical, or neosurrealist, but the "airport" makes perfectly logical sense as soon as one recognizes the implied punning between *plain*, the word that describes the unadorned monochrome and its ordinary paint, and the two different senses of *plane*: the aeroplanes of dust and the flat surface of the picture plane at the heart of Clement Greenberg's contemporaneous arguments about the essential nature of painting.[3] As "airports," the canvases are plain planes for planes. Rauschenberg himself took Cage's cue, explaining in retrospect: "They had to do with shadows and the projection of things in a room onto the blank whiteness."[4] As Branden Joseph has shown, these accounts echo Moholy-Nagy's description of Malevich's *White on White*: "The plain white surface, which constituted an ideal plane for kinetic light and shadow effects which, originating in the surroundings, would fall upon it. In this way, Malevich's picture represented a miniature cinema screen."[5]

The canvas, in these accounts, is a site of "projection" and intense visual focus; "why," Cage wondered, "did I not look at them with my magnifying glass?"[6] Rauschenberg's paintings give a concrete form to Moholy-Nagy's argument, and they translate the concept of the cinematic screen to the medium of paint. However, rather than presenting an obstacle to translation—something foreign or inherently removed from the concept of cinema—the material specificity at the heart of Rauschenberg's medium is in fact integral to the realization of that concept. In contrast to brushes or pallet knives or other modes of application, the operation of the roller on the paint encourages the effects of both shadow and dust, pulling the pigment toward the surface and emphasizing the adhesive tack and brilliant reflectance of its oil-glossed sheen.[7] Understood as translations of abstract ideas into formal particulars, Rauschenberg's white canvases can be seen as essentially cinematic paintings.

Translated from film to canvas to criticism to canvas, the concept of that blank canvas was then retranslated to music by Cage himself. The transformation of the cinematic into music resulted in a silent movie, to be sure, but it also produced a radical version of *cinéma pour les oreilles* and a preambient, protean "music for airports."[8] In 1952, after several years of contemplating similar compositions, Cage scored his landmark *4'33"*: empty staves partitioned into three movements adding up to the eponymous duration. What was tacit in that score became, in a later version, explicitly *"tacet"*: the musical directive for an instrument to refrain from playing during an entire movement.[9] Acknowledging the *White Paintings* as a precedent, Cage actively encouraged the comparison; his headnote to an essay on Rauschenberg in *Silence* abruptly announces: "To Whom It May Concern: / the white paintings came / first; my silent piece / came later."[10] In part, Cage's insight regarding the *White Paintings* derived from his ability to see through the concept to its material form, heeding Ludwig Wittgenstein's injunction: "Don't think, but look!"[11] Looking with a careful attention *at* the work, rather than *through* the work to its ostensible message, paradoxically permitted Cage to catch a better glimpse of the ideas at play in the *White Paintings*. If nothing else, Cage's patient watch revealed the surface of Rauschenberg's painted canvases to be far from purely or merely achromatic, but rather maculate, with minute *taches*.

Those small staining marks, moreover, are what permitted the series of inspired translations to continue. With a dumb literalism and obstinate misreading, Pierre Huyghe took a second look at the idea of the blank surface with the very magnifying glass Cage had forgotten to use the first time around. Reduplicating the move Cage himself had made when he transferred Rauschenberg's idea from painting to music, Huyghe translated Cage's own statement from the visual to the aural, from magnification to amplification. Using computer software to analyze a recording of one performance of Cage's ostensibly silent piece, Huyghe magnified the scale of the digital print, scrutinizing the enlarged surface of *4'33"* and dilating the ambient noises. Those distended patterns were then rescored using traditional staff paper and made newly audible as the 1997 flute sonata *Partition du silence*. At once understated and exaggerated, the sonata distorts only insofar as it pursues an impeccable fidelity, remaining faithful to the point of outrageous distortion. Huyghe's minutely detailed score, moreover, once again locates the most abstract limits of a concept in the most idiosyncratic material details of an object. The same paradox, wherein a seemingly abstract concept originates in the minute particulars of material media, obtains for Cage's *4'33"* as well. In a work that marks a key initial stage in Cage's thinking about the relation of silence and music (if not in fact an earlier version of *4'33"* itself), Cage proposed "a piece of uninterrupted silence" to be sold to the Muzak corporation; "it will be 3 or 4½ minutes long—these being the standard lengths of 'canned' music, and its title will be 'Silent Prayer.'"[12] The given commercial lengths ("3 or 4½ minutes long") recalls Marcel Duchamp's readymades, and the measurements of his *Trois stoppages étalons* (three uniform commercial mending stitches), which he described as "hasard en conserve [canned chance]"; yet that readymade duration was itself derived, as Kyle Gann importantly notes, from the media specificity of the Muzak network in the 1940s:

> Muzak was broadcast from 78 rpm vinyl records; a ten-inch disc held about three minutes of music and a twelve-inch disc about four and a half, thus accounting for the potential timings of the *Silent Prayer* Cage wanted to write. The length of *4'33"* itself owes something to the technology of the twelve-inch 78 rpm record.[13]

One of the most abstractly conceptual works in the history of music, as it turns out, derives from the molecular specifics of polyvinyl acetate—the parameters of its density and brittleness—and the speed of small rotary motors.[14]

Although Huyghe's *Partition* takes *4'33"* as its source, its procedure recalls a different Cage composition altogether. To produce his 1952 *Music for Piano*, Cage scrutinized an ostensibly blank sheet of manuscript paper for its inevitable imperfections and irregularities, looking for chromatic variations or loci of acute topographic relief, and then marking a predetermined number of the miniscule blemishes and bumps in ink. Overlaying a standard musical staff onto the field of the page then transformed that stochastic dispersal of dots into the related pitches of Western musical notation. Cage thus translated from the genre of drawing to the genre of music.[15] Following Cage's cue, *4'33"* has long been taken as the obvious intertext for the *White Paintings*, but I want to suggest that *Music for Piano*, dating from the same year, is just as closely related. Where *4'33"* restages the *White Paintings* as a musical performance—translating its neutral lack of intentional marking as a neutral absence of intentional sounds—*Music for Piano* takes as its starting point the lesson learned from the *White Paintings*: that seen from the right perspective, at the right distance, any ostensibly blank surface is in fact inconsistent, variable, fluctuant, and marked. Cage may have restaged the conceptual proposition of the *White Paintings* with his so-called silent piece, but with *Music for Piano* he restages his own activity in front of those canvases, noting—and ultimately notating—the small specks on a manuscript sheet just as he had noticed the flecks of dust on Rauschenberg's painting. *Music for Piano* treats the substrate of the score as if it were a monochrome white painting, to be gazed at with the intensity of a modern art connoisseur. Even more importantly, Cage recognizes that changes in social context produce changes in media. In more mundane circumstances, a dusty surface or an irregular page might provoke housecleaning or recycling, but under the sign of modernist abstraction, the facture of an otherwise blank surface generates visual interest, and under the sign of the musical score it generates pitch values. Each mote and macula may be a concrete particular, unique to the moment of viewing or the particular sheet of paper at hand, but how we understand those marks (indeed, whether or not we even register them in the first place) depends on the conceptual milieu in which they occur. Cage's writing in *Music for Piano* hinges on the placement of the dots on the page, just as the placement of the page itself within a musical environment (rather than framed on the wall, or stacked on an office desk) determines its meaning. *Milieux*—etymologically from the Latin *medius* and *locus*, a literal "middle ground"—can be accurately translated as *media*.

Cage ends his description of Rauschenberg's work with the sentence: "Not ideas, but facts."[16] "Say it," as William Carlos Williams wrote: "no ideas but in things" ("Even a long-playing record is a thing," as Cage pointedly said in his lecture on the idea of nothingness).[17] The fact of things might seem impervious to abstractions, an irreducible residuum that by definition remains unmovably itself; this may be the case, but we only recognize those things when they are enmeshed in the coordinates of some abstract theoretical map. Moreover, the dynamics of translation reveals the degree to which the conceptual relies on the material, the abstract relies on the minute particular, and the proclaimed "dematerialization of the art object" relies on a new appreciation of the materiality of substrates. Although these terms would seem to be mutually exclusive, defined in part through their opposition to one another, it turns out, again and again, that one term reveals itself as the essential core of the other, as requisite rather than banished. The closer one approaches the conceptual, the more palpably the material presses forward, even as that material, in turn, is only appreciable within a conceptual framework. Furthermore, this dynamic opens a situation in which the corporeal materiality of facts—the mere fact of a fact—can (in fact) be the idea: "What interests me is a *contact*," Rauschenberg explained with regard to the

White Paintings, "it is not to express a message."[18] "Translation must in large measure refrain from wanting to communicate something," Walter Benjamin argued accordingly, explaining:

> Wie die Tangente den Kreis flüchtig und nur in einem Punkte berührt und wie ihr wohl diese Berührung, nicht aber der Punkt, das Gesetz vorschreibt, nach dem sie weiter ins Unendliche ihre gerade Bahn zieht, so berührt die Übersetzung flüchtig und nur in dem unendlich kleinen Punkte des Sinnes das Original, um nach dem Gesetze der Treue in der Freiheit der Sprachbewegung ihre eigenste Bahn zu verfolgen.[19]

> [Just as a tangent touches a circle lightly and at but one point—establishing, with this touch rather than with the point, the law according to which it is to continue on its straight path to infinity—translation touches the original lightly and only at the infinitely small point of the sense, thereupon pursuing its own course according to the laws of fidelity in the freedom of linguistic flux.]

Benjamin's proposition accounts for the theoretical relation between the *White Paintings* and Cage's compositions *4'33"* and *Music for Piano* as translations. Not as translations that concern themselves with some represented meaning (at least not beyond an "infinitely small point"), but rather as translations that allow the fundamental logics of different media to inhabit one another. Seen in this way, such works are less like fixed objects and more like tactics. Additionally, translating the terms of Benjamin's account of translation "according to the laws of fidelity in the freedom of linguistic flux" permits it to be read as a description of the specific artworks we have been considering. Benjamin figures translation as "die Tangente [a tangent]," a word that derives directly from the Latin *tangere* (to touch) and so is intimately related to the participle *tactus* (touched): the technical musical term for the percussive pulse of repeating beats felt as points in time. Although a cyclic beat suggests the kind of repetitive segmentation that Cage's Bergsonian philosophy might reject in favor of a sense of continuous duration, the works by Cage and Rauschenberg measure time with a dynamic tension between continuous flux and discrete partition. They frame a durational experience of interconnected events, so that while their ultimate lessons are of the continuing flux of the world around us, the events they frame are always experienced as unique singularities: not just in the sense of some particular section of vertical space or some designated four-minutes-and-thirty-three-seconds of time, but in the sense of the particular particulate distribution of dust and ambient shadows on that space at any given moment; the specific ambients pervading any given performance of 4'33".[20] Those singularities are "the point [where] a circle begins and ends," as Rauschenberg initially described his *White Paintings*; or, as Benjamin underscores: the "tangent touches a circle . . . at but one point."[21] They may be unexpressive, but Rauschenberg's canvases and Cage's compositions are always quite *touching*. Moreover, Benjamin emphasizes that the tangent meets the singular point of the circle with a light touch. That is to say: discreet and thoughtful (as one would translate something with "tact"); softly, quietly, with the understated refinement of their tasteful minimalism; "tacet," as a musical description would read (from Latin *tacere*, to be silent). As one version of the tripartite score of Cage's composition reads: "I. Tacet / II. Tacet / III. Tacet." Following the same tack, with an implicit equation of silence and whiteness, the score for James Tenney's 1971 post-Fluxus composition *(night) For Percussion Perhaps, or . . .* reads, in its entirety: "very soft / very long / nearly white." Nearly, but not pure white; quiet, perhaps, but never silent—these are the nuances revealed by Cage's keen faculty of perception, his patient detailed scrutiny—in other words, his *tact*. "Die ungeheure und ursprüngliche Gefahr aller Übersetzung [The enormous danger inherent in all translations]," Benjamin feared, is that "daß die Tore einer so erweiterten und durchwalteten Sprache zufallen und den Übersetzer ins Schweigen schließen [the gates of language thus expanded and modified may slam shut and enclose the translator in silence]."[22]

Then again, Cage might have understood Rauschenberg's "contact" to be a kind of microphone. And Rauschenberg might always have retranslated Cage's composition back to canvas, with a 'pataphysical precision, as a six foot and nine inch extension: four feet and thirty-three inches, exactly. Both works, following Benjamin's argument, would have been true translations. Or, *pace* Frost, poems. Poetry may well be "what gets lost in translation," though that phrase should be understood not in the sense of elegiac ruination or privation, but of absorption and reverie—in the way one might be lost in thought. Which is precisely the way thought can be found in materials, ideas lodged in things.

7 SIGNAL TO NOISE

Je n'aspire qu'au silence.

[I hope only for silence.]

—FÉLIX FÉNÉON

Perhaps after all there is no message.

—JOHN CAGE

1966: The Beatles' last concert. Maria Callas's last concert. The final year of the ONCE Festival. The launch of the Monkees. Four Herb Alpert albums in the top ten. A series of singles from Simon and Garfunkel. The best-selling song in the United States all year: Staff Sergeant Barry Sadler's "Ballad of the Green Berets." There was nothing to listen to.

1966: A blank record might be heard as an elegy for the times, an epitaph, a cenotaph, *un tombeau*.

1966: Nothing to listen to. Not in the sense that there was nothing *worth* listening to: the Beach Boys release their unshakably strange (if not quite listenable) *Pet Sounds*; Frank Zappa debuts with *Freak Out!*; Cornelius Cardew joins AMM; the AACM issues *Sound*; Herbert von Karajan records the first installment of his *Ring* cycle; Miles Davis has his second great quintet in order; the Coltrane quintet is distending "My Favorite Things" to an hour of atonal improvisation; Steve Reich is phasing two tape players slowly out of sync; a mercurial quintet named The Hawks, later known as The Band, is warming up the tubes in their amps. . . . But with Ken Friedman's *Zen for Record* there is really finally nothing to listen to. After all the sheep bleating and bleary psychedelia; Sadler's jingoist snare drums and Zappa's deskilled jingles; Malachi Favors's "little instruments" and Simon Dupree's Big Sound; after Dylan's electric Judas kiss in Manchester and Rashid Ali's steel brushes shredding in Tokyo; after all the easy and difficult listening that year, you could have put on Friedman's disc and listened to nothing.

1966: But we might have guessed it, more or less. The title already dates the work squarely to its cultural moment and the intellectual climate of the postwar counterculture, with its distinctly Americanized understanding of Zen. More specifically, the title points to the pervasive alignment of Zen with Fluxus, that loose group of artists with whom Friedman was then in intimate dialogue. In part, the association between Fluxus and Zen was perhaps both inevitable and coincidental, given the congruous aesthetics of the "event score"—often presented in a haiku-like triplet—and the koan.

Ranging from a single word to a few paratactic sentences, the telegraphic noun phrases of the event score masquerade as imperatives, establishing a series of dynamic contrasts: between everyday vocabulary and the imaginative acts it might provoke; between the condensed language of grammatically contracted forms and the broadly abstract categories named; between the restricted verbal means of the score and the open-ended possibilities for its performance. In short, between minimal gesture and maximal potential; specificity and ambiguity; constraint and permission. "Permission granted," as John Cage was fond of saying, "but not to do whatever you want."[1]

Zen for Record might be thought of as a koan in the form of a phonograph disc: is it a version of the event score, or its performance? (The sound of the blackbird singing, or just after?)

1966: By now, however, Zen was also a quite explicit reference point for Fluxus, following the model of John Cage, who didn't meditate but for decades had mediated Daisetsu Suzuki's teachings of Zen, and who found a "taste of Zen" in anything that exhibited "the admixture of humor, intransigence, and detachment."[2] Nam June Paik, who had a far more contrary and critical understanding of Zen than the sunnily disposed Cage, had entitled a series of works with a formula that Friedman's record echoes: *Zen for Head*, *Zen for Street*, *Zen for TV*, *Zen for Film* . . .

1965: Friedman writes *Zen Is When*, an event score that reads, in its entirety:

A placement.

A fragment of time identified.

Brief choreography.

Which may be the koan, or the answer to the koan, depending on how clearly we hear *Zen for Record* as the performance of this score: the record placed on the phonograph, the needle placed in the groove, the duration measured by the playing time, the jitterbug dance of the needle and the circular sway of the disc.

1966: Another of Friedman's scores, like the contemporaneous *Zen for Record*, puts sound and silence into paradoxical play; the work reads, simply:

The sound of one shoe tapping.

Entitled *Zen Vaudeville*, the poem cleverly collapses form and content, not only suggesting vaudeville's main dance genre ("tap") but also enacting vaudeville's blunt punch-line humor with a slapstick pun. *Zen for Record*, again, makes a fine dance partner for this piece; its putative silence is easily imagined as a recording of "one hand clapping," and its actual sounds are more rhythmic than melodic: a high cymbal vinyl hiss and percussive phonograph pop, the mechanical taps of the turntable's idle.

Indeed, much of the interest of *Zen for Record* emerges precisely from that dialectic between the promise of pure silence and the minute particulars of surface and system noise. Or, in other words, between theory and practice. In the context of its title, the album suggests the Buddhist concept of *shunyata*: the dharmic silence of the fundamental void. But in the context of a turntable, that silence is always unattainable. Indeed, with *Zen for Record* the noises generated by the network itself are all the more pronounced. On the one hand, the expectation of a uniform experience (whatever you imagine the experience of silence to be). On the other hand, the reality of electric hum and mechanical rumble, the disruptions of unforeseen clicks and the startle of occasional popped reports. *Zen for Record* remains unenlightened, in this respect, a bodhisattva heretically proclaiming the illusion of illusion, the fact that we never get beyond the facts. In the context of the contact between two types of carbon—the diamond of the stylus and the chlorinated petroleum of the disc—it insists on the brute resistance of the material, the inescapable weight of even the most finely tuned and precision balanced world.

(But then again, perhaps Friedman's record wasn't ever so far from Zen to begin with. For all the images of emptiness and silence in some meditative void, Zen always had its noises too; beyond the bells and raspy flutes, you never knew when you might be startled with a suddenly shouted "Mu!" or when the crack of bamboo splints would sound the unsuspecting back of some drowsy disciple's skull.)

At the same time, the title may be more mimetic than anything else, and, like *Zen Vaudeville*, an enactment as much as a description. *Zen for Record*: the phrase itself is musical and classically weighted. Unemphatically trochaic, breaking into even feet, each with a short *e* and longer *or*, the words move forward and backward in the mouth, with the consonant *c* and *d* of the second half lending the phonetic sense of an ending, or the invitation to repeat. *Zen for Record*: a damped tapped beat; a soft tic-toc, tic-toc; the needle at the end of play sounding the cardiac shellac with a pulse of diastolic capture and release (a record always returns to the heart [Latin *re* (again) + *cor* (heart)]); centrifugal drift and quick collision; waver and knock; a clock set to thirty-three and one-half revolutions per minute.

Which brings us back to Cage. The point of his infamous 1952 composition *4'33"*, at least according to one of the readings Cage himself encouraged, was not of course the timed "silence" of the musician sitting for four minutes and thirty-three seconds, but rather the audience's realization during the performance that in fact "there is no such thing as silence."[3] Silence is always ideal, and illusory. Silence is a thought experiment, provocative and unverifiable. Although it is almost certainly apocryphal, Cage loved to tell the story of how he supposedly came to realize the fiction of silence while visiting the anechoic chamber of a Harvard laboratory and unexpectedly hearing sounds—a low pumped thump and a high electric whine—in what was advertised as a perfectly soundproof room. When he emerged, perplexed, the technician explained that Cage had heard his own heartbeat and the hum of his nervous system, recording itself recording.[4]

Had Cage played *Zen for Record* he would have had no need to travel to Harvard, or to invent any stories, because its lesson is the same: all inscriptive relays leave a trace of their own configuration. In other words, one can never find a perspective on a message free from the medium of its conveyance, because in the process of transmitting a message the network of recording and playback mechanisms always produce an account of their own instantiation as well. The media are always legible in the message (if not quite, *pace* McLuhan, the message itself). Michel Serres makes the same point when he declares that "noise is part of communication."[5] As does Wolfgang Iser, when he restates one of the basic axioms of information science: "There is always noise in the channel."[6] The same postulate might have been extrapolated from the tenets of Slavic Formalism, which understood poetic language as a language of diminished reference, oriented away from the communicative function and toward its other aspects (context, medium, structure, et cetera).[7] Indeed, *Zen for Record* is a perfect illustration of what the Russian formalists called "звукопись": the noise emitted by the surface texture (фактура) of a work; pure sonic inscription; the essence of "soundwriting" (a *phono-graph*). The strict formalism of an attention to the materiality of the media, regardless of any content, should not be mistaken as apolitical, however; Theodor Adorno extrapolated an entire ideology of musical reception from the "slight, continuous and constant noise" perceptible in the hum of the groove, the static of broadcast radio, and the dust and scratches of a cinematic soundtrack.[8] These a priori conditions of the medium, Adorno wrote, were "a sort of acoustic stripe," branding every mediated performance as a convict in the prison house of amplified sound.[9]

Under the sign of Jan Mukařovský, *Zen for Record* might be heard as an essay in linguistic theory. Under the sign of Serres, it might be heard as the field recording of rats rustling behind the kitchen door. Under the sign of Cage, it might be heard as a compilation album, with several equally good performances of *4'33"* run back to back (listeners with a stopwatch can figure out the interval between each performance). Under the sign of Paik, it might be heard as the soundtrack to *Zen for Film*.

1964: *Zen for Film*. The version I've seen, part of the *Fluxfilm Anthology* compiled by George Maciunas, opens with the title and signature, flashed in rapid blocky letters against a black ground. Otherwise, the work simply consists of a strip of clear 16mm leader. The dynamic is thus precisely the same as in *Zen for Record*. On the one hand, the premise holds out the prospect of a blank screen and the enlightened promise of seeing "nothing." On the other hand, actually screening the film instead brings to light all of the "visual noise" of cinema: any tremor of the projector; the slightest misregistration of image and screen; the barely perceptible blurring of the shutter's flicker; the sympathetic blinks of one's own strained eyes; all the opacities of dust and acetate. Above all, imperfections in the film or errors in optical printing—as well as any subsequent scratches—perform a magnified and animated dance. With an unpredictable foudroyance, like the flare of fleeting phosphenes, they start and twitch across the screen, erupting and disappearing as quickly as they eye can register them.

Zen for Film is sometimes described as an endless loop, sometimes as an hour long, or twenty minutes, often as an even ten. The version included in the *Fluxfilm Anthology* I saw runs to no more than eight. The discrepancies are surprising, because time, in Paik's work, is all to the point, and his film is a precision clockwork. Like *Zen for Record*, with its thirty minutes of long-play, Paik's film measures a certain duration at whatever length (even looped it establishes the duration of the cycle). Both works are thus related to the contemporaneous music of composers such as Cage and Christian Wolff, who were pioneering the use of time brackets in their scores: durational frames within which a variety of unspecified events might take place. The film also measures time in other ways, well beyond the frame of its running length. To begin with, it records the viewer's attention span at both a gross psychological level—how long until you get bored, look away, start to do something else—and a very local physiological level: the time between involuntary blinks or the spasms of the ciliary muscle. Moreover, the material of cinema inscribes time as well. The mechanism of the projector worries and wears the filmstrip, slowly disintegrating the film with each screening. As Paolo Cherchi Usai points out, any particular print has a limited number of runs through the projector—barely more than three hundred—before it must be abandoned as unusable.[10] The viewing of cinema is therefore inextricably intertwined with its slowly timed and inevitable destruction. The Fluxfilm edition of *Zen for Film* is an alarm set for forty hours. Long before the destruction of the print, however, the material of film inscribes time in a way that is particularly noticeable in Paik's work. The equation is simple and direct: the more often the film is screened, the more scratches and creases appear. Noise, in the technical sense, increases over time. The same is true of *Zen for Record*, which we might hear as a kind of audible chronograph, becoming noisier and noisier the more it is played, as scratches accumulate and the stylus slowly textures and widens the smooth groove of the lathe-cut channel, pocking the vinyl and etching miniature filigrees of dust and grit.[11]

Zen for Record thus teaches an important lesson about media. One could argue that Friedman's record and Paik's film are simply two different editions of a single work. Or, if not two formats for one and the same work, then at least that each is closer to the other than to the respective versions that might appear on DVD and CD. Indeed, the relation of *Zen for Record* to something like an imagined *Zen for Compact Disc* is worth considering. The comparison immediately raises a number of questions: would the CD consist of a digital recording of one play-through of a particular copy of *Zen for Record*? Or a PCM data file with all of the binary values set to one of the numbers reserved for null? A disc without any data recorded to it at all? The answers matter, because they decide between the technology's use as an archival preservation of sound (or silence) and its use as a source of sound, between the absence of sound as a cancellation of the disc's ability to record something else and the absence of sound as an indication of pure potential (the formatted but unrecorded CD, like an unpressed phonograph record, could hold any number of possible sounds).

Under the sign of Hegel, *Zen for Record* might be heard as an example of *Aufhebung*: a simultaneous preservation and cancellation.

That distinction between a record of an event and the means by which to record an event, or between the recording of events too small to register and the medium for their recording, brings us back to the issue of time: is the blank disc an index of the past, or an index of the future? In either case, the status of time in our imagined *Zen for Compact Disc* would be substantially different than in *Zen for Record*. One side of a standard compact disc (120 cm resolved at 16 bits and sampled at 44.1 khz per second) holds about seventy-four minutes of music—more than twice the thirty minute limit of a 12-inch microgroove record. Moreover, although compact discs are far from eternal (the foil pits and chips, the film separates, the plastic brittles over time), time does not accrue to compact discs in the same way that it does to phonograph records, and the decay is measured at a very different rate.

Of course many other distinctions between the compact disc and the phonograph might also inflect an attempt to read a work such as *Zen for Record* allegorically, to relate its "form" and "content." Does it matter, for instance, that the CD measures the totality of its potential time without the interruption of changing sides, like the LP (or a sheet of paper)? Or that its data are read outward from the center, rather than spiraling in? Or that its data are discrete rather than continuous? But instead of pursuing such distinctions here, I want to emphasize a more general point about the lessons that Freidman's disc—with its profound affinity to a film and its significant distance from a CD—teaches us about media.

First, it teaches us that "medium" is as unrealizable as "silence." The point becomes clear as soon as you try to locate the medium of *Zen for Record*. You could of course single out the disc of polyvinyl chloride, but to understand it *as a medium*—to make it legible as a medium *as such* and to distinguish it from home siding and credit cards and plumbing pipes and other instances of PVC—already inserts it into a network of material and technical supports that immediately disperse the notion of "medium" across an inextricable aggregate of distributed and differentiated forms: stylus, player, speakers, and all of their composite parts and points of connection (circuits and wiring, electromagnetic coils and regulating discs, foam and flexible membranes and resonant housings). Rosalind Krauss makes a similar point, directly applicable to *Zen for Film*, when she asks: "Is the 'support' of film the celluloid strip, the screen, the splices of the edited footage, the projector's beam of light, the circular reels?"[12] Such complex webs of overlapping technical support, as Krauss argues, fatally complicate any account of a single, pure, essential medium.[13] There are only ever media.

At the same time, as I have tried to demonstrate here, *Zen for Record* makes clear that even the most abstract and cerebral works of conceptual art cannot be separated from those material and technical supports. There is no single medium, to be sure, but media are inescapable. Friedman's record lays bare the structures that other audio works might seek to conceal, but which they can never elude or avoid. This is an important lesson, because after all the talk of the "dematerialization" of the art object in the 1960s, and after the futile challenge made by "idea art" and "information art" to the institutions they opposed, conceptual art has been too often imagined as immaterial (in both senses of the word).[14] *Zen for Record* proves both positions wrong.

Between these poles, *Zen for Record* resonates as ideal desert island listening, as music marooned or gone on holiday: a combination of cold deodorized intellect and the heat of machinic friction, a piece of obsidian sea glass polished from a message-sealing bottle tossed by waves of listed periodic motion and lofted by the wash of surface hiss.

2013: *Zen for Record* is the best album you've always never heard.

8 FURTHER LISTENING

Silence, I discover, is something
you can actually hear.

—HARUKI MURAKAMI

Heard melodies are sweet,

but those unheard are sweeter.

—JOHN KEATS

■ John Cage: *4'33"* (1952). The classic. In three movements. Premiered by David Tudor on piano, although it sounds pretty good even in transcriptions. Not to be confused with either the showier *0'00"* (1962), "to be performed in any way by anyone," "in a situation provided with maximum amplification," or the watered-down *Tacet* (1960), which "may be performed by (any) instrumentalist or combination of instrumentalists and last any length of time." Recommended recordings: following the world premiere recording by Aldo Orvieto on *Da Capo* (IB Office 3, cassette, 1985), try Frank Zappa's acoustic rendition on *A Chance Operation* (Koch 7238, 1993), or Lassigue Bendthaus's electronic version on *Render* (KK Records 115, 1994); the definitive recording of *0'00"* is by Peter Pfister (hat ART CD 2-6070, 1991). An attempt to game an annual UK song competition resulted in David Hilliard's waggish *Cage Against the Machine*, a minor alt-rock version of *We Are the World* with all the self-congratulation but none of the schmaltzy balladeering. The attendant MP3 compilation (Wall of Sound, 2010) includes one track of studio cleaning that sounds more like a revival of a Simone Forti dance piece than a Cage composition, and another documenting a television show played with the mute engaged that sounds more like a Nam June Paik sculpture. The best cut on the album is an addicting remix by Fake Blood (aka Theo Keating) that recalls the phonographic origins of Cage's composition. The other five tracks are inconsequential, and the title track performance of *4'33"* reveals the conductor doesn't take the tempi as marked; it clocks in a full 18 seconds too slow. For greater range and lots of artistic license (well, lots of license at least), check out Roel Meelkop's compilation of nine different performances on *45:18* (Korm Plastics 3005, 2002).[1]

■ Pavel Büchler: *3'34"* (installation, Kunsthalle Bern, 2006). Shrewdly collected silences from the lead-in tracks on ten John Cage albums from Büchler's record collection. These grooves are like the canine musicians in Franz Kafka's 1922 *Forschungen eines hundes*: "Sie redeten nicht, sie sangen nicht, sie schwiegen im allgemeinen fast mit einer großen Verbissenheit, aber aus dem leeren Raum zauberten sie die Musik empor [They did not speak; they did not sing; each of them remained silent—almost concertedly silent—but they conjured music from thin air]."[2] That thin air, as well as the music conjured from it, is what Marcel Duchamp would term "l'inframince [the thinner than thin; literally, 'below the thin']." Duchamp said that *l'inframince* could not be precisely defined but only approached by examples, such as "le bruit ou la musique que fait un pantalon de velours à côtes, comme celui-ci, quand on bouge [the noise or music made by corduroy pants like these rubbing when one moves]"; "Pantalons de velours— / leur sifflotement (dans la) marche par / frottement des 2 jambes est une / séparation infra-mince signalée / par le son [velvet trousers— / their whistling sound (in) walking by / brushing of the 2 legs is an / infrathin separation signaled / by sound]."[3] Kafka's dogs, accordingly, make their own silent music by moving their legs: "Alles war Musik, das Heben und Niedersetzen ihrer Fuße [Everything was music: the lift and lower of their limbs]."[4] In *3'34"* the lifting and lowering of the tone arm conjures the music: a barely audible phonographic hiss, whistling like fur or velvet, above the persistent crackles and the odd reports of needle-hopping pops that return the listener with a jolt to Duchamp's other example of the "séparation infra mince entre le bruit de *détonation* d'un fusil (très proche) et *l'apparition* de la marque de la balle sur la cible [infrathin separation between the detonation noise of a rifle (very close range) and the apparition of the bullet hole in the target]."[5] As this example suggests, the inframince is related, in Duchamp's lexicon, to "retard [delay]"—precisely what the lead-in track is meant to effect—and it is only the slight delay of the tone arm's descent, the inframince moment of deferral between the drop and the playback, that preserves the silence in this project, since the crunchy noise of scratch and wear becomes louder with every spin. Indeed, even the sounds of the original master are an index of how often Büchler listened to his Cage albums; the disc is as much confession, or proof, as concept. And as a concept, it is a nearly perfect gesture, in which even the flaws of deteriorating vinyl provide sonic interest. The only possible improvement to *3'34"* would be an adjustment to the total timing, which is tidily palindromic but not quite there. Had Cage been more sanguine about recordings of his work during the LP era, or Büchler more of a completist, he might have managed three more albums—enough for another 59 seconds of silence. Not to be confused with Conny Blom's more eclectic fusion piece

4:33 Minutes of Stolen Silence, which is built entirely from pauses within recorded compositions of rock, jazz, and classical music. Both works might be performances of one of George Brecht's "Gap Events," which reads, in its entirety: "between two sounds."[6]

Although the resulting track is of negligible musical interest, mashup enthusiasts should note that Matt Wand sampled Büchler's disc for his contribution to *Soundtrack for a Mersey Tunnel* (limited edition CD-R, *hors commerce*, 2008), a tribute album produced by Alan Dunn to honor the Number 433 bus, which travels the Mersey Tunnel between Liverpool and Birkenhead.

■ Alphonse Allais: *Marche funèbre pour les funérailles d'un grand homme sourd* (1897). The great-granddaddy of silent pieces. Allais—something of a cross between Erik Satie, Raymond Roussel, and Joel Stein—is probably best known for pioneering fiction structured on holorhymes, but he was also a composer. Sort of. The first movement of his *Funerary March* is simply nine empty measures, with the tempo marked "lento rigolando [slowly, jesting]."[7] No recording, to date, but a scaled-down version for string quartet was premiered at the FestivalManké (Nice) in 2000, under the direction of Ismaël Robert (who perhaps took a cue from Henry Flynt's 1961 Fluxus score, which reads: "The instructions for this piece are on the other side of this sheet"—the other side being, of course, blank).[8]

■ Stephen Vitiello: *Fear of High Places and Natural Things* (installation, SculptureCenter [Long Island City], 2004). Like a substantially more animated dance mix of Allais's *Marche*, Vitiello's installation at the Long Island City Sculpture Center visualizes sound in a mute choreography. An array of speaker cones hung from above in a semicircle pulse and bulge, deforming with the powerful sounds that they're making. But try as you might—head cocked, ear cupped—you can't hear a thing: the sounds are at such a low frequency they can't be heard by human ears. The huffs and puffs of expended air, however, can actually be felt as the woofers pant with the exertion, dancing on, without a sound, eternally suspended in the *grand jeté* of their aerial ballet.

■ James Whitehead (aka Jliat): *Still Life #5* (Edition . . . 011, 2000). "And perhaps, he thought further, there are several kinds of silence just as there are several kinds of noises?" the protagonist of Joseph Roth's *The Radetzky*

March speculates.[9] Right he was, as Jliat demonstrates with six types of silence, all sounding the same but all empirically different. And potentially damaging to boot. The medium is the message, and in the case of the 16 bit 44.1 khz compact disc the message can in fact have 65,536 types of silence, none of which are the same: different data but all sounding null. In *Still Life*, Whitehead wrote some of those data directly to a PCM file, creating six ten-minute pieces with all of the values in a given track set to the same binary values. As Whitehead explains:

> Pausing the playing of a track will show this to be so, for the data being played is halted and the CD system jumps back to zero—resulting in a click (if the value "playing" was not zero or near to it). Interestingly this click is heard but is not actually on the recording—it physically doesn't exist! It is the interference of the continuous stream of data which causes the sound.

The second track, "Swing" (+16383), is my favorite. Since the CD player translates every one of the continuous set of binary values to DC voltage, playing the disc can actually damage the speaker system coils and electronics in direct-current coupled equipment. Play at your own risk.

■ Ken Friedman: *Zen for Record* (1966). Blank phonograph record in homage to Nam June Paik's *Zen for Film* (1964): a 16 mm film consisting only of clear leader (often claimed to be an hour long, the screening I saw was advertised as 10 minutes, though it clocked in at closer to 8). Not to be confused with Christine Kozlov's *Transparent Film #2* (16 mm) from 1967, or Madison Brookshire's 2007 sound film *Five Times*, an audio update of Ernie Gehr's 1970 *History* ("five rolls of film, unedited, spliced one after the other," as Brookshire describes his version: "The only images and sounds come from the light that reaches the film when it is loaded into and taken out of the camera"). The incidental soundtrack to Paik's film is a lot louder than Friedman's disc. If you get a chance, sit near the projectionist; even after only eight minutes you'll never forget the nervous clack and twitter of the shutter, blinking like a blinded Cyclops in the noonday sun. . . .

■ Christian Marclay: *Record without a Cover* (Recycled Records, 1985; rereleased by Locus Solus in 1999). Issued without a sleeve or cover, and with the stern instruction "Do not store in a protective package," one side of the 12-inch 33 rpm disc contains music made by "manipulated records on multiple turntables recorded 4-track at Plugg New York City March 1985" (as the inscription on the verso of the grooved side reads). Though museums and collectors probably take pretty good care of their copies, the inevitable damage to the unprotected vinyl was intended to increase the nonmusical noises over time, in a collaborative duet between chance inscription and the carefully recorded turntable improvisations. On initial release, the former member of that duo is entirely silent. While the side engraved with written text remains silent, its legibility decreases in an inverse ratio to the audibility of the grooved side's aleatory duet. In contrast, Marclay's sophomore release, *Record without a Groove* (edition of 50; Ecart Editions, 1987), was issued in a swank suede protective package. In mint condition it reportedly sounds a lot like a Coil B-Side.

■ W. Mark Sutherland: *Scratch* (Koffler Gallery, 2002). Piero Manzoni meets Christian Marclay. In a more articulate version of John Berndt's neoist performance at the Berlin Apartment Festival (1986), in which he vandalized a blank record with intentional scratches, Sutherland ruined a perfectly good metal master by scratching the word "scratch" into the plate, from which two hundred phonograph records were pressed. With no recorded sound to guide it, the needle skates across a frozen vinyl lake, tripped up by written ruts in need of resurfacing, as the LP spins to an unpredictably post-bop syncopated set of skips and pops. Recursively iconic, the work repeatedly performs its title: a hastily written (*scratched*) word canceling (*scratching*) the master and producing chance (*scratch*) music, with oblique references to the cultural history of the phonograph as it cut across musical genres, all the way from jazz (the *scratch*, or money, that commercialized recording prom-ised and too frequently denied to the players and composers themselves) to hip-hop (the DJ's *scratching* of the phonograph in a quick manual shuffle for cross-faded rhythmic effect).

■ Steve Reich: *Pendulum Music* (1968). Like your high school physics lab, but without fudging the results. Several microphones (no input) are sus-pended from a cable over a loudspeaker, with amplifiers arranged so that they generate feedback only when the microphone and loudspeaker are in alignment. The mics are set swinging along their pendular paths, honking briefly each time they pass the speaker and coming naturally to a droning stop. Premiered in Boulder by Reich and William Wiley, the performers for the 1969 Whitney concert were Reich, Bruce Nauman, Michael Snow, Richard Serra, and James Tenney. Two good recordings from the Ensemble Avantgarde (two versions) (Wergo 6630-2, 1999) and Sonic Youth on *Goodbye 20th Century* (SYR4, 1999).

■■ Milan Knížák: "Confrontation No. 3" (1964). The performance score reads: "Keep silent all day long." While it might be mistaken for an extended performance of *Tacet*, the title clearly distances this confrontational silence from Cage's pacifist quietism. Confrontations 1 and 2, respectively, involved sword fighting and riding the train without a ticket (no idle dare in Communist Prague, as anyone who has been asked to produce documents by the undercover transit police knows).

■■ La Monte Young: *Piano Piece for David Tudor #2* (1960). Opening with a quotation from the premiere of *4'33"*, the score instructs the performer to "open the keyboard cover without making, from the operation, any sound that is audible to you." Harder than it sounds, Young anticipated failure; the score continues, in part: "Try as many times as you like. The piece is over when you succeed or when you decide to stop trying." Young's *Composition # 5*, from the same year, insists on the musicality of sounds inaudible to the human ear (what Seth Kim-Cohen would term "noncochlear sound"); the performance involves letting slip one or several butterflies into the auditorium.[10] Young was forbidden from performing the piece inside Berkeley's Hertz Hall, but it was likely to have been included in Philip Corner's 1974 concert of a dozen silent music pieces, and it would have made a fine addition to Brian Lane's proposed concert of silent pieces—though with over a score of scores already assembled, Lane had so many works that he planned to stage several of them simultaneously in order to keep the performance time to a reasonable length and might not have wanted to wait around for the butterflies to find their way out of the hall.[11]

■■ Matmos: "Always Three Words" (*Quasiobjects*, Vague Terrain 001, 1998). First word: 4-channel tape recorder. Second word: walkie-talkie (no input). Third word: another walkie-talkie (no input). Both of the handheld walkie-talkies are put in transmit mode and moved over the recorder, producing interference that can be manipulated with gestural sweeps. Last word: smart and funny and it's got a beat.

■ Jarrod Fowler: *70'00"/17* (limited edition CD-R, JMF 002, 2004). A precision stopwatch without that irritating ticking noise nagging at you constantly—or any noise at all, for that matter—Fowler's disc is a template with which the compact-disc player functions merely as a clock, without any sonic decoding. With seventeen tracks timed to exactly four minutes each, it's intended to explore bounded aspects of space and extension, but it's also handy for timing a brunch's worth of perfect soft-boiled eggs when they come cold from the fridge. Similarly silent chronographic projects by Fowler have included audio-file translations of texts, in which one page of the source equals one second of playing time, and a mashup audio translation of Heidegger's *Being and Time* and Sartre's *Time and Nothingness*, which results in an empty file. Clicking on the link from Fowler's website provokes Quicktime into placing a transparent question mark over its clocklike logo *Q* in an angst-ridden existential shrug of the MPEG-1 Audio Layer 3 shoulders. The result is probably a lot like what Jacques Cégeste was listening to while composing *Nudisme* at the Café des Poètes in Cocteau's *Orphée*. "Aucun excès," as Orpheus is admonished, "n'est ridicule!"

■ Danger Mouse and Sparklehorse: *Dark Night of the Soul* (self-released, 2009). Brian Burton and Mark Linkous collaborated with over a dozen singers for a concept album of trippy, moody self-regard. Fortunately, a dispute with EMI kept the music from being included in this release, which instead offered a booklet bloated to over one-hundred hard-backed pages of David Lynch photographs and a recordable disc with the explanation: "For Legal Reasons, enclosed CD-R contains no music. Use it as you will." Sadly, the dispute was quickly resolved and the songs were officially released the following year. Not to be confused with a Jarrod Fowler project.

■ Haco: *Stereo Bugscope 00* (IMJ 523, 2004). Like ripping the pickups out of Taku Sugimoto's guitar and running them over Toshimaru Nakamura's no-input mixer. The avant-pop chanteuse gives up her surreal, after-dinner crooning and '80s fashion frock, dons a crisp white lab coat and grabs a couple of induction microphones to amplify the normally unheard electromagnetic noises generated from common consumer electronics: a cell phone's hibernating heartbeat clicking off the seconds even in the sleep mode; a wire-less router sending out its fluttering protocol pulse; cooling fans and minidiscs in spin; the tug and stretch of bootstraps as computers start themselves up and shut themselves down, still in constant hum even when dataless and asleep; the interior integrated circuits of motherboards and lithium-driven real-time clocks oscillating with nearly silent currents. Unplugged and idle, the electronic world surrounding us on standby is in constant whine and chat-ter, tiny poltergeists and banshees and lorelei with luring whispers in the near dark night of small red indicator lights.

■ Mattin and Taku Unami: *Shyrio No Computer* (h.m.o./r 01, 2004). Haco may have taken her inspiration from Basque artist Mattin, who has been playing the computer in that manner for years, and Taku Unami may well be doing much the same thing on his disc *Intransigent toward the Detectives of Capital* (w.m.o./r 08, 2004), though to be honest I can't really hear what's going on over the noise of my own computer. On *Shyrio* (the Shinto term for the spirit of the dead acting on the living), Mattin and Unami facilitate the studio improvisation between a speaker cone and the computer feedback that drives it, self-generated when the input and output ports of the same machine are connected in one of Mattin's trademark perverse loops. The result is like the placid burble of electric brooks, barely audible inside a slumbering laptop dreaming of Arcadian runnels. Twigs snap now and then, there's a rustle in the leaves just beyond the field of vision, from somewhere a panting picks up, too late the dreamer and the nightmare inextricably meld, prey and pursuer merge, the pacific pastoral shatters, awakened by out-bursts of autophagic choke and failed squelch, the electric ouroboros gagging in an outraged roar and leaving you shaking with the unshakable dream of an inhuman silence we can never attain. Compare with the earlier Mattin and Unami duet *Attention* (h.m.o./r 03, 1997), on which they turn up the volume on what it means to listen to a CD in the first place.

■ Mike Batt: "One Minute of Silence" (EMI 5 57316 2, 2002). The kind of thing that gives the avant-garde a bad name. Third-rate excerpt from Cage's *4'33"*, impatiently arranged by British impresario Batt and included on the album *Classical Graffiti* by The Planets. An imposter child of Silence and slow Time, Batt was promptly sued by Cage's publisher for copyright infringement. The suit was eventually settled out of court for an undisclosed six-figure sum.[12]

■ Leif Elggren, Per Jonsson, and Kent Tankred: "60 Seconds of Silence for Per Jonsson" (*UGN/MAT*, Ash International 5.3, 2004). Far superior to Batt's similar-sounding composition, decidedly quieter than Hoyland's equally timed minute, and less maudlin than Semper's, Per Jonsson's piece plays as a deep sigh of recuperation, relief, and fortification programmed between two works of loud theatrical absurdity. Collectors should note that, in an inversion of The Phantom Pregnancy's technophobia, the steely studio digital silence is available only on the CD release and is not included on the 12-inch record from which the opening Fylkingen performance was remastered (*UGN*, radium 226.05 RAFE01646, 1986).

■ No Noise Reduction: "0'0,060" for a Rock and Roll Band" (*The Complete No Noise Reduction*, Moneyland records, MR0495, 1995). Rowdy post-punk thrash from Tina and the Top Ten, featuring the enthused guitars of Johnny Santini and Paulo Feliciano, with all the amps set to 11. The precision edit by Portuguese conceptualist Rafael Toral captures the band at their top-volume full-blast blowout for exactly sixty milliseconds—just long enough to jolt you up out of the mosh pit and give a palpable sense of the band's early exuberance and deskilled attack. The rest of the piece is an ironically skillful fifteen seconds and forty milliseconds of silence. Careful listening reveals that band member Mimi is sitting those milliseconds out, and unfortunately is not heard on this track.

■ Yves Klein: *Symphonie Monoton-Silence* (1957). Meant to provide a sonic equivalent of his monochrome paintings, the second movement of Klein's *Symphony* consists of twenty minutes of silence—just enough time to give the audience a chance to shake the sense of ringing from their ears: the first twenty minutes consist of a sustained D-major chord. The work was originally conceived for full Wagnerian orchestra, but performed in 1960 at the Galerie Internationale d'Art Contemporain by a small chamber group who memorized the score on short notice (though perhaps after peeking at the scrupulously notated version prepared by Pierre Henry a few years earlier). There is also a later, atmospheric version scored for mixed choir, strings, flutes, oboes, and horns. Not to be confused with the similar-sounding con-clusion to Guy Debord's film *Hurlements en faveur de Sade* (1952), which stretches aggressively on for a full four minutes longer. Though he denies any influence, Klein, not coincidentally, was present at the premiere screening.

There are rumors that Klein also issued a completely silent recording, in 1959, of a *Concert de vide* (Concert of vacuum) (not to be confused with Sir Malcolm Arnold's roughly contemporaneous concert of vacuum *cleaners* [op. 57, 1956]).

■ David Hoyland: "A Minutes Silence for the Queen Mum" (*A Call for Silence*, Sonic Arts Network SA301-2, 2002). The inverse of Klein's *Symphonie*, in some respects. Or disrespects. The unpatriotic Brits at this football match cheat the Queen out of about 12 seconds, but the pompous anthem that follows, with its slightly sour brass, makes one nostalgic for every second of preceding quiet. The unshielded mic picks up a lot of wind noise, so this lo-fi recording is primarily of documentary historical interest.

■ Jonty Semper: *The 1 Minute Silence from the Funeral of Diana, Princess of Wales* (Charrm CH060997, 2001; limited to 250 copies on 7-inch vinyl). Mawkish tabloid silence captured in Hyde Park on 6 September 1997. Ecou-teuristic document of private emotions put on public display as they aspire to the bathos of private tragedies published as national spectacle, with every second scripted and conscripted in turn. Semper's *Minute Silence* stands as a contemporary free-verse lyric proem to his historic epic *Kenotaphion* (joint production between Charrm and Locus+, CH060887 / KENO1, 2001). Tak-ing the long view of Matt Rogalsky's one-day sample, *Kenotaphion* fills two CDs with absences culled from seventy years of BBC, British Movietone, and Reuters broadcasts of the annual two-minute silences during Britain's Armi-stice Day ceremonies. Each year, while telephone and telegraph exchanges idled, trains braked to a stop, and factory machines powered down, the BBC did not just cut its signal but continued to broadcast what at any other time would be the journalistic sacrilege of dead air (a state that is in fact finable in the UK at a rate of £25,000 per minute for stations that continue in silence without alerting their listeners). Unlike the Cenotaph at Whitehall, these recordings are far from empty, with Big Ben drowning out the coughs and uncomprehending children of the reverent, amid atmospheric weather effects, broadcast static, startled birds, and rifle reports. The only truly silent Armistice minutes occurred during the Second World War, from 1941 to 1944, when the ceremony was suspended. Absent from Semper's discs, those years speak the loudest and are by far the most moving. Released in funereal black and clear plastic versions.

■ Jean-Luc Godard: *Bande à part* (1964). In a moment of boredom, unable to think of how to entertain themselves and too agitated to indulge in a true French *ennui*, Franz (Sami Frey) proposes that the *bande* take "une minute de silence." Godard obliges by cutting the soundtrack (*la bande sonore mise à part*). "Une vraie minute de silence, ça dure une éternité [A real minute of silence can last forever]," Franz notes, but Godard's lasts only 33 seconds. The discrepancy provides an accessible, funny, narrative reprise of the acerbic, mean-spirited abstract silence from the final twenty-four minutes of Guy Debord's *Hurlements en faveur de Sade* (1952). The situationists would denounce Godard's techniques as "tardivement plagié et inutile . . . prétentieuses fausses nouveautés [tardily plagiarized and useless . . . pretentious false novelties]," but they were never known for their sense of humor, and it's really pretty funny.[13] A similar and even shorter composition, presumably by Michel Legrand, accompanies the tabletop finger performance of the film's iconic dance scene, in which Odile and Arthur negotiate the steps they'll soon dance to Legrand's hipster swing number "Le Madison," itself interrupted by parenthetical excerpts from the earlier minute of silence. In mono.

■ John Cage: *Silent Prayer* (1948, unrealized). Hints at the neo-Dada origins of *4'33"* and its latent corporate critique. Cage's plan was to "compose a piece of uninterrupted silence and sell it to Muzak Co. It will be three or four and a half minutes in length—those being the standard lengths of 'canned music.'"[14] Cage, that still unravished *mariée*, would have *mise à nu* canned music—a kind of sonic readymade—and translated it into a Duchampian "hasard en conserve [canned chance]."[15] Always seemed to be playing in the elevator in my old building.

■ Dick McCann: *Three Minutes of Silence* (1952). Just as Cage plotted to insert a blank record into the Muzak playlist, a New York humor columnist imagined blank records inserted into jukeboxes for shy dates who could avoid the latest jump hit by Louis Jordan in favor of discs "that play absolutely nothing, nothing but silence."[16] A follow-up release anticipated ambient minimalist electronica by decades; it was said to incorporate "a beep tone which will sound ever so gently every 15 seconds so that people will know the machine is playing."[17] After his death, it was discovered that John Cage had carefully saved a clipping of the article, which had been published in the same year as *4'33"*.

■ Coil: "Absolute Elsewhere" (*How to Destroy Angels*, L.A.Y.L.A.H. Antire-cords LAY05, 1984ff.). Reichian music (though that's Wilhelm, not Steve), Coil's EP is the sonic equivalent to the architecture of an orgone box: a lot of attitude and BS with nothing inside. In this case, BS stands for B side: the verso of the 12-inch with the full title *The Soundtrack to the Program HOW TO DESTROY ANGELS: Ritual Music for the Accumulation of Male Sexual Energy* (a long way of saying what T. Rex summed up with "bang a gong; get it on"). Unlike the gong-show A side, "Absolute Elsewhere" manifests itself—depending on the particular pressing—as a track of sheer noise, a constant quarter-hour tone, a series of lock-groove test tones, or a smooth grooveless slab (that is, a record with no "coil" at all). The CD version (Threshold House, LOCI CD5, 1999) consists of one second of silence.

■ Telium Group: *Record 1* (MGT 700-7, 1991). Occasionally listed as "self-titled" or "t" (from the retro lowercase letter encircled on the silkscreened cover), this Magnatone Records release is a grooveless 7-inch (edition 354). And I mean *grooveless*: George Clinton would be mortified.

■ Reynols: *Blank Tapes* (TrenteOiseaux 002, 1999). Yep. Pieces made by the digital and analog processing of blank magnetic tapes. But special blank tapes, some of which had been saved, with a kind of touching sen-timentality, since 1978. A lot noisier than the Argentine trio's first release, *Gordura Vegetal Hidrogenada*, which was a "dematerialized cd" (it came as an empty jewel case, reprising Psychodrama's 1984 release *No Tape*, a cassette shell that did not, as promised, contain any tape [the band's best release to date]). That (lack of a) debut CD was appropriate for a group whose leader, Miguel Tomasin, occasionally asserted that they don't exist. Tomasin, whose Down's syndrome misprisions were taken as oracular pronouncements by his partners Alan Courtis and Roberto Conlazo, also regularly announced that the United States doesn't exist either, which substantially cut down on his touring there. Though they did make it to Sweden: a live version of *Blank Tapes* (not audible on Büchler's disc) was recorded in Malmö, at the Rooseum, in 2003. As Tomasin also says: "Todo afrazarmo de lo soplido cintas."[18]

■ Linear Regressionists: *Living on the Regression Line* (rrr 02, 1990; edi-tion of 50). The statistical tool of linear regression analyzes the relation of independent variables for some quantity of interest. Here the variables include an unrecorded compact disc (X) drilled with holes (Y). The quantity of musical interest rapidly approaches zero (O), while the quantity of collectors' interest rises over time. Observable data plots the current value to collectors at $30 (+/-$10). Find the sum of squares who will make the purchase (HINT: the slope is downward and the intercept rare).

■ Peeter Vähi: *Supreme Silence* (CCnC 182, 1999). The third movement of this Estonian composer's piece is indeed scored for silence, which was probably a nice break for Kristjan Järvi and the men of the Estonian National Choir. Not to mention the listener who has to sit through the New Age orientalist mysticism of the other movements (the first of which, just to give you an idea, is entitled "Mandala Offering"). Fine silence, to be sure, piping to the spirit ditties of no tone, and it's nicely recorded on this disc, but "supreme" is probably overstating the case.

■ *0: 0.000* (Mu-Label 002, 2002). Actually not so rigorous as the title (or the pseudonym of Nosei Sakata) suggests, but rather the subtle hum and the molecular waver of air from frequencies just beyond the threshold of human perception: an ultrasonic 20,200 hz and a subsonic 14 hz (or, in the case of one raucous track, the overtone produced when the two are combined). Though even that relatively lower frequency isn't likely to be reproduced on most sound systems. If you've got a good stereo, turn it up really loud and see how the neighbor's dog reacts.

■ Mieko Shiomi: *A Musical Dictionary of 80 People Around Fluxus* (? Records 10, 2002). Music worthy of the OuLiPo, in which Shiomi "describes" each of those people either by realizing one of their works, putting a signature compositional method into practice, or through a general pastiche of technique or timbre, but in all events using only the pitches available from the letters in the dedicatee's name. The disc from Galerie Hundertmark doesn't match the rigor of its concept with musicianship—a few selections feature Shiomi's lackluster keyboard work, while others are left to an equally impassioned computer-driven synthesizer. After a few tracks one wishes Shiomi had waited a few years and instead recorded a performance of her 2008 piano score consisting of a fermata over a single measure rest—a pause of indefinite duration sustained by the instructions to "repeat indefinitely" and tempered with a tempi of *grave*. As it is, the best piece is #56, for Yoko Ono, whose name wisely refused to supply any notes.

■ Yoko Ono and John Lennon: *Unfinished Music 2: Life with the Lions* (Zapple ST-3357, 1969). On this follow-up to *Two Virgins*, taped in the Queen Charlotte's Maternity Hospital (London) where Ono was staying, one can hear a version of her 1963 event scores "Beat Piece" ("Listen to a heart beat") and "Pulse Piece" ("Listen to each other's pulse by / putting your ear on the other's / stomach").[19] The second track on the B side records the *in utero* heartbeat of her child, just before its miscarriage. At twice the length of the pro-forma memorial tribute, the following "Two Minutes Silence" is certainly long enough to provoke uncomfortable reflection, but not so sustained that it drifts beyond its subject into expressionless avant-garde territory. To record is to return to the heart (Latin *re* + *cor*), and here recording is abjured. Genuinely sad.

■ Though no definitive recording ever emerged, the anti-expressivist wing of the Japanese *onkyo-kei* (sound reverberation school) brand of minimal gesture had been moving toward working entirely with non-networked equipment before the moment passed. The musicians themselves would object, but you might think of it as applied Zen. More ascetic than spiritual, some performances matched Otomo Yoshihide and Akiyama Tetzui on empty turntables with Sachiko Matsubara at the sampler, but with no samples (only its sine wave test)—all mixed together by Toshimaru Nakamura's mixer without any input. For reference, audition *Good Morning Good Night* (Erstwhile 042-2, 2004), which sounds like an old grade-school hearing test, deep in some cinderblock nurse's office, misadministered with faulty war-surplus equipment. Then again, it may be better to meditate on the idea than to actually listen; try to imagine the hand of one clap sounding (in applause).

■ Institut für Feinmotorik: *Penetrans* (Staubgold 25, 2002). Following Martin Tetreault's minimalist work directly with tone arm pickups, this southern German collective of turntablists spin their machines without any records. The record players, however, are very well prepared (in the Cagean sense of the term) with household items: rubber bands, tape, a toothbrush, et cetera. As the hearts of the *hochwertige Discoplattenspielers* beat away, a few wheeze and cramp with the repetitive stress, some begin to click and thrum, and before you know it the resultant low-tech techno creates a wry roots electronica. Most astonishing of all, though, is that what might have been an inspired conceptual gesture or a 'pataphysical investigation into "precision motoricity" has been going on for years now and led to ten (!) albums. Put on your narrow black-rimmed glasses and check one out.

■ Ervín Schulhoff: "In Futurum" (1919). Manic, anxious silence. The influence of early jazz and Dada cabaret songs is palpable in the third movement of the Czech modernist's *Fünf Pittoresken* (Five picturesques) for piano. Though entirely silent, the score—marked "Zeitmaß-zeitlos [Timeless tempo]"—bristles with notation: from long, angst-filled tacets to jittery quintuplet rests. The counting is tricky, and with any but the most accomplished pianist it can detract from the work's potential for emotional outpouring; according to the composer's headnote, the piece is to be played with "as much heartfelt expression as desired—always, all the way through [tutto il canzone con espressione e sentimento ad libitum, sempre, sin al fine]!" The reference recording is by Steffen Schleiermacher (*Czech Avant-Garde Piano Music: 1918–1938* [MD&G 613 1158-2, 2003]).

■ Richard Eigner: *Denoising Noise Music* (Wald 01, 2007). The laboratory findings of Eigner's master's thesis at the Fachhochschule Salzburg, these two discs document the use of noise-reducing technologies on a range of soi-disant "noise music"—from Iannis Xenakis and Merzbow to Luigi Russolo's *Risveglio di una città* and Lou Reed's *Metal Machine Music*. Intended to clean up nonmusical sounds and restore damaged audio signals, the denoising algorithms set diligently to work on an entire genre. With few structural clues or melodic sequences to alert the denoising software to the presence of "music," the original compositions were carefully erased and only a few stray signals survived the cleansing. Occasional and soft, squeegeed squeaks and muted bleeps break unpredictably from the granulated quiet like sonar pings from the sunken impulse of the avant-garde, stifled under the slowly shifting sands of some abysmal oceanic basin. The once desperately deafening SOS broadcasts of the most strident musical extreme barely break the surface of Eigner's discs in dreamy liquid echoes, a few drops of cleanser still clinging from the scrub.

■ Emilio Villa: *Karnhoval* (1969; edition of 100). Described as a "disco muto," the record is silent only to the ears; the surface of the disc is printed with multicolored greens and whites in the Futurist tradition with a riot of swirled text, varied typefaces, and chaotic font changes from letter to letter within words. The cover is even more colorfully distressed. Printed in Macerata, Italy, on the occasion of the Carnevale Internazionale degli Artisti di Rieti.

■ Edgardo Antonio Vigo: *Poemas (in)sonoros* (Diagonal Cero, 1969). The cover of Vigo's record announces it as "Un Disco para mirar [An album to watch]." The statement is ironic, since the record is square, and not properly a disc at all, but it's also sincerely ingenuous, since the inaudible sound poetry is quite literally something to see rather than hear. The center labels sport nine concentric rings around the spindle hole (side A in light green, side B in period orange); printed with subtly varying widths and slightly off-center, they spin hypnotically like one of Marcel Duchamp's rotoreliefs, as the sharp edges of the square record blur to a circular black void that serves as a kind of signature for the publisher's imprint: Diagonal Cero (diagonal zero).[20] Mesmerizing.

■ Pavel Büchler: *LIVE* (FACT, 2003; edition limited to 351 copies). The audience applause from the 351 "live" albums in Büchler's collection, with none of the music. Although anyone can hear the occasional rowdy rock crowds and stoned '70s country-folk fan inclusions, connoisseurs will note that most of the audiences seem to be composed of avant-jazz hipsters, with a number of distinctive acoustics discernible among the open seaside spaces of Newport and Antibes: the heavily curtained converted hockey rink in Victoriaville, Canada; the wood-beamed and paneled concert hall in Willisau, Switzerland; the concrete and flagstone band shell in Montreux; the deep-echoing cave created by the balcony at the old Fillmore East. Ranging from 1957 to 1998, the recordings utilized by Büchler, not coincidentally, correspond to the major historical shift in jazz audiences and their responses, as the gin-soaked swingers who rallied the band for certain tempi and communal intensity gave way to the more intellectual responses of the post-bebop era, when jazz fans stopped being alcoholic dancers, eager for entertainment and hoping to hook up, and instead became frowning brow-creased introverts, more inclined to subtle, aloofly knowing head nods than any sort of vulgar foot stomping. Ross Russell pinpoints the moment when the demographics shifted from the dancers to

> the "alligators" of the late swing period, those serious types, self-styled students of American jazz, who used to edge up to the orchestra shell and remain there all night, indefatigably listening. . . . They gave the impression that they had never danced a step in their lives, nor had any intention of so doing.[21]

Despite the historic sweep of *LIVE*, certain key jazz recordings are absent. At the beginning of *Charles Mingus Presents Charles Mingus* (America Records AM6082, c. 1961), the authoritarian eponym admonishes: "Ladies and gentlemen . . . restrain your applause . . . don't even take any drinks, or no cash register ringing, et cetera." The audience compliance was perfect, and so can't be heard on *LIVE* (although I suppose *Mingus Presents* wouldn't have made the cut anyway, since despite the bandleader's chatter it was actually a studio album, which made it a lot easier for the chastened audience to keep themselves in line). An album such as Pharoah Sanders's *Live at the East* (Impulse! AS-9227, 1972) presents a trickier decision, since— *pace* the title—it was actually recorded in the studio when the logistics of transporting recording equipment to The East Afrocentric cultural center in Brooklyn proved too costly; but the habitués did tramp across town from the center to the studio instead. Similarly, The Cannonball Adderley Quintet's *Live at "The Club"* (Capitol ST-2663, 1966) was also recorded in the studio with an imported audience, this time paid with free alcohol. Putting the "lie" back in "live," the disingenuous album title was a favor to Adderley's friend, club owner E. Rodney Jones (beautifully enough, unbeknownst even to jazz insiders, the Quintet had indeed been recorded live at The Club a few months earlier, although that album wasn't released until 2005 when the forgotten tapes were discovered, and so it isn't on *LIVE* either). However Büchler might resolve these conceptual issues, the result is visceral: the waves of collaged applause are giddying. With all the emotional triggers of anticipation and catharsis but never a recognizable moment for cathexis, the listener is continually buffeted from an eager expectation that builds but never climaxes to *dénouements* that always ring false. *LIVE*, in this respect, is thus a thorough and rigorous anticlimax. The ultimate effect, however, is euphoric: all the optimism of crowds expecting a good performance to come and all the gratitude for the performance just past, but with none of the wrong notes, botched timings, or annoying feedback. The album, however, is also a philosophical proposition posing as conceptual art: what does it mean to be (a)live? The title prompts one to wonder what might constitute a recording that was *not* live. But then again, on reflection, as the cheers and whistles and clapping continue, one starts to wonder what recording might ever in fact be truly "live": experienced for the first vibrant time and not merely a recorded document of something always already terminated, of some guaranteed past in which the performers, however vital at the moment of registration, might now no longer be living. Büchler's disc, like his *3'34"*, would seem to answer both questions at once: prerecorded sounds reanimated in their unprecedented new context, as they have never been heard before. A paradox that resolves itself, *LIVE* now lives as a not-live live album.

■ Pavel Büchler: *Encore* (Kunsthalle Bern, 2005). Once more, from the top, with feeling: a 7-inch vinyl reprising *LIVE* by including the audience responses on the opening and closing tracks of the fifty-two live albums added to Büchler's record collection since October 1999 (when the *LIVE* project was produced). Arranged in the order of acquisition over a playing time of four minutes and thirty-three seconds, this is a collector's edition of collected editions, limited to a pressing of 433 discs. Put it on before going to the next big stadium show and practice shouting out requests for "Free Bird."

■ Christopher DeLaurenti: *Favorite Intermissions: Music Before and Between Beethoven—Stravinsky—Holst* (GD Stereo, 2007). Illegal, undercover surveillance as musical composition. DeLaurenti went wired to classical music concerts, making bootleg binaural recordings of everything but the programmed music: laughter and footsteps and the scrape of chairs on a largely emptied stage, the audience mill and mumble, the returning musicians' arpeggiated warm-up scales, all sorts of noodlings and tunings and autistic snippets of melodic lines. Heavy on percussion, woodwinds, and low brass, one wonders what the string players are all doing backstage during these breaks. The result, in all events, often sounds suspiciously like a composition by Carl Alessandro Landini. The album ends with a public-address announcement: "Ladies and Gentlemen, the maestro and orchestra will not stop between the Ravel and Strauss, please hold your applause." Such programming not only prevents DeLaurenti from sneaking in a bonus track from that concert, but it also ensures that the recording won't show up as part of an encore to Büchler's *Encore*. Two editions (neither of which should be mistaken as the audiobook version of the eponymous Victor Borge memoir): the first with a cover designed in the mode of classic Deutsche Grammophon albums, the second redesigned to satisfy the lawyers at Universal Music Group (DG's parent corporation).

■ *The Best of Marcel Marceao* (MGM SE-4745, 1971). Two identical sides (each bearing a different matrix number from the pressing) consisting of 19 minutes of silence followed by a minute of applause. While it might be misheard as the abridged audiobook version of *The Wit and Wisdom of Spiro T. Agnew*, which had also been published in L.A. the previous year, Agnew kindly supplies one of the endorsements on the back cover of the LP sleeve, calling it "the quintessence of euphony, cacophony and salacious ecstasy. I found this record to perfectly represent the position of the silent majority until I materialized onto the scenic expanse." Those still tempted to hear it as a novelty record, despite Agnew's enthusiasm, should remember that the routines of the album's obvious eponym depended on the same sort of humor; a gag, after all, is both an amusing skit and also something that prevents one from speaking. Produced by Michael Viner, the album originally retailed at $4.98.[22] Though self-recommending to silence completists, this is admittedly not an essential recording. But then again, to recall another slogan from 1971, a mime is a terrible thing to waste.

■ *The Wit and Wisdom of Ronald Reagan* (ABRA 1, from Stiff Records released under the name of Magic Records, 1981). Seventeen equally silent tracks divided over two sides of a commercially pressed LP. Not to be confused with *The Best of Marcel Marceao*, despite nearly identical timings (the Reagan recording, tellingly, omits the applause). A quarter of a century later, James Humes published the book version, *The Wit and Wisdom of Ronald Reagan* (Washington: Regnery, 2007), ruining perfectly good blank pages with quotes and anecdotes from the former president.

■ Les Petites Bonbons in Hollywood (1972–1974). With coverage in *Newsweek*, *People*, *Record World*, and other pop culture magazines, Jerry Dreva, Bob Lambert, and Chuck Bitz achieved more fame with their short-lived glam-rock group than most bands ever do. And they did it all without recording even a single, or ever making any music at all for that matter.[23] Competing respectably for coverage with War's *The World Is a Ghetto* and Elton John's *Goodbye Yellow Brick Road*, the Bonbons wisely disbanded before having to compete with the juggernaut double disc *Frampton Comes Alive!* Dreva, admittedly, took it all too far (but boy could he play guitar).

■ The Phantom Pregnancies: "Project P.KO" (*Hey Mom, the Garage Is on My Foot*, DAMGOOD 102, 1996). Riot Grrl meets Mike Batt. Nearly a minute of pregnant silence, the phantom sound on this contribution to the Damaged Goods comp is apparently not the result of some deskilled mastering oversight but rather a manifestation of the PP's hatred of digital technology: a refusal to contribute anything other than mardy silence to a CD project. By far the best track on the compilation—garage punk never sounded so good, and here it finally lives up to the pretenses of its attitude.

■ Nick Thurston: *Erased Motion Poems* (self-released MP3 file, 2008). In the audio equivalent of airbrushing a photograph to remove blemishes, Thurston edited out the poems of England's Poet Laureate from the 2005 Poetry Archive CD *Andrew Motion Reading from His Poems*, evacuating the vacuous verse and leaving only Motion's introductory explanations of what the poems are about: "This next poem is called 'A Blow to the Head,' and is about just that. . . . This poem is called 'The Spoiled Child.' . . . This next poem is called 'Goethe in the Park' and is a kind of miniature biography of a bit of wood." The best erasure here is a poetic retelling of Jonty Semper's *1 Minute*: "A short poem about the death of Princess Diana." The great paradox of the project comes from what Cleanth Brooks called "the heresy of paraphrase": if poetry, by definition, is what cannot be paraphrased, then Thurston hasn't really removed any poetry at all.[24]

■ Language Removal Service: *Static Language Sampler* (promotional CD, 2003). State of the art in speech elimination, LRS cleans and purifies recordings of all language. Sources from their archive include entries from various categories: "divas" (Callas, Monroe, Dietrich), "critics" (Sontag, Chomsky), "musicians" (Mingus, Monk, Cage), "artists"—well, I guess they're actually all divas once you think about it. In every case, LRS takes out the words but leaves all the other sounds untouched: air whistling in buccal cavities, the pool and drain of saliva and phlegm, the glottal pops and deglutinations that punctuate the inframince spaces between even the most rapid speech. With that speech liberated from the distracting clamor of language, the cleansed recordings let ye soft pipes play ever on. With a good pair of headphones you can almost imagine the aeolian echo of inspiration and the calcinated drip off stalactites in the caverns of bucolic grottos. . . .

■ Matt Rogalsky: S (2002). Like the LRS but even cleaner. Rogalsky plays Doktor Murkes with this project, actually collecting the *gesammeltes Schweigen* (collected silence) that Heinrich Böll's character supposedly splices together on tape.[25] Doktor Murkes works in a radio studio, and S, not coincidentally, compiles all of the silences in one day of BBC radio broadcast. Testing both the proposition that "the tedium is the message" (as Darren Wershler has phrased it) and that "silence is golden," the result was released as a limited edition boxed set (24 audio CDs and a CD-ROM documentation) priced at £300. No doubt feeling some pressure from the masses, Rogalsky later used filtering software to distill the set into a single disc of excerpts—a "best of" album, of sorts, containing only the quietest silences—which was later released in a more democratic unlimited edition—though still kind of pricey at £15 (S [The Archers], ARiADA, Sonic Arts Research Archive CD1, 2003). Although they congratulated themselves on treating the whole project lightheartedly, the BBC did assert its rights to the silences, risking a show-down with Cage's publisher.[26]

■ Tac: *Lapse of Silence* (taccdr 006, 2003). A project of such conceptual integrity that the already very quiet recordings are not compromised by audible events. The result is a sort of "virtual aurality" untainted by sound. A distinctly romantic pastoralism, however, can nonetheless be felt, echoing Fluxus works such as Takako Saito's *Silent Music* (1999), for blown airborne plant seeds (think of milkweed, dandelion, or cottonwood), and Yoko Ono's 1963 *Tape Piece I* ("Stone Piece: Take the sound of the stone aging") and *Tape Piece III* ("Snow Piece: Take a tape of the sound of snow falling. / This should be done in the evening. / Do not listen to the tape . . .").[27] The seven brief tracks on *Lapse* document the sounds of shadows moving, sun shining, ice melt-ing, water evaporating, grass growing, candles burning, and—in a nice nod to Cage—mushrooms dropping spores. With this do-it-yourself kit, Tom Cox takes the *tac* out of *tacet*. Where Ono sold her "Soundtape" of the *Snow Falling at Dawn* (in three versions: snow of India; snow of Kyo; snow of Aos) at the rate of 25 cents per inch in 1965, *Lapse* comes in an edition limited to only 50 copies, each 3-inch self-released CD-R encased in a unique, delicate, sound-damping sculptural container of *papier-mâché* and eggshells.[28]

■ The Haters: *Wind Licked Dirt* (RRR 033,1988). Betraying traces of the band's distinctive early blend of punk and Fluxus, this entropic release by former Survival Research Labs technician GX Jupitter-Larsen sounds like a concert bootleg of The Haters amplified *intonarumori*—with the audience just beginning to rip up the club—but played back at the geologic speed of the dirt and pebbles that come packaged with the unlathed disc. The sleeve states: "This record is played by rubbing dirt on it." *Wind Licked Dirt* is especially convenient for when you want to listen to a record but don't have a turntable handy. For those willing (or unwilling) to embrace the digital, but without a CD player, a self-released CD reissue, with no noticeable remaster-ing, followed in 1993, also to be "played by rubbing dirt against it." As an agitated shuffle reveals, sufficient dither will mask the granulation noise (the technical term for the distortion that follows from quantization errors intrud-ing at very low input levels as sinusoids decay—and the input levels here, remember, are *very* low).[29] The 2008 cassette edition from Hanson Records (HN205) came out just in time to accommodate a world in which cars no lon-ger come equipped with cassette decks (the last factory-installed dash deck appeared in the 2010 Lexus).[30] Keeping with its gritty DIY aesthetic, the tape release is appropriately low-fi: no chromium dioxide; no cobalt-doped iron oxide; no dobly; and with abrasion substantially increasing print-through. Hard to hear over the engine noise, but while idling at a stoplight it sounds something like a rainstick. Performances tend to be messy, but you can clean all the dust and dirt from your hands while listening to The Haters' 1990 *Oxy-gen Is Flammable* (self-released)—a piece of broken plastic packaged like a CD that is played by running water over it (water not included)—and then dry off listening to Larsen's quietest release to date: *Shear* (self-released, 1991), a wad of boxed cotton batting meant to be played by squeezing the fluff between the fingers. Recommended.

■ Jens Brand: *Stille-Landschaft* (Silence landscape) (2002). Real, authen-tic, documentary silence. The soundtrack to Brand's video installation (a full-circle pan across a desert landscape) is almost as empty as the view, which records a spot in Botswana that is one of the few places in the world where, at certain times, there is indeed almost absolute silence. Since the only way to really hear what was there is to not hear it, a full appreciation of the soundtrack requires its site-specific installation in an anechoic chamber. Brand's video art is less in the tradition of nineteenth-century landscape painting or the spectacle of the panorama than the philosophical proposition: if there are no trees in the forest to fall . . . ?

■ Joseph Beuys: *Grammophon aus knochen* (Record Player of Bone) (1958). A longer-playing, higher-fidelity version of Beuys's *tonband in filz-stapel* (audio tape in stacked felt), the *stummes Grammophon* (mute phono-graph) displays a covered phonograph record, perhaps with a recording of Beuys's felt-wrapped piano (felt, of course, is a material known for damping sound, as it's used around the hammers *inside* a piano). Though we'll never know, because the swing arm and needle have been replaced by a bone, bluntly inverting Rainer Rilke's hallucinatory dream of playing the jagged coronal suture of the skull with a phonograph cartridge.[31] Beuys also invokes the early history of the phonograph's spiritualist associations, since the spirit, as Hegel famously said, is a bone ("ein Knochen ist").[32]

■ Baudouin Oosterlynck: *Variations du silence*, Opp. 73–104 (1990–1991). Twenty-three preludes, five oratorios, three overtures and a sonata—a quarter-century of confessional, romantic, egotistically autobiographical silence. Following extensive research covering 15,000 kilometers over west-ern Europe, Oosterlynck documents silent locations that were of particular importance to him. Not sufficiently outsider to excuse the visionary preten-tiousness, Oosterlynck is like Joseph Beuys without all the dead rabbits and schmaltz (but keeping the goofy haberdashery in a silent tip of the hat to the German master). Reference recordings on the four-disc set 1975–1978 (Metaphon 001, 2008).

■ Pierre Huyghe: *Partition du Silence* (Score of silence) (1997). Who says you can't get something for nothing? Huyghe took a digital recording of Cage's *4'33"* and used computer software to enlarge the scale of the digital print. Like blowing up a photograph to reveal what couldn't be seen, the result of Huyghe's magnification amplified what was previously inaudible. Huyghe then scored those sounds using traditional musical notation to create a playable transcription of Cage's piece. Like a map drawn to a scale that's greater than one to one, the *Score* is thus simultaneously a grossly inaccurate distortion and a minutely faithful facsimile. "Silence," as Mark Rothko said, "is so accurate."[33]

■ In 1953, Robert Rauschenberg convinced Willem de Kooning to give him a drawing, which Rauschenberg promptly and studiously erased. Now you can hear the conversational version. Finding that he had accidentally erased an interview he'd just conducted with J. G. Ballard, Jeremy Millar exhibited it as the *Erased JG Ballard Interview* (Nothing Exhibition, Rooseum, 2001), with just enough metallic hiss to make Reynols reunite and head back to the studio. While it's nice to see a dumb mistake transformed into a smart installation, it would have been better if he'd wiped out a specially commissioned electroacoustic composition from someone at Dartmouth, or given a full performance of Maciunas's *Homage*.

■ George Maciunas: *Homage to Richard Maxfield* (1962). A student in John Cage's composition course at the New School for Social Research (and the first professor of electronic music in America when he took over the class as Cage's successor), Richard Maxfield must have heard the story Cage liked to tell about his own student days: "One day when I was studying with Schönberg, he pointed out the eraser on his pencil and said, 'This end is more important than the other.'" Maxfield, who seems to have taken good notes, was best known for using the erase button on the tape machine as a compositional tool. Maciunas's *Homage*, accordingly, instructs the musician to follow a performance of one of Maxfield's compositions by flippantly flipping the erase switch while rewinding Maxfield's master tape. There is no record that Maciunas's piece was ever performed, although he did provide a "chicken variation on the same theme" ("just rewind the previously played tape of R. Maxfield without erasing"), thus exponentially increasing the likelihood of a performance and opening the possibility for an encore. Maciunas's self-canceling composition became a kind of *tombeau* in 1969 when Maxfield performed a fatal defenestration.

■ Wandelweiser Group. New York (School) by way of Vienna, on a direct flight with one of those noise-canceling headphones on. Founded in the early 1990s by Burkhard Scholthauer and Antoine Beuger (later joined by Jürg Frey, Michael Pisaro, Radu Malfatti, and Manfred Werder among others), the group has recorded seminal performances of John Cage's *Branches* and Christian Wolff's *Stones*. Given the formal conceits of their own compositions (works with durations extending from only four seconds to more than a week, compositions for two CD players, nine minutes of lead-in silence, et cetera), one might mistake them for post-Fluxus avant-garde pranksters (minus the squeaky toys and smashed instruments). But despite the overuse of tubas and accordions, these guys really seem to mean it. These are not just silences, but rigorous, deliberate, purposive silences. Dissertations on phenomenology, architecture, and memory, Wandelweiser compositions come off as philosophical investigations into the negative ontology of silence. And yet, in the patiently controlled quiet of the performances they manage to end up as more weighed than weighty, more studied than studious. Taken together, their recordings are arguments for musical planning (along the lines of "family planning"): none of the pauses here are pregnant.

■ Robert Watts: non-vinyl records (1969–1972). Starting with the *String Record*, Watts began manufacturing records with various groove depths and material properties, but with no sound reproduction, to be played at a number of speeds. As Watts explains:

> I began experiments with the manufacture of a series of records in different materials such as metals, plastics, wood, clay and latex. Most of these were made on a machine lathe at Rutgers University, and I thought of them as being sound portraits of this machine.[34]

At 20 rpm, with lots of ripping scratches breaking the drone, the *String Record* sounds like the cabin noise of a jumbo jet as its aluminum skin suffers a catastrophic structural failure.

■ Tim Ulrichs: Schleifpapier-Schallplatten (1968). A series of monaural discs made from thirteen grades of commercial sandpaper in a nuanced mood-music suite orchestration of V. A. Wölfli's industrial noise composition "Pferd/Horse/Elastic," named after the Pferd company's steel-cutting discs. Wölfli apparently just slapped a hundred of the construction-duty grinding wheels inside record covers (safe to 5,100 rpm if you can crank the player that fast, but try only at your system's risk). Putting the dust in industrial,

the anarcho-duchampian Dust Breeders (Michael Henritzi with Thierry Del-
lès and Yves Botz, aka Mickey H and Youri Potlatch) issued their first single,
"Sandpaper Mantra" (1989), as a 7-inch piece of sandpaper guaranteed to
produce some *élevage de poussière* when run under a diamond stylus. Their
1995 dance classic "I'm Psycho 4 Yur Love" then swapped the materials, so that vinyl was housed inside a sandpaper record sleeve, making
the psychedelic noise even noisier every time the disc is removed (rrr062/
EPP02). An anonymous release in 1980 had used the same strategy on a
microhouse track, issuing a blank grooved disc inside a sandpaper sleeve
of Adolor/Norton P80 G21 abrasive sheets; starting as minimal techno,
the track becomes increasingly glitchy with repeated play (variable speed).
These discs are all introverted and considerate versions of various antisocial
packaging for albums from The Durutti Column (*The Return of the Durutti
Column* [FACT14, 1979]); Feederz (*Ever Feel Like Killing Your Boss?* [Steal 1,
1984]); and Illusion of Safety (*Illusion of Safety* [Mort Aux Vaches 2, 1999]).
Housed in sandpaper covers with the abrasive surface on the outside, in
homage to Verner Permild's design for Guy Debord and Asger Jorn's book
Mémoires, they deface the albums next to them with every reshelving.

■ Alvin Lucier: "Quiet Coffee" (*A Call for Silence*, SA301-2, 2004). Under-
caffeinated composition by the master of conceptual music. I suppose it's
the sonic equivalent to those sleepy early morning moments lost staring at
the steam rising from the coffee mug, but to be honest, I can't hear much
going on here—even wide awake with headphones and the volume turned
up all the way. But it does give an excuse to mention the collection *A Call
for Silence*, curated by Nicolas Collins for Sonic Arts Network. Though it
often confuses quiet with silent, the compilation highlights include Christian
Marclay's *Unused Space,* which would make a good encore for an Institut für Feinmotorik show, and Matt Rogalsky's "Two Minutes and Fifty-Five
Seconds . . . ," in which he bullies George W. Bush into rushing through a
patriotic performance of Cage's masterpiece and gets him to say a lot more
than usual in the process. The CD also contains a couple of tracks in homage
to Lucier's famous *I Am Sitting in a Room*: the Kapital Band's raucous party
game "How Many People Are in This Room" and Richard Beard's contrarian
"I Am Not Sitting in a Room." The latter is not quite silent either—you can
hear the tick-tock allusion to Lucier's *Clocker* as well as some shuffling and

fidgeting—but it demonstrates with conviction that Beard isn't going to take this kind of avant-garde nonsense sitting down.

■ John Levack Drever: "Pastoral Pause" (*A Call for Silence*, SA301-2, 2004). Yet another track of note from the *Call for Silence* CD ("The art of our time," as Susan Sontag recognized, "is noisy with appeals for silence"), this is ominous, edge-of-your-seat silence recorded on location in Dartmoor.[35] A sudden epic opening, *in medias res*, just moments after a car has passed over a cattle grid in the sonic foreground: the drumroll clang and reverb of the grating die with a quick decay and the motor fades into the distance, replaced with some solitary birdcalls, the sluice of a rill, and the sound of wind over an unimpeded expanse (Drever's work is not for the agoraphobic). But wait, what was that? A noise in the distance? The approach of another car? Who could be coming? Et in Arcadia ego? The suspense builds, but we never hear what happens when it gets to the crossing. With an echo of the crop-duster scene in *North by Northwest,* this is environmental art reimagined as a horror movie. Terrifying.

■ Jacob Kirkegaard: *Four Rooms* (Touch Tone 26, 2006). Alvin Lucier meets Andrei Tarkovsky. Sounding at first like the title-menu cue music to a creepy science fiction film—with slowly pulsing drones, metallic-tape abrasions, disquieting high-frequency crackles, and ominous echoing pings reverberating like inhuman cries in empty space—the looping of Kirkegaard's tracks comes not from failing to press Play but from the recursive logic of their own construction. The spaces summoned by the sounds, however, are indeed haunted. Kirkegaard made his recordings in four of the silent, evacuated public spaces of Pripyat (and neighboring Krasno), Ukraine, ground zero for the nuclear reactor that served Chernobyl until 1986. Recording the silent spaces deep inside the deserted Alienation Zone for ten minutes, he then played back the tape inside the same space, recording again; the result was played back again, recorded, and so on, proceeding like Lucier's *I Am Sitting in a Room*, but without the narration and in rooms where no one can sit for long. The results sound like the gravely static of a Geiger counter, stretched to the thirty-year duration of a cesium half-life. The narrative pull of the increasingly laminar sonic spaces is compelling, and suspenseful, but the tracks would have been just as effective without their irradiated *mise-en-scène*: all spaces are haunted by their own interiority.

■ Braco Dimitrijević: *Njeqove dovke glas* (His pencil's voice) (Galerija Studentskog Centra i Muzicki Salonteatre ITD Zagreb, 1973). Pre-posthistorical work from the Sarajevo-born conceptualist, who has written: "Je veux un style aussi neutre que possible, une sorte d'écriture de l'univers [I want a style as neutral as possible, a kind of writing of the universe]."[36] In this case, the neutral style takes the form of a stylus, the carbon of the diamond transformed into a softened graphite: the universal phonography here was done with a sharpened pencil on a piece of white cardboard, creating a unique variable-speed phonograph record (16, 33, 45, or 78 rpm). I've never heard this one (well, you know what I mean), but apparently the album was exhibited in Zagreb and Chicago in the '70s. Whereof one cannot speak . . .

■ Nick Thurston: *33 1/3* (self-produced, 2009). Like machine-age assembly-line versions of Dimitrijević's Old-Master, hand-sketched artisanal craft object, Thurston's concentrically ridged paper records, each pressed from a precision, laser-etched template, play the paper itself rather than transmitting any prerecorded sound. While the matrices are smooth and hard-edged, the irrepressibly rough grain of the paper is an order of magnitude larger than the clean die of the template pressed into it (not to mention the minute wavers of a typical phonograph groove), and so it offers itself up as a source of amplified variance and vibration. With its recording filter larger than any information it might be required to record, the substrate of the phonograph is manifest as "noise" in both the audio and media-theory sense. The medium itself, in the absence of any information from the matrix, gladly supplies the message. With a similar turn, Thurston's project establishes a mode of mechanical reproduction in which the original master cannot make replicas: each disc sounds distinctly different, depending on the chance arrangement of its pulp's pressed fibers and the type of paper used. Like Apollinaire's Merlin, the enchanted needle makes "des gestes blancs parmi les solitudes [some motions among white solitudes]," spinning like a desert dervish toward a centrifugal collapse as the stylus surgically incises, slowly abrades, and ultimately cuts through with sufficient playings, revealing the black humor of Ubu's spiraled *gidouille* beneath.[37] Sized so that the needle completes its course in exactly sixty seconds (when spun at the eponymous thirty-three and one-half revolutions per minute), these inflexibly flexible pages are little clocks each timing a perfect minute waltz.

■ Vasilii (Vasilisk) Gnedov: смерть искусству (*Smert' iskusstvu*, Death to art) (St. Petersburg: Peterburgsky Glashatay, 1913). Sound poetry reduced to the blank page. "Silence in this sense, as termination, proposes a mood of ultimacy," as Susan Sontag would write about the rhetoric of silence in 1967, framing the postwar aesthetics of silence as a *reductio* of modern art: the logical conclusion of Greenbergian modernism arriving at a "point of final simplification."[38] As James Sherry has observed, a blank sheet of paper is worth about 4 cents, but as soon as you print a poem on it, it's rendered economically worthless; смерть искусству, accordingly, keeps its value and is worth every cent. While one might consider Jason Kahn and John Müller's *Papercuts* (Crouton 22, 2004) or Steve Roden's *Forms of Paper* (Line_007, 2005) to be versions, the definitive recording of Gnedov's page was realized by Miguel Molina in 2007 and pressed by ReR Megacorp in 2009 in an edition of 150 personalized copies, strictly *hors commerce*. An historically informed production that would make all three Kuijken brothers proud, that disc records playback from an unregistered wax cylinder, re-creating the sound of silence circa 1913. Molina's realization thus transforms Gnedov's poem into a cenotaph for the particular silence of wax, which was replaced by amberol celluloid plastic in 1912, just as Gnedov composed his text. Following the recitation of Gnedov's alternate title, "Поэма конца" (Poem of the end), the disc hisses and pops with the vacuum squall of a brittle wax wind for ninety-three minutes and fifty-five seconds. As Molina's CD-R evinces, Sontag's vanishing point is always a point of departure as well; Gnedov designated his work as an epic poem (поэма), rather than a lyric (стихотвореные), and his histrionic declamations of the work were immensely popular with audiences who clamored for renditions at poetry readings and brought down the house with their applause. All of which must have sounded a lot like a Pavel Büchler album.

Notes

1   THE LOGIC OF SUBSTRATE

1. John Cage, "Lecture on Nothing," in Cage, *Silence* (Middletown: Wesleyan University Press, 1961), 105.

2. In particular, *Le rien* would also have recalled Flaubert's famous letter (16 January 1852) in which he writes the frequently cited parenthetical:

   > Ce qui me semble beau, ce que je voudrais faire, c'est un livre sur rien, un livre sans attache extérieure, qui se tiendrait de lui-même par la force interne de son style, comme la terre sans être soutenue se tient en l'air, un livre qui n'aurait presque pas de sujet ou du moins où le sujet serait presque invisible, si cela se peut.

   > [What seems beautiful to me, what I would like to make, is a book about nothing, a book without exterior link, which supports itself by the internal force of its style, like the earth suspended in space, a book which would have almost no subject, or at least where the subject would be almost invisible, if that is possible.]

   Gustave Flaubert, *Correspondance*, vol. 2, ed. Jean Bruneau (Paris: Gallimard, 1980), 31.

3. Nor are any of these possibilities as far-fetched as they might sound. Jiří Valoch published a small, blank, fifty-five-page *Book about Nothing* (Brno, 1970); Barrie (bp) Nichol responded with *A Condensed History of Nothing*, treating the same subject in the same manner, but in only eight pages and a reduced format (Toronto: Ganglia Press, 5 cent mini mimeo series No. 39, 1970). In Mladen Stilinović's *Oduzimanje nula* (To subtract zeroes) (Ljubljana: Zavod Parasite, 2006), the blank upper portions of the booklet's translucent pages appear to be illustrations of the hand-drawn equations at their bottom: arithmetical equations involving only zeroes. The otherwise unmarked pages seem to figure either the "nothing" that results from adding, subtracting, or multiplying zero with itself, or the impossibility of illustrating division by zero. Applying the principle of subtracting nothing from nothing to the sequential structure of the book itself, each page subtracts from the number of written

zeroes until eventually even the notation of nothing, the zero itself, is subtracted—leaving only a final, entirely blank page as its remainder.

Such books are a positive version of the genre of humorous writing based on stereotyped insults: the blank page in Len Shackleton's autobiography under the chapter heading "The Average Director's Knowledge of Football," or Victor Dinnerstein's *The Wit and Wisdom of Spiro T. Agnew* (Los Angeles: Price Stern Sloan, 1969), or any number of frequently racist or sexist variations. Perhaps the most interesting example of this genre is Ed Sanders's *A Valorium Edition of the Entire Extant Works of Thales! The Famous Milesian Poet, Philosopher, Physicist, Astronomer, Mathematician, Cosmologist, Urstoff-Freak, Absent-Minded Professor & Madman* (New York: Fuck You Press, 1964); after a brief introduction by Aristotle (in Greek), the following page of the four-page pamphlet is blank. Thales of Miletus—typically considered the first figure of Western philosophy—left no writings.

With a more complicated and belabored dynamic, blank pages also serve as an aggressive retort in Marcel Broodthaers's edition of Charles Baudelaire's *Pauvre Belgique!* (Poor Belgium!) (Brussels: Daled, Gevaert & Lebeer, 1974); behind a new cover and jacket, Broodthaers replicates the covers of Baudelaire's *Œuvres complètes* (Bibliothèque de la Pléiade), within which he frames one hundred and forty-two pages from the Pléiade, paginated 1315 to 1457, with running titles ("Sur la Belgique" and "Pauvre Belgique," respectively) but with all of Baudelaire's text eliminated. (For details on the publication, see Yves Gevaert with the collaboration of Émile van Balberghe, "*Pauvre Belgique*: 'An Asterisk in History,'" trans. John Shepley, *October* 42 [1987]: 182–195.) Censoring Baudelaire's mean-spirited travel notes in this way, Broodthaers also literalizes the terms of his predecessor's condescending cultural critique. Seeing his subject as an essay "du rien [on nothing]," Baudelaire weighs the prospective title "La Belgique toute nue [Belgium naked]" against "La Belgique déshabillée [Belgium unclothed]." Baudelaire's Belgium is characterized (or caricatured) by absence: "pas de trottoirs" (no sidewalks); "pas de ruisseaux" (no gutters); "pas de toilettes" (no toilets); "pas d'étalages" (no stalls); et cetera. Although there are, in contrast, "beaucoup de balcons [many balconies]," there is "personne au balcon [no one on them]." That pervasive architectural emptiness is matched by a cultural void; Belgian cuisine is "absente dans les Restaurants—ou plutôt pas de restaurants [absent from the restaurants—or, rather, there are no restaurants]"; there are no women ("pas de femmes"); nor is there love ("pas d'amour"), which is conspicuous in its absence ("L'amour brille par son absence")—in short: "pas de vie [no life]." Among "le néant belge [the Belgian nothingness]," "tous les Belges, sans exception, ont le crâne vide [all Belgians, without exception, have empty skulls]." More recently, Ara Shirinyan's *Your Country Is Great: Afghanistan—Guyana* (New York: Futurepoem, 2008) contains chance restagings of this national commentary, halfway between Baudelaire and Broodthaers. Following the constraint that the language of the poems must come from Internet searches for the name of a country followed by the statement "is great," the pages following the titles "Antigua and Barbuda," "Burkina Faso," "Burundi," "Central African Republic," and "Equatorial Guinea" are blank. Apparently, no one anywhere on the World Wide Web had ever said those countries were great.

Like Broodthaers, Jessica Smith offers a rebuke in the form of blank pages. Smith's book *Zen* forms its title by eliminating most of the letters in the title of Friedrich Nietzsche's *Also sprach Zarathustra: ein Buch für Alle und Keinen*, and it finds its format defined by Smith's edition of Nietzsche's book, which supplied the number of pages to be included in her publication. While her blank book might be read as a commentary on any number of Nietzschean themes, the capricious method of generating the title (why one particular *e* or *n* rather than another? Why the distributed "zen" rather than "rat," say?) points to the target of her critique: the mania for *soi-disant* erasure poems that followed the success of Tom Phillips's *A Humument* books and Jen Bervin's *Nets* (Brooklyn: Ugly Duckling Presse, 2004). By erasing the entirety of its source text, *Zen* flaunts the *reductio ad absurdum* of the genre. At the same time, the bite of Smith's cynicism hinges on the possibility of a more sincere reading of the blank pages in relation to the title. From this perspective, her book mocks the mystical associations cultivated by blank books such as Idries Shah's *The Book of the Book* (London: Octagon Press, 1969), which follows a dozen pages of prefatory text with blank pages, as a lesson in Sufi mysticism. Similarly, Anne Mœglin-Delcroix reads Herman de Vries's series of blank books as manifestations of the same heady mix of D. T. Suzuki's Buddhism and Meister Eckhart's German mysticism that captivated John Cage (*Herman de Vries: les livres et les publications* [Saint-Yrieix-la-Perche: Centre de Livres d'Artistes, 2005]).

Further documentation of the surprisingly copious subgenre of the blank book can be found in Michael Gibbs's *All or Nothing: An Anthology of Blank Books* (Cromford: Research Group for Artists Publications, 2005) and Anne Mœglin-Delcroix's "Neither Word nor Image: Blank Books," in *Voids: A Retrospective* (Zurich: JRP|Ringier, 2009). Several examples of literary blank pages may be found in Louis Lüthi, *On the Self-Reflexive Page* (The Netherlands: Roma Publications, 2010), 23–45.

4. The rejoinder from Orpheus's companion looks forward to the line from Caetano Veloso's "O Estrangeiro": "Tudo cala frente ao fato de que o rei é mais bonito nu [Everything is silent before the fact that the emperor is much more beautiful nude]" (Caetano Veloso, *Estrangeiro* [London: Mango CIDM1028, 1990]).

5. Jacques Derrida, *La Carte postale: de Socrate à Freud au-delà* (Paris: Flammarion, 1980), 443.

6. Ibid., 446.

7. Ibid., 443.

8. The audience for *Orphée*, one should recall, would likely have seen the cur-tained movie screen unveiled, so that the blank pages of *Nudisme* figure their own cinematic ground to some extent: the blank space of the screen itself *mise-en-abîme* and visible in the unshadowed wash of the projector's light. In any event, the blank page as a site for projection—whether cinematic or psychological—resonates with surrealist cinema.

9. Jean Baudrillard, *L'Autre par lui même* (Paris: Éditions Galilée, 1987), 20.

10. Ibid.

11. Ibid.

12. Ibid.

13. Heinz Gappmayr, *Raum* (Munich: Edition UND, 1977; 2nd ed., Aachen: Ottenhausen Verlag, 1983); cf. Gappmayr's *Quadrat* (1981).

14. John McDowall's artist's book *Still Life* (Bradford, 2005) makes a similar point by printing the shape of the shadows cast by the curving pages as they are read under particular conditions.

15. In the Kulchur Foundation Records archived at Columbia University, the book is catalogued as untitled (as Saroyan himself refers to it); in *Contemporary Poets* (Detroit: St. James Press, 1970) it is listed as "(An untitled book)" (369). The biographical note in Paul Carroll's *The Young American Poets* (Chicago: Follett, 1968) describes it as "an untitled wrapped ream of typing paper stamped © Aram Saroyan 1968" (369). Alternately, in contemporaneous advertise-ments it is titled "1968" (see, for example, *Evergreen Review* 12, no. 58 [September 1968]: 100). That advertisement also indicates a "four dollar" hardback, but I can find no other record of such a binding. Saroyan recalls the edition size was one thousand copies (Aram Saroyan, "Contretemps: A Minimalist Parable," *Jacket* 33 [July 2007]: n.p.). As a set of five hundred sheets, the form of Saroyan's book looks forward to Robert Grenier's boxed set of five hundred index cards, *Sentences* (Cambridge: Whale Cloth, 1978).

16. See the contributors' notes to *Poetry* 110, no. 6 (1967): 435.

17. Lita Hornick, *The Green Fuse: A Memoir* (New York: Giorno Poetry Systems, 1989), 45. Alternately, Hornick might have suspected that the proposal was a commentary on whether even the small readership for avant-garde poetry actually reads the books at all. Contemporaneously, a not particularly funny humor column proposed that since most professors never really read the dis-sertations they claim to vet, prospective doctoral candidates might "merely attach a Deluxe Title to a ream of blank typing paper and turn it in" (Rudolf

Harvey, "What to Do until the Doctorate Arrives," *Music Journal* 25, no. 4 [1967]: 62).

18. William Saroyan, "Perhaps You Know Ann Danford," in Saroyan, *Where the Bones Go*, ed. Robert Setrakian (Fresno: Press at California State University, Fresno, 2002), 50.

19. William Saroyan, *The Daring Young Man on the Flying Trapeze and Other Stories* (New York: New Directions, 1997), 66.

20. Harlan Hatcher, "William Saroyan," *English Journal* 28, no. 3 (March 1939): 175.

21. Aram Saroyan, *Coffee Coffee* (New York: 0 to 9, 1967); *Aram Saroyan* (New York: Random House, 1968); *Pages* (New York: Random House, 1969). For an archaeology of the typewriter, see Darren Wershler-Henry, *The Iron Whim: A Fragmented History of Typewriting* (Ithaca: Cornell University Press, 2007).

22. Kulchur Foundation records, 1936–1994, Columbia University Libraries Special Collections; Series I: Correspondence, 1961–1993; Box 5: Folder 23, Letter No. 10, Aram Saroyan (12 November 1967).

23. One should note that within *Pages* the fonts are varied (or, more probably, the typescript was photographically enlarged to varying degrees). Additionally, although both are typewritten texts enlarged to the point of revealing the imperfections of the metal letterforms' inked impressions, the cover of *Pages* is in "another style" than *Aram Saroyan*; indeed, the style of the cover text differs from the typeface of its own back-cover copy and interior poems. Presumably the designers at Random House worked from their own mock-up of the title page, typed on a different brand of typewriter. The typeface, significantly, is different again for the collection of these works in Saroyan's *Complete Minimal Poems* (Brooklyn: Ugly Duckling Presse, 2008).

24. Saroyan, *Pages*, back-cover copy. In her memoir, Theodora Bosanquet, James's amanuensis, recalls:

> Indeed, at the time when I began to work for him, he had reached a stage at which the click of a Remington machine acted as a positive spur. He found it more difficult to compose to the music of any other make. During a fortnight when the Remington was out of order he dictated to an Oliver typewriter with evident discomfort, and he found it almost disconcerting to speak to something that made no responsive sound at all.

Theodora Bosanquet, "Henry James at Work," *The Hogarth Essays* (London: Hogarth Press, 1928), 248.

25. Saroyan, "Contretemps." The Kulchur archives indicate the other possibilities Saroyan initially entertained: "1. A completely visual book, employing larger than standard type face. This is my favorite idea so far. 2. A chronological

selection of my work—from early 'regular' poems on out, and out. . . . 3. A book of short poems and visual works from the last year or so." Kulchur Foundation records, 1936–1994, Columbia University Libraries Special Collections; Series I: Correspondence, 1961–1993; Box 5: Folder 23, Letter No. 8, Aram Saroyan (21 October 1966).

26. Quoted in Paul Goldberger, "The Sky Line: Charles and Ray Eames, Multimedia Pioneers," *New Yorker* 75, no. 11 (24 May 1999): 98. Eames's position recalls Ludwig Wittgenstein's aphorism: "In der Kunst ist es schwer etwas zu sagen, was so gut ist wie: nichts zu sagen [in art, it is hard to say something better than saying nothing]" (*Vermischte Bemerkungen* [Frankfurt: Suhrkamp, 1977], 50). Or, as Ulises Carrión would write: "The most beautiful and perfect book in the world is a book with only blank pages, in the same way that the most complete language is that which lies beyond all that the words of a man can say. / Every book of the new art is searching after that book of absolute whiteness, in the same way that every poem searches for silence" (Carrión, "The New Art of Making Books," *Kontexts* 6–7 [1975]). Carrión, in turn, echoes Mallarmé: "L'armature intellectuelle du poème se dissimule et tient—a lieu—dans l'espace qui isole les strophes et parmi le blanc du papier: significatif silence qu'il n'est pas moins beau de composer que les vers [The intellectual armature of the poem disguises itself and takes place—posits itself—in the space that isolates the stanzas among the white of the paper: significant silence which is no less beautiful to compose than verse]."

27. Arthur C. Danto, *Andy Warhol* (New Haven: Yale University Press, 2009), 52. In *Smithsonian Depositions* (New York: Vehicle Editions, 1980), 10, Clark Coolidge brings the rectangular ream into proximity with the cardboard box, emphasizing the mass and weight of the paper in the process: "500 sheets of Substance 20 8½ X 11 Sphinx Aristocrat Mimeo Bond (white stock) lain on a slab of plywood propped on cardboard moving-boxes in a corner."

28. Aram Saroyan, *Friends in the World: The Education of a Writer* (Minneapolis: Coffee House, 1992), 84. Saroyan specifically recalls being impressed by the Warhol *Brillo Box* in Ted Berrigan's apartment (ibid., 38).

29. Lyn Hejinian and Craig Dworkin, "Roughly Stapled: An Interview with Lyn Hejinian," *Idiom* 3 (Berkeley, 1995): unpaginated.

30. See Marcel Duchamp, *Notes*, ed. Paul Matisse (Boston: G. K. Hall, 1983): "Séparation infra mince entre / le bruit de *détonation* d'un fusil / (très proche) et l' / *apparition* de la marque de / la balle sur la cible" (Note 12); "La chaleur d'un siège (qui vient / d'être quitté) est infra-mince" (Note 4); "Quand la fumée de tabac sent aussi de / la bouche qui l'exhale, les 2 odeurs / s'epousent par infra-mince" (Note 11; cf. Note 33); "La différence / (dimensionnelle) entre / 2 objets faits en / séries [sortis du / même moule]" (Note 18); "différence entre

les volumes d'air déplacés par une chemise propre (repassée et pliée) et la même chemise sale" (*London Bulletin* 13 [15 April 1939]: 12).

31. Quoted in Denis de Rougemont, *Journal d'une époque* (Paris: Gallimard, 1968), 567. Cf. Duchamp, *Notes*, Notes 17–20.

32. Duchamp, *Notes*, Note 45. Although it is not a flat surface, the same practice of aligning surfaces underlies Friedman's untitled 1990 work, an unspooled roll of toilet paper, with its cardboard spine removed, which has been smoothly rerolled to its original state; in the context of the other works under discussion here, one should note that this sculpture is essentially a series of perforated blank pages. Indeed, Friedman has frequently used blank pages for their sculptural properties, exploiting their *inframince* depth and tendency to curl in ellipsoid curves under typical conditions of atmospheric humidity and gravitational pull: the shadowed surface facture of two identically wrinkled sheets of paper (1990); a paper pierced by a pin so often that it loses its structural integrity, softening and sagging but not tearing (1991); a suspended sheet of paper torn almost completely in half but still connected by a single fiber (1992); a piece of paper cut and curled into bursts of blistered stars (1997).

33. Although Asher left the decision to the editors' discretion, the glued pages were not entirely blank; the journal's standard headers—noting the pagination and Asher's name—were printed as usual, although they obviously cannot be easily read. See Michael Asher, *Writings 1973–1983 on Works 1969–1979* (Halifax: Press of the Nova Scotia College, 1983), 108–109. Compare Asher's gesture to the extended procedure undertaken by Les Coleman's *Glue* (London: In House Publishing, 2002), a small-format (12.5 x 17 cm) booklet with around thirty pages. At once less precise and more materially specific than Asher's piece, Coleman lists the dozen different types of glue—Coccoina, Pritt Copydex, PVA-UHU, et cetera—used to affix the pages to one another, with a slight cumulative creasing and puckering that rimples the stiffened interior pages.

One might consider Asher's work to be less as a version of Robert Barry's magazine pieces than his proposal in *Art & Project Bulletin* 17 (December 1969): "During the exhibition the gallery will be closed." Concurrently, the Galleria Sperone (Turin) hosted a show by Barry that was announced with the following advisory: "For the exhibition the gallery will be closed—per la mostra la galleria sarà chiusa." Accordingly, Asher's piece announces, in essence: for the publication the pages will be closed.

For a history of empty galleries and evacuated exhibitions see the extraordinary catalogue *Vides: une retrospective*, edited by Mathieu Copeland with John Armleder, Laurent Le Bon, Gustav Metzger, Mai-Thu Perret, Clive Philpot and Philippe Pirotte (Paris: Éditions du Centre Pompidou, 2009). The book contains extensive documentation of modern artistic concerns with nothingness, immateriality and the void relevant to a more metaphysical and existential reading of the works under discussion here. Related catalogues include an ironically diminutive one to accompany "The Big Nothing" at the ICA (Ingrid Schaffner, Bennett Simpson, and Tanya Leighton, eds., *The Big Nothing* [Philadelphia: University of Pennsylvania, 2004]) and Martina Weinhart and Max Hollein, eds., *Nichts*, following a 2006 exhibition on "nothing" at the Shirn Kunsthalle Frankfurt (Ostfildern: Hatje Cantz Verlag, 2006). For evidence of continued interest in the topic, see *Cahier Louis-Lumière* 6 (Spring 2009), edited by Gérard Pelé, devoted to "vide, vacuité, désœvremnet [void, emptiness, idleness]."

34. Asher, *Writings*, 108.

35. "Serious Playboys: Tom Friedman in Conversation with John Waters," *Parkett* 64 (2002): 82.

36. Sterne's modes of direct address to the reader in *Tristram Shandy* are varied; for a considered analysis, see Barbara M. Benedict, "'Dear Madam': Rhetoric, Cultural Politics and the Female Reader in Sterne's *Tristram Shandy*," *Studies in Philology* 89, no. 4 (Autumn 1992): 485–498. Because of Tristram's instructions to the reader to draw the portrait "as unlike your wife as your conscience will let you," Benedict glosses the blank page as "a test of the 'gentle' reader's aesthetic talents and taste, not an opportunity for unmonitored day-dreaming" (494). The female reader, she continues, "is banished from the text. This exclusionary rhetoric reasserts the value of social control." Earlier, her discussion of curiosity is particularly apposite (491–492).

37. Laurence Sterne, *Tristram Shandy*, new ed. (London: T. Becket and P.A. Dehondt, 1769), vol. 6, 146–147. Davis Schneiderman's *Blank* (n.p: Jaded Ibis Press, 2010) extends the conceit to the level of narrative, simultaneously inviting the reader to imagine the events unfolding in each of its twenty chapters and underscoring the extent to which novelistic cliché's have already anticipated and determined the scope of what the reader is supposedly free to fantasize. Contrary to its title, the book is far from blank, with summary chapter titles ("a character"; "another character"; "they meet"; et cetera), page numbers, obtrusively smudged running heads, and a gratuitous suite of similarly smeared abstract illustrations (by Susan White) that hint at the ominous headings of the final chapters but ultimately cannot be accounted for by the narrative.

38. *Merriam-Webster Collegiate Dictionary*, 11th ed. (2004), 764.

39. Bruce Hainley, ed., *Tom Friedman* (New York: Phaidon, 2001), 9.

40. Michel de Certeau, *L'invention du quotidien*, vol. 1: *Arts de faire*, rev. ed. (Paris: Gallimard, 1990), 71; trans. Steven Rendall as *The Practice of Everyday Life* (Berkeley: University of California Press, 1984), 43.

41. Teresa de Lauretis, "Calvino and the Amazons: Reading the (Post) Modern Text," in de Lauretis, *Technologies of Gender: Essays on Theory, Film, and Fiction* (Bloomington: Indiana University Press, 1987), 75; Susan Gubar, "'The Blank Page' and the Issues of Female Creativity," in Elizabeth Abel, ed., *Writing and Sexual Difference* (Chicago: University of Chicago Press, 1982), 77. On the sexual psychology of the figure of the "virgin page," see also Sandra Gilbert and Susan Gubar, *The Madwoman in the Attic: The Woman Writer and the Nineteenth-Century Literary Imagination* (New Haven: Yale University Press, 1984), 6. For just one example of the figure, which puts some pressure on the metaphorization of a solitary manual activity as copulation, recall Thomas Moore's "Take Back the Virgin Page," which was written, the subtitle tells us, on the occasion of "returning a blank book": "Take back the virgin page, / White and unwritten still; some hand, more calm and sage, / The leaf must fill."

42. A similar dynamic obtains in Frédéric Laé's *Une épreuve vierge* (A blank copy) (Brest: Zédélé, 2004), a book of blank pages taken, so the author attests, from the warm-up run of the offset press for the Nantes newspaper *Presse-Océan*; the discarded sheets have passed through the press as its settings are adjusted, but they remain unprinted. The title translates, literally, as "a virgin proof."

43. Jacques Derrida, *De la grammatologie* (Paris: Éditions de Minuit, 1967), 203ff.

44. Isak Dinesen (pseudonym of Karen Blixen) narrates the blank page as a sign of potential in her short story "The Blank Page," in which a famous bard proclaims:

> Who then tells a finer tale than any of us? Silence does. And where does one read a deeper tale than upon the most perfectly printed page of the most precious book? Upon the blank page. When a royal and gallant pen, in the moment of its highest inspiration, has written down its tale with the rarest ink of all—where, then, may one read a still deeper, sweeter, merrier and more cruel tale than that? Upon the blank page.

Compare this valorization of the blank page with Wassily Kandinsky's assertion that a blank canvas is "full of expectation" (*Complete Writings on Art*, ed. Kenneth Lindsay and Peter Vergo [New York: Da Capo, 1994], 780); he continues: "Wonderful is the empty canvas—more beautiful than some paintings."

45. Volume 3, no. 6.

46. Without challenging the underlying terms of fecund female space, Gubar realigns the sexual metaphors of the blank page with "a revisionary female theology" ("'The Blank Page,'" 92; cf. 91). For Gubar, accordingly, the blank pages of the *Little Review* become an assertion of a distinctly female creativity in place of a masculine inking: "The female divinity for the male god, the womb for the penis" (ibid., 92). Basing her reading on Margaret Anderson's

The Unknowable Gurdjieff (London: Routledge, 1962), rather than on the journal itself, Gubar misstates the number of blank pages; Anderson writes, "We brought out a number made up of sixty-four blank pages" (75). The discrepancy is surprising, since the journal rarely ran to half as many pages at the time, but beyond the missed opportunity for a punctilious accounting Gubar's mistake is telling, since it suggests the common supposition—contrary to the argument I am making here—that one does not need to actually read blank pages, and that the idea of their blankness rather than their physical particulars are sufficient.

47. "We Also Await," Little Review 3, no. 7 (November 1916): 27.

48. "So Did We," ibid.

49. Jacques Derrida, La Verité en peinture (Paris: Flammarion, 1993), 63.

50. I have only seen reproductions of the cover and have not seen the journal myself, drawing corroborating information from the following: "Issue no. 10 consists of blank pages, with information on the issue printed on a separate sheet of paper inserted into the magazine" (Dubravka Djurić and Miško Šuvaković, Impossible Histories: Historic Avant-Gardes, Neo-Avant-Gardes, and Post-Avant-Gardes in Yugoslavia, 1918–1991 [Cambridge: MIT Press, 2003], 318). "In issue number 10, the pages are completely blank—all information (title, publisher, issue no., year) is printed on a separate piece of paper the size of a calling card, inserted among the empty white sheets" (Laura J. Hoptman and Tomás Pospiszyl, eds., Primary Documents: A Sourcebook for Eastern and Central European Art since the 1950s [Cambridge: MIT Press, 2002], 132).

   More reductionist still, another issue of Gorgona was proposed by Dimitrije Bašičević, who "designated an issue that was not to be published" (Gwen Allen, Artists' Magazines: An Alternative Space for Art [Cambridge: MIT Press, 2011]: 263).

51. Quoted in Djurić and Šuvaković, Impossible Histories, 316.

52. Kozlov's pages were presented at the "Number 7" show, Paula Cooper Gallery (New York), 18 May–15 June 1969; cited in Lucy Lippard, Six Years: The Dematerialization of the Art Object from 1966 to 1972 (New York: Praeger, 1973), 101. More tentatively, one could consider Martin Kippenberger's melodramatic No Drawing No Cry (Cologne: Walther König, 2000), a book reproducing hundreds of pages of (mostly) blank hotel stationery—materials that had served as the basis for two previous books of drawings.

53. Undertaken between June 1981 and October 1987, these events were subsumed under the collective title Nightsea Crossing (Mary Richards, Marina Abramović [New York: Routledge, 2010], 22, 48; Charles Green, The Third

Hand: Collaboration in Art from Conceptualism to Postmodernism [Minneapolis: University of Minnesota Press, 2001], 171–172).

54. Adrian Heathfield and Tehching Hsieh, *Out of Now: The Lifeworks of Tehching Hsieh* (Cambridge: MIT Press, 2009), 48. The previous year (1985–1986), Hsieh had set out to "not do ART, not talk ART, not see ART, not read ART" (ibid., 46).

55. Center for Conceptual Art Bukovje (Slovenia), http://www.cac-bukovje.com/pastevents1000.html.

    Blom's performance highlights the element of intentionality. Can one say, following Blom's equation, that the indecisive shopper at an office supply store has performed the "rationalized re-enactment" of *1,000 Hours of Staring* by staring for a minute at one hundred and twenty reams of copy paper on the shelf?

56. Malevich's painting is 31.25 inches square.

57. Thierry de Duve, *Kant after Duchamp* (Cambridge: MIT Press, 1998), 251; although it goes unremarked in *Kant after Duchamp*, de Duve does interrogate the sexual vocabulary of the "virgin canvas" elsewhere; see *Nominalisme pictural: Marcel Duchamp, la peinture et la modernité* (Paris: Minuit, 1984), 35–36.

58. De Duve, *Kant after Duchamp*, 255–257ff.

59. Ibid., 252.

60. Although no poem follows Gnedov's title, because it is the last page in the pamphlet the page does contain the paratextual information for the book as a whole, advertising the printer and the date of publication.

61. Two earlier poems in the book, numbers 11 and 14, consist of only a single letter each.

62. Lisa Gitelman, *Always Already New: Media, History, and the Data of Culture* (Cambridge: MIT Press, 2006), 7.

63. Ibid.

64. Mark Hansen, *Embodying Technesis: Technology beyond Writing* (Ann Arbor: University of Michigan Press, 2000), 4.

65. Overlapping terminology can lead to apparent contradictions; John Guillory emphasizes JoAnne Yates's premise "that one must not confuse media and genre" because "the *generic* feature of written communication" evolved in response to institutional pressures "and not initially to the creation of new media" (John Guillory, "The Memo and Modernity," *Critical Inquiry* 31, no. 1 [Autumn 2004]: 115; Guillory is summarizing JoAnne Yates, *Control through*

Communication: The Rise of System in American Management [Baltimore: Johns Hopkins University Press, 1989]).

66. herman de vries: vijf manifesten over taal—en een gedicht = fünf manifeste über sprache—und ein gedicht . . . (Bern: artists press, 1975), n.p.

To continue to read in the absence of that meaning would adhere to what Michel Foucault (L'Ordre du discours [Paris: Gallimard, 1971], 55) designated "la règle de l'extériorité [the rule of exteriority]":

> ne pas aller du discours vers son noyau intérieur ou caché, vers le coeur d'une pensée ou d'une signification qui se manifesteraient en lui; mais, à partir du discours lui-même, de son apparition et de sa régularité, aller vers ses conditions externes de possibilité, vers ce qui donne lieu à la série aléatoire de ces événements et qui en fixe les bornes.

> [not to go from a discourse toward its interior or hidden core, toward the heart of a thought or a meaning which manifests itself in that discourse, but rather to go away from discourse itself—from its appearance and its regularity—to seek its external conditions of possibility, to seek out what provides a space for the chance series of its events and which establishes its limits.]

One direction for external readings would lead to the antihermeneutic impulse in German media studies; see, to begin with: Hans Ulrich Gumbrecht, "A Farewell to Interpretation" and K. Ludwig Pfeiffer, "The Materiality of Communication," in their jointly edited collection Materialities of Communication, trans. William Whobrey (Stanford: Stanford University Press, 1994), 389–402, 1–14; David E. Wellbery, "The Exteriority of Writing," Stanford Literature Review 9 (1992): 11–23; Friedrich Kittler, Discourse Networks 1800/1900, trans. Michael Metteer with Chris Cullens (Stanford: Stanford University Press, 1990).

67. Darren Wershler has drawn my attention to the correspondence between my thinking here and recent scholarship on what Will Straw has called the "circulatory turn" in media theory; following that turn, "the principal question concerning media is not their action in relation to some prior substance (like social discourse, knowledge, or subjectivity) to which they give form. Rather, the turn to circulation comes with an understanding of media as mobile forms circulating within social space" (Will Straw, "The Circulatory Turn," in Barbara Crow, Michael Longford, and K. Sawchuk, eds., The Wireless Spectrum: The Politics, Practices and Poetics of Mobile Media [Toronto: University of Toronto Press, 2010], 23).

Following the antihermeneutic German scholarship referenced in the note above, "the nature of this intervention is an anti-interpretive one, intended to challenge a concern with cultural forms which sees them principally as bearers (however mobile) of meaning" (Straw, "The Circulatory Turn," 23). Such work sees circulation not as the transmission of some prior meaning, but as itself creating meaning: "Circulation is a cultural process with its own forms of abstraction, evaluation, and constraint, which are created by the interactions between specific types of circulating forms and the interpretive communities built around them" (Benjamin Lee and Edward LiPuma, "Cultures of Circulation: The Imaginations of Modernity," *Public Culture* 14, no. 1 [Winter 2002]: 192).

68. For example, "Non-Cochlear Sound," curated by Seth Kim-Cohen, Diapason Gallery, Brooklyn, October 2010.

69. Charles Bernstein frames the same point this way: "As James Sherry noted years ago in $L=A=N=G=U=A=G=E$: a piece of paper with nothing on it has a definite economic value. If you print a poem on it, this value is lost" (Charles Bernstein, *My Way: Speeches and Poems* [Chicago: University of Chicago Press, 1999], 150). Taking that bibliographic potlatch to an extreme, Jean Keller proposes publication as an economic calculus with his print-on-demand project *The Black Book*:

> Ink used for digital printing is one of the most precious substances in the world. A single gallon of ink costs over four thousand dollars and this is one reason why digitally printed books are so expensive.
>
> However, the price of a book is not calculated according to the amount of ink used in its production. For example, a Blurb book of blank pages costs an artist as much to produce as a book filled with text or large photographs. Furthermore, as the number of pages increases, the price of each page decreases. A book containing the maximum number of pages printed entirely in black ink therefore results in the lowest cost and maximum value for the artist.

> Combining these two features, buyers of *The Black Book* can do so with the guarantee that they are getting the best possible value for their money (http://www.blurb.com/bookstore/detail/1768873, accessed 15 April 2011).
>
> Even beyond these instances, one should be alert to the economic sense of the word *medium*, as in the idiom "medium of exchange," which remains strong. The example of a "Swiss bank" as a medium in the *Oxford English Dictionary* illustration does not appear by chance.

70. Robert Morris, "Blank Form," in Peter Osborne, ed., *Conceptual Art* (London: Phaidon, 2002), 195.

71. De Duve, *Kant after Duchamp*, 250. From another perspective on the picture haunting even the most abstract artwork, Walter Benn Michaels identifies the very idea of substrate as the fundamental problem for minimalism (*The Shape of the Signifier: 1967 to the End of History* [Princeton: Princeton University Press, 2004], 85).

72. Quoted in Matthew G. Kirschenbaum, *Mechanisms: New Media and the Forensic Imagination* (Cambridge: MIT Press, 2008), 233. In arguing that media are dynamic procedures rather than static objects, I have the benefit of several conceptual models in addition to Abby Smith's. Jerome McGann argues, for instance, that "a 'text' is not a 'material thing' but a material event, or set of events" (*The Textual Condition* [Princeton: Princeton University Press, 1991], 21). N. Katherine Hayles, similarly, argues that "rigorously speaking, an electronic text is a *process* rather than an object, although objects (like hardware and software) are required to produce it," and further: "Materiality should be understood as existing in complex dynamic interplay with content . . . as *the interplay between a text's physical characteristics and its signifying strategies*" ("Print Is Flat, Code Is Deep: The Importance of Media-Specific Analysis," *Poetics Today* 25, no. 1 [Spring 2004]: 79, 71, 72). Hayles will later identify that interplay as an "emergent property": something "created through dynamic interactions between physical characteristics and signifying strategies," so that "the materiality of an embodied text is the interaction of its physical characteristics with its signifying strategies" (*My Mother Was a Computer: Digital Subjects and Literary Texts* [Chicago: University of Chicago Press, 2005], 2, 104 and passim, 103; cf. 9). More recently, John Bryant has conceived of the literary "work" as a process rather than a product, arguing that literary works are not things but rather flows of energy—work, that is, in the sense of *travaille* rather than *oeuvre*, as the scientific measure of force over a distance (*The Fluid Text: A Theory of Revision and Editing for Book and Screen* [Ann Arbor: University of Michigan Press, 2002], 61).

73. Kirschenbaum, *Mechanisms*, 129.

74. Guillem de Peiteus, in Robert Kehew, ed., *Lark in the Morning: The Verses of the Troubadours* (Chicago: University of Chicago Press, 2005), 24.

2   CENOGRAPHY

1. Blanchot's *L'Espace littéraire* (Paris: Gallimard, 1955) was translated into English as *The Space of Literature* by Ann Smock (Lincoln: University of Nebraska Press, 1982); Thurston's text is based on this translation.

2. *Reading the Remove of Literature* (York: Information As Material, 2006) is set in a digital ITC Garamond, designed by Tony Stan in the 1970s, while *The Space of Literature* is set in Garamond #3, a face drawn for the Linotype Company in the 1920s. Both descend from an American Type Founders face, designed by Morris Benton and Thomas Cleland in the late teens, which was an influential modern revival of punches mistakenly attributed in the nineteenth century to Claude Garamond. Those matrices and punches were in fact

seventeenth-century designs by Jean Jannon (although the confusion is understandable, since Jannon's face is itself based loosely on Garamond's originals). See Paul Beaujon (pseudonym of Beatrice Warde), "The Garamond types: XVIth and XVIIth Century Sources Considered," *The Fleuron* 5 (1926): 131–179.

3. Blanchot, *L'Espace littéraire*, 51.

4. Michael Camille, *Image on the Edge: The Margins of Medieval Art* (Cambridge: Harvard University Press, 1992), 18.

5. Ibid., 21. Punctuation slightly modified.

6. *Adversaria* denotes, literally, what is written on one side of a sheet of paper. Relevant to the current project, however, the phrase also carries unintended suggestion of a writing turned toward or against itself. For a general introduction to the subject of marginalia, see H. J. Jackson, *Marginalia: Readers Writing in Books* (New Haven: Yale University Press, 2001).

   One specific genre of marginalia comes from copyeditors. Charles Gute, in a project that resonates with Thurston's book, has repurposed the discarded files from his freelance job copyediting art publications; with the original typescript source texts removed except for noted mistakes, Gute leaves his electronically marked-up corrections and suggestions floating over the page, in the diagrammatic format of Adobe's stylized geometric graphics: tight circles and narrow ovals; angled lines; horizontal brackets closing gaps and the hash of space; curlicues of deletion; cryptic phrases. Displaying only the errors, Gute's pages preserve the features of texts on the verge of disappearance—remainders from the subtraction of the galleys from the proofs.

7. Susan Howe, "Melville's Marginalia," in Howe, *The Nonconformist's Memorial* (New York: New Directions, 1993). Susan Howe Papers, MSS 0201, Series 3, Subsection F. Mandeville Special Collections Library, University of California at San Diego, Archive for New Poetry. Cowen's two-volume work was reprinted as part of the Harvard Dissertations in American and English Literature series (New York: Garland, 1987).

8. John Cage read Rauschenberg's work as a response to Marcel Duchamp's model: "Duchamp showed the usefulness of addition (mustache). Rauschenberg showed the function of subtraction (De Kooning)" (John Cage, "26 Statements Re Duchamp," in Cage, *A Year from Monday* [Middletown: Wesleyan University Press, 1967], 71). A less telegraphic argument connecting the two artists is made by Benjamin Buchloh, "Allegorical Procedures: Appropriation and Montage in Contemporary Art," *Artforum* 21, no. 1 (September 1982): 46 and passim. Duchamp may have been countering Rauschenberg's "function of subtraction" with his 1965 work consisting of a readymade image of *La Gioconda* (a playing card, as it happens) mounted on a sheet of paper with the caption "rasée / L.H.O.O.Q."; seen in the wake of Duchamp's iconic,

mustachioed version of the *Mona Lisa* from 1919, the unassisted image now appears as having been shaved (*rasée*).

9. Rauschenberg explains: "I erased the de Kooning [*sc.* the drawing] not out of any negative response. I was working on the all-white and all-black paintings. I loved to draw and I did erasure drawings. It just didn't make much sense for me to erase my own marks" (quoted in Stephanie Rosenthal, ed., *Black Paintings* [Otsfildern: Hatje Cantz, 2006], 30).

    In contrast to Rauschenberg's disavowal of any hostility to his source, Thurston admits that the gesture of his 2008 *Erased Kosuth Concept (Art as Idea as Idea as Art)* is equal parts "homage" and oedipal "patricide" (private correspondence, 4 November 2010). The work is another instance of textual elimination that has obvious similarities to *Reading the Remove of Literature*, although it substitutes the censoring black of cancellation for the white page of erasure. The *Erased Kosuth* replicates the 48-inch-square format of Kosuth's signature reproductions of dictionary definitions, as well as their mode of black and white silver printing. Thurston's work rephotographs one of Kosuth's 1966 "water" definitions (sourced from *Artists and Photographers Box*, ed. Lawrence Alloway [New York: Multiples, Inc., 1970]). During the process of photographic enlargement, however, Thurston permitted a sustained spill of light from the enlarger to eventually burn the image into an unreadable, uniform monochrome black. Kosuth's distinctive prints, with their white texts against a black background, were originally a result of the material particulars of the photostatic machines of the 1960s, which happened to make their first image in negative. Similarly, Thurston's black square takes its form not in imitation of the philosophical concerns of Ad Reinhardt or the spiritualist concerns of Kazimir Malevich, but rather from the technical particulars of its media: the unexpected and usually unwanted degree of refraction permitted by the enlarger set to produce a four-foot-square image.

10. John Cage, "Indeterminacy," in *Silence: Lectures and Writings by John Cage* (Middletown: Wesleyan University Press, 1961), 270.

11. As Cage writes in "45' for a Speaker": "There is no / such thing as silence. Something is al- / ways happening that makes a sound" (Cage, *Silence*, 91).

12. Although the veracity of the story is doubtful, Cage claimed to have learned this lesson when he heard the low percussive sound of his heart beat in what was otherwise the perfectly soundproof space of an anechoic chamber. See Cage, *Silence*, 8. For skepticism about the story, see Branden W. Joseph, "White on White," *Critical Inquiry* 27 (Autumn 2000): 105–106; Kyle Gann, *No Such Thing as Silence: John Cage's 4'33"* (New Haven: Yale University Press, 2010), 164ff.; and Seth Kim-Cohen, *In the Blink of an Ear: Towards a Non-cochlear Sonic Art* (New York: Continuum, 2009), 160–161.

13. Michel Foucault, *La pensée du dehors* (Paris: Fata Morgana, 1986), 56; translated by Brian Massumi as "Maurice Blanchot: The Thought from Outside," in *Foucault / Blanchot* (New York: Zone Books, 1987), 54.

14. Maurice Blanchot, *Le Pas au-delà* (Paris: Gallimard, 1973), 12–13.

15. Maurice Blanchot, *Le Très-Haut* (Paris: Gallimard, 1948), 233. For an interesting discussion of this scene, see Allan Stoekl, *Politics, Writing, Mutilation: The Cases of Bataille, Blanchot, Roussel, Leiris, and Ponge* (Minneapolis: University of Minnesota Press, 1985), 31. In *Au moment voulu* (Paris: Gallimard, 1951), Blanchot writes in similar terms of "tous les bruits silencieux qui attaquaient l'épaisseur de cette nuit [all the silent noises that attack the thickness of the night]" (56).

16. Maurice Blanchot, "La littérature et le droit à la mort," *Critique* 20 (January 1948): 37; trans. Lydia Davis as "Literature and the Right to Death," in *The Station Hill Blanchot Reader: Fiction and Literary Essays* (Barrytown: Station Hill, 1999), 387.

17. *Oxford English Dictionary.*

18. John Keats, *Hyperion* I.15.

19. Blanchot, "La littérature," 37 / "Literature," 387.

20. Maurice Blanchot, *L'Entretien infini* (Paris: Gallimard, 1971), 622; trans. Susan Hanson as *The Infinite Conversation* (Minneapolis: University of Minnesota Press, 1993), 424.

21. Blanchot, "La littérature," 37 / "Literature," 387.

22. Blanchot, *L'espace littéraire*, 9–10; trans. Lydia Davis from *The Station Hill Blanchot Reader*, 401.

23. Modified from Maurice Blanchot, "The Absence of the Book," trans. Lydia Davis from *The Station Hill Blanchot Reader*, 473.

24. Blanchot, *L'Entretien infini*, 622 / *Infinite Conversation*, 424; Blanchot, "La littérature," 35 / "Literature," 384; Blanchot, *L'Entretien infini*, 565 / *Infinite Conversation*, 385.

25. Denis Hollier, "Poetry . . . up to Z," *Yale French Studies* 81 (1992): 65–66. Cf. "Mais comme toute production, celle de l'abîme venait saturer ce qu'elle creuse [But like all *production*, that of the abyss came to saturate what it hollows out]" (Jacques Derrida, *La Vérité en peinture* [Paris: Flammarion, 1978], 40; translated as *The Truth in Painting*, trans. Geoff Bennington and Ian McLeod [Chicago: University of Chicago Press, 1987], 33).

26. Derrida, *Vérité*, 21 / *Truth*, 17.

27. Blanchot, "La littérature," 34, 37 / "Literature," 387. As Derrida puts it, the central text is now "à la fois puissant et impuissant, puissant de son impuissance même, tout en puissance dans son inégalité à soi. Tout ici résonne et se répercute dans le sublime dynamique [both potent and impotent, potent to its very impotence, all potential in its unequalness to itself. Everything here resounds and echoes in the dynamic sublime]" (Derrida, *Vérité*, 167 / *Truth*, 146).

28. Blanchot, *L'Entretien infini*, 620 / *Infinite Conversation*, 422.

29. Blanchot, *Le Pas au-dèla*, 107; trans. Lycette Nelson as *The Step Not Beyond* (Buffalo: SUNY Press, 1992), 76–77.

30. Blanchot, *L'Entretien infini*, 389 / *Infinite Conversation*, 168; Foucault, *Pensée*, 56 / *Thought*, 54.

31. Blanchot, *L'Entretien infini*, 564 / *Infinite Conversation*, 384.

32. Ibid., 442 / 422.

33. Maurice Blanchot, *The Work of Fire*, trans. Charlotte Mandell (Stanford: Stanford University Press, 1995), 322.

34. Maurice Blanchot, *Lautréamont et Sade*, 2nd ed. (Paris: Minuit, 1963), 89.

35. Blanchot, *L'espace littéraire*, 11; translation from *The Station Hill Reader*, 402.

36. Roland Barthes, *Œuvres Complètes*, vol. 1, 218; trans. Annette Lavers and Colin Smith as *Writing Degree Zero* (New York: Hill and Wang, 1968), 78.

37. William Warner, *Albion's England, The third time corrected* (1592), VII. xxxix.193.

38. See Blanchot, "La littérature," note 1.

39. Ronald Bates, "Shakespeare's 'The Phoenix and Turtle,'" *Shakespeare Quarterly* 6 (1955): 19–30; see, for examples, *Julius Caesar* I.iii.26–28; *3 Henry VI* V.vi.44; *Macbeth* II.ii.3; *Richard II* III.iii.183; *Venus and Adonis* I.531.

40. Blanchot, *L'Entretien infini*, 622 / *Infinite Conversation*, 422.

41. *Hamlet* IV.v.81.

42. Jacques Derrida, *Monolinguisme de l'autre: ou, la prothèse d'origine* (Paris: Galilée, 1996), 98; trans. Patrick Mensah as *Monolingualism of the Other, or, The Prosthesis of Origin* (Stanford: Stanford University Press, 1998), 83.

43. Blanchot, "La littérature," 41 / "Literature," 391–392.

44. Hollier, "Poetry . . . up to Z," 66.

45. Maurice Blanchot, "Le regard d'Orphée," in *L'espace littéraire*, 221–227 passim.

1. Gérard Genette, *Seuils* (Paris: Éditions du Seuil, 1987), trans. Jane E. Lewin as *Paratexts: Thresholds of Interpretation*, series in Literature, Culture, Theory, number 20 (Cambridge: Cambridge University Press, 1997), 3–4. For slightly different formulations of the idea of the literary paratext, see Genette's *Palimpsestes: la littérature au second degree* (Paris: Éditions du Seuil, 1982); Susan Vanderborg's *Paratextual Communities: American Avant-Garde Poetry since 1950* (Carbondale: Southern Illinois University Press, 2002); and Vincent Colonna's nicely titled "Fausses notes," in *Colloque de Cerisy: juillet 1984*, Cahiers Georges Perec, 1 (Paris: POL, 1985).

2. The proliferation of varied books under the same title pushes the distinction between different editions and entirely different books to the limit, as even the briefest bibliography will suggest. The first version of the *Topographie anecdotée du hasard* was published as a catalogue of sorts for one of Spoerri's exhibitions (Paris: Éditions Galerie Lawrence, 1962), with text by Spoerri and collaborative additions by Robert Filliou. The book was apparently translated into Dutch in 1964, although I have been unable to locate a copy. An expanded English edition, *an anecdoted topography of chance* (New York: Something Else Press, 1966), with sketched pen and ink illustrations by Roland Topor, was translated and annotated by Emmett Williams, with an excerpt appearing the same year in the *Paris Review*. A German edition, *Anekdoten zu einer Topographie des Zufalls* (Neuwied: Luchterhand, 1970), was expanded yet again, though with the illustrations omitted, and translated—from the text of the first French edition and the notes of the English edition—by Dieter Roth (then "Diter Rot"), who added his own annotations. A facsimile of the original French edition was published by the Archives of the Centre national d'art contemporaine (Paris, 1972), and that version of the book was subsequently reprinted in a new edition, with a new introduction by Topor (Paris: Centre Georges Pompidou, 1990). Most recently, a newly expanded and reannotated English edition, with the illustrations restored, was published in an oversize format as a sort of genetic text that brings all of the earlier variants together: Daniel Spoerri, Robert Filliou, Roland Topor, Emmett Williams, Dieter Roth, and Alastair Brotchie, *An Anecdoted Topography of Chance*, Atlas Arkhive Four, Documents of the Avant-Garde (London: Atlas Press, 1995); all citations in the present essay are to this edition. In addition to a trade edition, Atlas also published a limited deluxe edition, and one might note that there was both a hard- and soft-cover version from Something Else Press. The map of the table was printed differently by each of the presses. On the significance of the format of the Something Else edition, with implications for the reading of the new Atlas edition, see Paulo Silveira, *A página violada: da ternura à injúria na construção do livro de artista* (Porto

Alegre: Editora da Universidade do Rio Grande do Sul, 2001), 169. Additionally, compare the new schematic layout of the Atlas edition with Thomas McFarland's description of Eduard Fraenkel's book on Horace as "one giant footnote of 460 pages, with footnotes to that footnote cascading magnificently down the bottoms of those pages" (Thomas McFarland, "Who Was Benjamin Whichcote? or, The Myth of Annotation," in Stephen A. Barney, ed., *Annotation and Its Texts* [Oxford: Oxford University Press, 1991], 159).

3. Henry St. John, Viscount Bolingbroke, "A Letter Addressed to Alexander Pope, Esq.," in *A Letter To Sir William Windham* . . . (London: Printed for T. Cadell, 1787), 337.

4. Evelyn B. Tribble, "'Like a Looking-Glas in the Frame': From the Marginal Note to the Footnote," in D. C. Greetham, ed., *The Margins of the Text* (Ann Arbor: University of Michigan Press, 1997), 229–230.

5. Peter W. Cosgrove, "Undermining the Text: Edward Gibbon, Alexander Pope, and the Anti-Authenticating Footnote," in Barney, *Annotation and Its Texts*, 130–131.

6. The recurrent dairy products mentioned in the *Topographie*—a "half-litre bottle of milk," a "quarter of a pound of butter," "the corner of a half-litre container of milk," an empty milk carton—may not be incidental. "Note," the English translator of the *Topography* might have noted, is a dialect term for cow's milk (*Oxford English Dictionary*).

7. Spoerri et al., *An Anecdoted Topography of Chance*, 50, 61–62.

8. Ibid., 149.

9. Johanna Drucker, *The Century of Artists' Books* (New York: Granary, 1995), 335ff.

10. Alexander Pope, *The Dunciad . . . Variorum* (London: M. Cooper, 1743); Henry Fielding, *The History of Tom Jones, a Foundling* (Edinburgh: J. Dickson and P. Hill, 1792); Laurence Sterne, *The Life and Opinions of Tristram Shandy, Gentleman*, 2nd ed. (Dublin: Henry Saunders, 1765–1767); T. S. Eliot, *The Waste Land* (New York: Boni & Liveright, 1922); Samuel Beckett, *Watt* (Paris: Olympia, 1955); James Joyce, *Finnegans Wake* (London: Faber & Faber, 1939); Vladimir Nabokov, *Pale Fire* (New York: Vintage, 1989); Manuel Puig, *El beso de la mujer araña* (Barcelona: Seix Barral, 1976); Nicholson Baker, *The Mezzanine: A Novel* (New York: Weidenfeld & Nicolson, 1988); Mark Danielewski, *Mark Z. Danielewski's House of Leaves, by Zampano*, 2nd ed. (New York: Pantheon, 2000).

    For a discussion of the literary footnote in romantic poetry, see Jacqueline Labbe, "'Transplanted into More Congenial Soil': Footnoting the Self in the Poetry of Charlotte Smith," in Joe Bray, Miriam Handley, and Anne C. Henry, eds., *Ma(r)king the Text: The Presentation of Meaning on the Literary Page* (Aldershot: Ashgate, 2000).

11. Georges Perec, "Notes concernant les objets qui sont sur ma table de travail," *Nouvelles Littéraries* (February 1976); trans. John Sturrock as "Notes Concerning the Objects That Are on My Work-Table," in *Species of Spaces and Other Pieces* (London, 1997), 140–143.

12. Thomas Pynchon, *Gravity's Rainbow* (New York: Penguin, 1995), 18.

13. Spoerri et al., *An Anecdoted Topography of Chance*, 25.

14. Ibid., 29; quoting the *Oxford English Dictionary* at "anecdotic."

15. Compare this practice with Jackson Pollock's roughly contemporaneous "drip" paintings, as well as the reverse procedure of Marcel Duchamp's 1917 *Trébuchet* (snare; literally, a "stumbler"; the word is also a *terme de métier* in chess for placing a pawn in the opponent's path): a set of mounted coat hooks taken off the wall and affixed to the floor to create a sort of sculptural trap.

16. *Oxford English Dictionary*.

17. Hans H. Wellisch, *Indexing from A to Z*, 2nd ed. (New York: H. W. Wilson, 1995), 206.

18. Malcolm Beckwith Parkes, *Pause and Effect: Punctuation in the West* (Berkeley: University of California Press, 1993), 139.

19. Ibid., 57.

20. Tribble, "'Like a Looking-Glas in the Frame,'" 231; H. J. Jackson, *Marginalia: Readers Writing In Books* (New Haven: Yale University Press, 2001), 55; Parkes, *Pause and Effect*, 57.

21. Parkes, *Pause and Effect*, 57. Before the coining of the word "footnote," Samuel Johnson would speak of notes "subjoined to the text in the same page" (Samuel Johnson, *The Lives of the English Poets: and a Criticism on their Works* [Dublin: Whitestone et al., 1779–1781], 3: 112; quoted in Jackson, *Marginalia*, 60).

22. Jackson, *Marginalia*, 55–56; Cosgrove, "Undermining the Text," 139.

23. Quoted in Tribble, "'Like a Looking-Glas in the Frame,'" 232.

24. Tribble, "'Like a Looking-Glas in the Frame,'" 232, 231ff.

25. Simon Morris, with Forbes Morlock, Liz Dalton, Tim Brennan, and Cindy Smith, *Interpretation*, 2 vols. (York: Information as Material, 2002).

26. Stéphane Mallarmé, "Variations sur un sujet: l'action," *Revue Blanche* 7, no. 40 (February 1895): 98.

27. Roland Barthes, *S/Z* (Paris: Éditions du Seuil, 1970); trans. Richard Miller (New York: Hill and Wang, 1974); Walter Abish, "Ardor, Awe, Atrocity," *New Directions* 35 (1977): 57–73; rpt. in Abish, *In the Future Perfect* (London: Faber and Faber, 1984), 45.

28. In Shari Benstock's distinction, "critical" footnotes are essentially exophoric, while "fictional" footnotes are anaphoric: pointing back to the text to which they are keyed rather than outward to another, cited work (Benstock, "At the Margins of Discourse: Footnotes in the Fictional Text," *PMLA* 98, no. 2 [March 1983]: 209; cf. 205, 207–208, and passim). That schematization is useful to a point, but even "critical" footnotes are doubly articulated indices, hinged between the text they note and the one they cite, looking—Janus-faced—simultaneously at both.

    One further complication of this scheme would be a case such as the numbered endnotes to an essay by Jean-Marie Gleize, which are not keyed to any particular section of the article. The first note slyly explains: "Les notes renvoient à n'importe quel endroit du texte [The notes refer to any place in the text]." Gleize's apparatus would be not quite clever enough save for the flair with which he then exponentially multiplies the possibilities, doubling the stakes of his scholarly parlor trick: "Aussi bien à n'importe lequel de ses blancs [And to any of the white spaces as well]" (Jean-Marie Gleize, "Il n'y a pas un instant à perdre," *TXT* 17 [1984]: 29). I am grateful to Genette for bringing Gleize's essay to my attention.

29. Viktor Shklovsky, "Art as Technique," in Lee T. Lemon and Marion J. Reis, ed. and trans., *Russian Formalist Criticism: Four Essays* (Lincoln: University of Nebraska Press, 1965), 22.

30. Ibid., 12.

31. Abish's numbering was almost certainly not a strictly retrospective revision, since one suspects that "xenophile" did not merely happen to occur but was generated by the formal need to include at least three words beginning with the letter *x*. The general principle, if not a strict procedure, is still indeterminate.

32. The excess of annotators is legendary, and the Reverend John Hodgson's *History of Northumberland*, a heavily anecdoted "topographical enquiry" (v), is one of the most infamous. Chuck Zerby overstates the case considerably when he claims that an entire volume is given over to a footnote on the Roman Wall, while Grafton downplays the margin by which Hodgson sets the record for "the longest footnote in English" (Zerby, *The Devil's Details: A History of Footnotes* [Montpelier: Invisible Cities, 2002]; see Anthony Grafton, *The Footnote: A Curious History* [Cambridge: Harvard University Press, 1997], 120); in the third volume of the second part of Hodgson's *History* (edited by James Raine), the subtitle "Roman Barriers in Britain" is followed by a footnote that

runs for 264 pages. The main text continues to squeeze along at the top of the page in a trickle two or three lines wide for seventeen pages, but then gives over entirely to the note—and to the series of notes within that note—for the remainder of the volume.

The satiric impulse behind Rabener's book has more recently taken form in a series of essays mocking the ossified conventions of law review articles. Although it is excessively footnoted, the main text of Erik M. Jensen's "The Shortest Article in Law Review History" can be easily quoted in full: "This is it" (Jensen, "The Shortest Article in Law Review History," *Journal of Legal Education* 50, no. 1 [March 2000]: 156). Two responses, also fully footnoted, set the record (straight): Grant H. Morris's rebuttal "Not so!," and Thomas H. Ohom's subsequent query "Why?" (Morris, "Reply," *Journal of Legal Education* 50, no. 2 [June 2000]: 310; Ohom, "Reply," *Journal of Legal Education* 50, no. 2 [June 2000]: 311). Beaten at his own game, Jensen's "Comments in Reply" is simply a blank page, without notes (Erik M. Jensen, "Comments in Reply," *Journal of Legal Education* 50, no. 2 [June 2000]: 312).

33. Phillip Gallo, *Captions from Animals Looking at You* (Minneapolis: Hermetic Press, 1981).

34. "Nonsense [is] the essential sense of the Marginal Note" as Edgar Allan Poe wrote (quoted in Lawrence Lipking, "The Marginal Gloss," *Critical Inquiry* 4 [1977]: 609). With a phrase that resonates with the works considered in this essay, Lipking argues that, for Poe, the ultimate attraction of marginalia was its "complete independence from the text," "glossing the white space of nothingness" (ibid., 610, 611).

For a discussion of the new sentence, see Ron Silliman, *The New Sentence* (New York: Roof, 1987), 63–93 and passim.

35. Antin must have used Matheson's two-volume Epictetus (*Epictetus: The Discourses and Manual: Together with Fragments of His Writings*, ed. P. E. Matheson, 2 vols. [Oxford: Clarendon Press, 1916]). His procedure might be seen as a riff on Whitehead's often quoted (and rarely footnoted) remark that "the safest general characterization of the European philosophical tradition is that it consists of a series of footnotes to Plato" (Alfred North Whitehead, *Process and Reality: An Essay in Cosmology*, Gifford Lectures [Cambridge: Cambridge University Press, 1929], 63).

Following Antin's slip of the tongue (a mis-placed *gloss*, as it were) that his volume of Epictetus was "open to the footnotes" (David Antin, *Selected Poems: 1963–1973* [Los Angeles: Sun & Moon Press, 1991], 19), one scholar has also referred to the source of the separations as footnotes rather than endnotes (Loss Pequeño Glazier, "Our Words Were the Form We Entered," *Witz* 4, no. 2 [Summer 1996]: n.p.). I recognize that this is an exceedingly pedantic distinction, and what must sound like a lot of fuss over *Fussnoten*, but I hope that the small force of the difference will be clear by the end of this chapter.

36. More pedantry, just for the record: in his introduction to the *Selected Poems*, Antin illustrates the origin of his first line as a verbatim transcription, but note the slight final inversion.

37. David Antin, *Meditations* (Los Angeles: Black Sparrow, 1971), 70.

38. Jacques Derrida, "This Is Not an Oral Footnote," in Barney, *Annotation and Its Texts*, 196.

39. Antin, *Meditations*, 68.

40. Ibid., 66, 70.

41. Ibid., 66.

42. Ibid.

43. Silliman, *The New Sentence*, 109ff.

44. Antin, *Meditations*, 68.

45. Ibid.

46. See, in particular, *Discourses*, book I, chapter VII.

47. Drucker, *The Century of Artists' Books*, 2.

48. Ibid.

49. Ibid., 4, 3. Vincent Colonna argues that Georges Perec's use of notes "s'attaque à la matérialité du livre, à la dénégation de son support matériel mais parce qu'en exploitant des possibilités paratextuelles inusitées dans les œuvres de fiction, elle déplace ce qui fait notre logique de la lecture, en particulier pour ce qui est de l'instanciation du discourse littéraire [grapples with the materiality of the book, with the denial of its material support, but by taking advantage of the unexploited paratextual possibilities in fictional works, it displaces that which constitutes our logic of reading, specifically that which is the instantiation of literary discourse]" (Colonna, "Fausses notes," 108).

50. Jack Spicer, *My Vocabulary Did This to Me: The Collected Poetry of Jack Spicer*, ed. Peter Gizzi and Kevin Killian (Middletown: Wesleyan University Press, 2008), 249–280; Bruce Andrews, *Getting Ready to Have Been Frightened* (New York: Roof, 1988).

51. Tyrone Williams, *c.c.* (San Francisco: Krupskaya, 2002).

52. Critical Art Ensemble, *Cronicas Brazileiras / Annotations to Cronicas Brazileiras* (n.p., 1989).

53. Jennifer Martenson, *Xq28*[1] (Provincetown: Burning Deck, 2001), 5.

54. Ibid., 8.

55. Ibid., 9, 8, 14, 13, 15, 6, 17, 13.

56. Ibid., 14, 11, 16, 6–7.

57. Ibid., 6–7.

58. Ibid., 7. The phrase appears in one of the concluding sentences to the research article that sparked the debate of Xq28: "Our experiments suggest that a locus (or loci) related to sexual orientation lies within approximately 4 million base pairs of DNA on the tip of the long arm of the X chromosome" (D. H. Hamer, S. Hu, V. L. Magnuson, N. Hu, and A. M. L. Pattatucci, "A Linkage between DNA Markers on the X Chromosome and Male Sexual Orientation," *Science* 261 [1993]: 327).

59. Rosmarie Waldrop, *Lawn of the Excluded Middle* (Providence: Tender Buttons, 1993); *The Reproduction of Profiles* (New York: New Directions, 1987).

60. Martenson, *Xq28*[1], 13. *Xq28*[1] is anticipated by Martenson's earlier poems such as "Gene Expression" (*How2* 1, no. 2 [September 1999]: n.p.), which could serve as a proem of sorts to *Xq28*[1], and "Cast" (*How2* 1, no. 2 [September 1999]: n.p.), which has the visual form of a glossed text such as S. T. Coleridge's *Rime of the Ancient Mariner* or Lyn Hejinian's *Gesualdo* (Berkeley: Tuumba, 1978).

61. Martenson, *Xq28*[1], 16.

62. Ibid., 5–6. See, for a further elaboration of the issue, S. Hu et al., "Linkage between Sexual Orientation and Chromosome Xq28 in Males but Not in Females," *Natural Genetics* 11 (1995): 248–256.

63. Denise Bazzett, untitled review of *Xq28*[1], in *New Pages Reviews* (http://www.newpages.com).

64. Benstock makes this claim more strongly when she asserts that the discourse of the footnote is "inherently marginal" ("At the Margins of Discourse," 204).

65. Derrida, "This Is Not an Oral Footnote," 193.

66. Cosgrove, "Undermining the Text," 139. Or as Grafton puts it, in rhyming sestets, the footnote has the power to "buttress and undermine, at one and the same time" (*The Footnote*, 32).

67. Quoted in Labbe, "'Transplanted into More Congenial Soil,'" 79.

68. The metaphoric association of the "body" of the text can also influence our understanding of the notes against which it is defined; "marginal notes,"

according to Valéry's Cartesian schema, "are part of the notes of pure *thought*" (Lipking, "The Marginal Gloss," 610).

69. Martenson, *Xq28*[1], 13, 8.

70. Gérard Wajcman, *L'Interdit: roman* (Paris: Denoël, 1986).

71. The phrasing is Wajcman's: "silence inexplicable" and "acte silencieux" (*L'Interdit*, 23).

72. Wajcman, *L'Interdit*, 114.

73. Ibid., 37–38, 170.

74. Ibid., 67, 204.

75. Ibid., 37, 234.

76. Ibid., 225.

77. Ibid., 50.

78. Ibid., 97.

79. Ibid., 36–37; cf. 122, 52. The note is a quote from Paul Claudel's *Le philosophie du livre*, which itself echoes Freud's description of psychic disturbances: "One way [to resolve such disturbances] would be for the offending passages to be thickly crossed through so that they were illegible . . . best of all, the whole passage would be erased." (Sigmund Freud, "Notiz über den 'Wunderblock,'" *Internationale Zeitschrift für Psychoanalyse* 11, no. 1 [1925]: 1–5; trans. James Strachey as "A Note upon the 'Mystic Writing Pad,'" *International Journal of Psycho-Analysis* 21, no. 4 [1950]: 469–474; rpt. in *The Standard Edition of the Complete Works of Sigmund Freud*, vol. 19 [London: Hogarth Press, 1959], 236.)

80. Wajcman, *L'Interdit*, 140.

81. Ibid., 188.

82. Hugh Kenner, *Flaubert, Joyce and Beckett: The Stoic Comedians* (London: W. H. Allen, 1964), 40.

In Genette's typology, the essence of the note is its always local character; unlike a preface, for instance, notes refer to only a partial portion of a text. Moreover, there is a social version of this logic of collage: notes tend to be addressed to a more specific audience and to anticipate only certain readers (Genette, *Seuils*, 319).

83. William Hanks, *Intertexts: Writings on Language, Utterance, and Context* (Lanham: Rowman & Littlefield, 2000), 19.

84. See, for instance, "Irony," in X. J. Kennedy and Dana Gioia, eds., *Literature: An Introduction to Fiction, Poetry, and Drama*, 5th ed. (New York: Longman, 1999).

85. Jenny Boully, *The Body* (Raymond: Slope Editions, 2002), 59.

86. Ibid., 18, 26, 75.

87. The quotation is from chapter 6 of Stevenson's *Treasure Island* (London: Cassell & Company, 1883), 50.

88. Ibid., 32.

89. Boully, *The Body*, 27, 45.

90. Ibid., 36.

91. Parkes, *Pause and Effect*, 57.

92. James G. Ballard, "The Index," *Bananas* (1977); reprinted in *Re/Search* 8/9 (1984): 84–87.

93. Peter Greenaway, *The Falls* (Paris: Éditions Dis Voir, 1983); Charles Finlay, "Footnotes," *Fantasy and Science Fiction* 101, no. 2 (August 2001): 85–88. In addition to Paul Violi's poem "Index" (in Michael Lally, ed., *None of the Above: New Poets of the USA* [New York: Crossing Press, 1976], 208–209), one might note two other books in this context. Niels Nielsen's *Biografisk Skygge Leksikon: "Pedersen"—"Poulsen"* (Copenhagen: Biblioteket Øverste Kirurgiske, 2000) is a work of mad genius that purports to be the volume covering "Pedersen" to "Poulsen" in a fictitious biographical dictionary. *The Dictionary of Traumatic Signs*, an alphabetized reverse dictionary of Freudian dream symbolism, appears as the appendix to Stefan Themerson's *Cardinal Pölätüo* (London: Gaberbocchus, 1954); this reference work is intended to prove the Cardinal's innocence: if the Freudian system interprets the most innocuous everyday images as ciphers for secret sexual desires, then sexual desires—in the Cardinal's logic—must merely be signs of innocuous everyday objects.

94. Finlay, "Footnotes," 88, 86.

95. Ibid., 85, 87.

96. Terrence Gower and Mónica de la Torre, *Appendices, Illustrations & Notes* (Los Angeles: Smart Art Press, 1999).

97. Kenner, *Flaubert, Joyce and Beckett*, 39.

98. Paul Fournel, *Banlieue* (Bibliothèque Oulipienne, 46); reprinted in *La Bibliothèque oulipienne*, vol. 3 (Paris: Seghers, 1990), 183–214; trans. Harry Mathews as *Suburbia*, in *OuLiPo Laboratory: Texts from the Bibliothèque oulipienne* (London: Atlas, 1995), vi, 5, 9, and passim.

99. Alastair Johnston, *Heath's German Dictionary* (Minneapolis: Poltroon, 1975).

100. Ludwig Wittgenstein, *Philosophische Untersuchungen / Philosophical Investigations*, trans. G. E. M. Anscombe, 2nd ed. (Oxford: Blackwell, 1997), 198.

4	HARD CORE / SOFT FOCUS

1. Oscar Sugar, "How the Sacrum Got Its Name," in James Doty and Setti Rengachary, eds., *Surgical Disorders of the Sacrum* (New York: Thieme Medical Publishers, 1994), 1–2.

2. *Oxford English Dictionary.*

3. *Jacobellis v. Ohio*, 378 U.S. 184 (1964).

4. Peter Blum Editions; quoted by Susan Tallman, "Meltdown," *Arts Magazine* 64, no. 8 (April 1990): 25.

5. *Oxford English Dictionary.*

6. Ibid.

5	THE DATIVE OF FORM

1. Tom Gunning, "To Scan a Ghost: The Ontology of Mediated Vision," *Grey Room* 26 (Winter 2007): 99.

2. See, for just one discussion of these issues, the chapter on "Mechanical Objectivity" in Lorraine Daston and Peter Galison, *Objectivity* (Brooklyn: Zone Books, 2007), 133.

3. The agon of media and representation, fought out on the field of the obliterated human face, was the subject of some of Michael Fried's most exciting work from the 1980s, in the book *Realism, Writing, and Disfiguration: On Thomas Eakins and Stephen Crane* (Chicago: University of Chicago Press, 1987) and in the long essay "Almayer's Face: On 'Impressionism' in Conrad, Crane, and Norris," *Critical Inquiry* 17, no. 1 (Autumn 1990), which analyzed "the irruption of mere (or brute) materiality within the scene of writing" (200).

4. Susan Stewart, *On Longing: Narrative of the Miniature, the Gigantic, the Souvenir, the Collection* (Baltimore: Johns Hopkins University Press, 1984), 127.

5. *Oxford English Dictionary.*

6. On the impossible nature of the ghost, see Derrida's argument that "le spectre est une incorporation paradoxale, le devenir-corps, une certaine forme

phénoménale et charnelle de l'esprit [the specter is a paradoxical incorporation, the becoming-body, a certain phenomenal and carnal form of the spirit]"
(Jacques Derrida, *Spectres de Marx: L'état de la dette, le travail du deuil, et
la nouvelle Internationale* [Paris: Galilée, 1993], 25).

7. Židlický's defaced nudes inevitably recall one set of E. J. Bellocq's photographs
    of New Orleans prostitutes that have had their faces scratched black (see John
    Szarkowski, ed., *Bellocq: Photographs from Storyville* [New York: Random
    House, 1996]). The circumstances of those hasty scrapings are unknown,
    but as with Židlický's photographs, the vandalism not only suggests a psy-
    chosexual narrative but also draws attention to the other instances of surface
    distress. The photographs record a number of similar surfaces—the crumpled
    folds of drapery and decorated pillowcases, tained mirrors, marks and scrapes
    on the paint and paper of the brothel's worn interior walls. At the same time,
    the photographs themselves have come down to us with their own visible
    imperfections: cuts on the glass plates; dehiscent striations; bright droplet
    pocks and graduated pools of evaporated liquid with fractal salted shores;
    black splatches and grayed abrasions; the lichenous spread of slow chemical
    breakdowns in the decomposed and corroded bromide-resistant gelatin; the
    nitrate flake and jagged craquelure of thin film foil chipping around the edges
    of the image like a shattered antique mirror.

8. Meghan Morris offers the smart analogy that with regard to the argument in
    Mille plateaux "a human face can, but certainly need not, entail 'faciality,'
    just as in psychoanalysis the penis can, usually does, but need not, represent
    the phallus" (Morris, "Great Moments in Social Climbing: King Kong and the
    Human Fly," in Beatriz Colomina, ed., *Sexuality and Space* [New York: Prince-
    ton Architectural Press, 1992], 4).

9. Gilles Deleuze, *Francis Bacon: la logique de la sensation* (Paris: Éditions de
    la Différence, 1981), 19; trans. Daniel Smith as *Francis Bacon: The Logic of
    Sensation* (London: Continuum, 2005), 15.

10. Gilles Deleuze and Félix Guattari, *Mille plateaux* (Paris: Éditions de Minuit,
    1980), 208.

11. As Brian Massumi summarizes the concept: "'Faciality' organizes systems of
    binary opposition operating on different levels, and functions as their dynamic
    point of contact: an abstract plane with which they all intersect, and by virtue
    of which they can communicate with each other and with the world at large"
    (Massumi, *A User's Guide to Capitalism and Schizophrenia: Deviations from
    Deleuze and Guattari* [Cambridge: MIT Press, 1992], 173).

12. For the equation of the faceless head to the body without organs, see Deleuze,
    Francis Bacon, 33.

13. Deleuze and Guattari, *Mille plateaux*, 209–210; trans. Brian Massumi as *A Thousand Plateaus: Capitalism and Schizophrenia* (Minneapolis: University of Minnesota Press, 1987), 171.

14. Jean Khalfa, "An Impersonal Consciousness," in *Introduction to the Philosophy of Gilles Deleuze* (London: Continuum, 2003), 82.

15. Deleuze, *Francis Bacon*, 11 / 4.

16. Ibid., 9 / 2.

17. Ibid., 19 / 16, 24 / 22, 19 / 15.

18. See Emmanuel Levinas, *Totalité et infini: essai sur l'extériorité* (The Hague: Martinus Nijhoff, 1961), trans. Alphonso Lingis as *Totality and Infinity: An Essay on Exteriority* (Pittsburgh: Duquesne University Press, 2001); see also Jacques Derrida, *Adieu à Emmanuel Levinas* (Paris: Galilée, 1997).

19. Levinas, *Totalité*, 21 / *Totality* 50–51.

20. Jill Robbins, *Altered Reading: Levinas and Literature* (Chicago: University of Chicago Press, 1999), 23.

21. Levinas, *Totalité*, 173 / *Totality*, 199.

22. Emmanuel Levinas, *Difficile liberté* (Paris: Albin Michael, 1976), 21; cf. Levinas, *Totalité*, 41; Robbins, *Altered Reading*, 11. As Françoise Mies points out: "Le Littré précise que 'autrui' dérive d'alteri, c'est-à-dire d'alter au datif [The Littré specifies that "others" derives from altered, which is to say alter in the dative]" (Mies, *De l'autre: essai de typologie* [Namur: Presses Universitaires de Namur, 1994], 50).

6 TANGENT

1. Quoted in Louis Untermeyer, *Robert Frost: A Backward Look* (Washington: Library of Congress, 1964), 18.

2. Branden Joseph's more nuanced and sophisticated reading concludes that "Rauschenberg's *White Paintings* differ from their historical avant-garde counterparts as well as from their formalist or minimalist understandings" (Branden W. Joseph, "White on White," *Critical Inquiry* 27, no. 1 [Autumn 2000]: 113). See, for comparison, Thierry de Duve, "The Monochrome and the Blank Canvas," in Serge Guilbaut, ed., *Reconstructing Modernism: Art in New York, Paris, and Montreal, 1945–64* (Cambridge: MIT Press, 1990), 244–310.

3. In addition, as Joseph astutely records ("White on White," 97), the association suggested between Cage's quasi-surrealist notice of dust on the *White*

Paintings and the photograph of "élevage de poussière [dust breeding]" on Marcel Duchamp's *Grand verre* is corroborated by the caption that accompanied the iconic image when it was published in *Littérture* 5, no. 1 (October 1922): "Vue prise en aéroplane par Man Ray [As seen from an airplane by Man Ray]."

4. Quoted in Kirby Gookin, "Robert Rauschenberg," *Artforum* 31, no. 8 (April 1993): 97.

5. Joseph, "White on White," 98; see László Moholy-Nagy, *The New Vision* (New York: Wittenborn, 1946).

    The figuration of the monochrome canvas as a kinetic, vibrant, animate object recurs in Wassily Kandinsky's description of the blank canvas. Dumb and dull at a distance, under the close scrutiny that characterizes Moholy-Nagy's imaginative stare and John Cage's magnified attention he senses the canvas thrumming with potential energy: "An empty canvas, apparently really empty, that says nothing and is without significance. Almost dull, in fact. In reality crammed with thousands of undertone tensions and full of expectancy. Slightly apprehensive, lest it should be outraged. Yet docile enough. Ready to do what is required of it, and only asking for consideration. It can contain anything, but cannot sustain everything. . . . An empty canvas is a living wonder—far lovelier than certain pictures." (Quoted in Paul Overy, *Kandinsky: The Language of the Eye* [New York: Praeger, 1969], 118.) One might compare the conception of a monochrome oil painting as animate with Henri Michaux's description of an "ineffable vide [indescribable void]": "violant, actif, vivant. Nappe . . . [violent, active, alive. A swirled film of oil . . .]" (Michaux, "Ineffable vide," in *Œuvres complètes* [Paris: Gallimard, 2001], 777).

6. John Cage, "On Robert Rauschenberg, Artist, and His Work," in Cage, *Silence: Lectures and Writings* (Middletown, CT: Wesleyan University Press, 1968), 108.

7. See Anthony Bond, "Fragility and Impermanent Materials," *Parallaxe: Conservation and Interpretation*; proceedings archived at <http://www.parallaxe. net/conservationandinterpretation.htm>. Clement Greenberg, in retrospect, described the *White Paintings* as "familiar looking and even slick" (Greenberg, "Recentness of Sculpture," in Gregory Battcock, ed., *Minimal Art: A Critical Anthology* [Berkeley: University of California Press, 1995], 181), a term that indicates both the glibly déclassé social register of house paint on an artist's canvas as well as the sebaceous reflectance of the commercial-grade paint; the word "tacky" would similarly cover both a class-inflected social register and an objective material description.

8. Cf. the phonograph by Brian Eno, *Ambient 1: Music for Airports* (Polydor AMB001, 1978).

9. The textual status of *4'33"* is complicated, and its instability is all to the point for understanding the relation of conceptual music to the material fact of writing. David Tudor, who premiered the work in 1952, recalls the first manuscript (now lost): "The original was on music paper, with staffs, and it was laid out in measures like the *Music of Changes* except there were no notes. But the time was there, notated exactly like the *Music of Changes* except that the tempo never changed, and there were no occurrences—just blank measures, no rests—and the time was easy to compute. The tempo was 60." (Quoted in William Fetterman, *John Cage's Theater Pieces: Notations and Performances* [Amsterdam: Harwood, 1996], 72.)

Tudor produced two subsequent reconstructions of the score (Fetterman, *John Cage's Theater Pieces*, 75), and a second manuscript score was written by Cage in 1953 (collection Irwin Kremen), but in a graphic notation of proportional duration that divides the half-dozen pages of the score into vertical bands of varying width; this drawing—which visually echoes Rauschenberg's canvases—served as the basis for at least two different printed editions (*Source: music of the avant-garde* 2 [July 1967] and Peters Edition 6777a [1993]). The score quoted above, which repeats "tacet" for each of its three sections (suggesting, as Kyle Gann has noted, a classical sonata structure; Gann, *No Such Thing as Silence: John Cage's 4'33"* [New Haven: Yale University Press, 2010], 167), is clearly a related piece, though whether in the final analysis one should consider it to be a variation, an edition, or an entirely different work altogether is not immediately clear. The three injunctions to silence are followed by a discursive note describing the premiere and stipulating that the work "may be performed by any instrumentalist or combination of instrumentalists and last any length of time." To complicate matters (or matter) further, this work (or version of a work) was itself published in two slightly but significantly different editions (Peters 6777 [1960] and Peters 6777 [1986]). The latter, in a typeface reproducing Cage's distinctive handwriting, states that the timing of the original movements was 30", 2'23", and 1'40". The former states those times as 33", 2'40", and 1'20". Once again, one must decide whether that discrepancy is merely error or the indication of two distinct compositions. Similarly, the program for the 1952 premiere lists "4 pieces" by John Cage: one entitled *4'33"* and then three other movements adding up to *4'33"*—in sum, a good nine minutes of silence. Do the facts belie the concept? Does the concept trump the facts? In either case, the most elegantly simple composition in the history of music has one of the most convoluted and mysterious textual histories.

10. Cage, "On Robert Rauschenberg," 98.

11. Ludwig Wittgenstein, *Philosophical Investigations*, trans. G. E. M. Anscombe (Oxford: Blackwell, 1953), 66.

Surprisingly, looking thoughtfully at painted canvas is, presumably, what was to be expected of every viewer of the *White Paintings*, just as being silent and listening attentively were already an ingrained part of classical music concert protocol when *4'33"* was premiered (see Douglas Kahn, *Noise, Water, Meat: A History of Sound in the Arts* [Cambridge: MIT Press, 1999], 165–166). Kahn argues that the encouragement Cage received from Rauschenberg's paintings should not be mistaken for influence (168).

12. John Cage, "A Composer's Confession," in *John Cage: Writer: Previously Uncollected Texts*, ed. Richard Kostelanetz (New York: Limelight, 1993), 43.

13. Douglas Kahn also makes a passing connection between *Silent Prayer* and Duchamp (Kahn, *Noise, Water, Meat*, 178); his reading of the labor politics informing *Silent Prayer* is more sustained and of particular interest (175–178); see also Gann, *No Such Thing as Silence*, 128.

14. Ironically, those particular material configurations developed in turn because of their ability to produce certain audible pitches; although "silent," Cage's *Prayer* is based on technologies precision-tuned to vibrate at certain frequencies; the work thus repurposes machines designed to generate sound into clocks or timers. To the extent that it ignores recording in order to exploit a seemingly incidental or supplemental aspect of recording technology, one might consider Cage's work in relation to Jarrod Fowler's *70'00"/17*, a compact disc with no audio but with tracks delineated in order to engage the timing function of CD players. Although blank in terms of music, it is not blank "as far as time is concerned" (quoted in Seth Kim-Cohen, *In the Blink of an Ear: Towards a Non-cochlear Sonic Art* [New York: Continuum, 2009], 241; cf. 232–233).

15. In its first iteration, Cage tried to find as many blemishes as he could in a set amount of time; in subsequent iterations the number of notes to be marked were determined beforehand by *I Ching* operations, which also determined subsequent details, such as key, dynamics, and attack (see James Pritchett, *The Music of John Cage* [Cambridge: Cambridge University Press, 1993], 94). Cage continued to work on compositions under the same title for a decade, concluding in 1962 with *Music for Piano 85*.

16. Cage, "On Robert Rauschenberg," 108.

17. William Carlos Williams, *Paterson*, rev. ed. (New York: New Directions, 1992), 6; John Cage, "Lecture on Nothing," in Cage, *Silence*, 126.

18. Quoted in Branden W. Joseph, *Random Order: Robert Rauschenberg and the Neo-Avant-Garde* (Cambridge: MIT Press, 2003), 267–278.

19. Walter Benjamin, "Die Aufgabe des Übersetzers," in *Illuminationen* (Berlin: Suhrkamp, 1977), 60; trans. Harry Zohn as "The Task of the Translator," in

Benjamin, *Selected Writings*, vol. 1, *1913–1926*, ed. Michael Jennings (Cambridge: Harvard University Press, 1996), 260–261.

20. On Cage's interest in Henri Bergson's philosophy of temporal flux in duration, and its relation to *4'33"*, see Joseph, "White on White," 21–23 passim. For the importance of the durational score, see Liz Kotz, *Words to Be Looked At: Language in 1960s Art* (Cambridge: MIT Press, 2007).

21. Quoted in Walter Hopps, *Robert Rauschenberg: The Early 1950s* (Houston: Fine Arts Press, 1991), 230.

22. Benjamin, "Die Aufgabe des Übersetzers," 62 / "The Task of the Translator," 262.

7   SIGNAL TO NOISE

1. John Cage, *A Year from Monday* (Middletown: Wesleyan University Press, 1967), 28.

   Liz Kotz provides a far more comprehensive account of the event score in *Words to Be Looked At*. Importantly, for the claims I am making here, Kotz's patient and perceptive argument finds the origin of the genre of the event score in John Cage's *4'33"*. Moreover, she finds Cage's "silent" piece in turn derived from the specifics of media; Cage's "complete rethinking of the nature of sound" was "made possible by the new technologies of amplification, microphony, radio, and magnetic tape" and his rethinking of the nature of the musical score was abetted by "the introduction of electric, electronic, and computer-based means into experimental music" so that "anything from circuit diagrams to punch cards to simple drawings and verbal instructions could arguably function as scores or notational devices" (Liz Kotz, *Words to Be Looked At: Language in 1960s Art* [Cambridge: MIT Press, 2007], 31, 5). Most importantly, perhaps, "Cage's work with audiotape altered his understanding of the nature of sound and time, and decisively transformed his use of notation" (43), but Kotz also locates his "license to free up the relationship between simultaneous elements in order to permit unplanned superimpositions and chance encounters" in the material properties of magnetic tape media (specifically, their inability to synchronize with precision) (46).

   For another sustained consideration of the event score that also reads it in relation to the tension between singularity and abstraction, see Julia Robinson, "From Abstraction to Model: George Brecht's Events and the Conceptual Turn in Art of the 1960s," *October* 127 (Winter 2009): 77–108. Robinson's conception of "seriality without repetition" (108) would be another way to understand the chronological dimension of *Zen for Record* discussed above.

2. John Cage, "An Autobiographical Statement," *Southwest Review* 76, no. 1 (Winter 1991): 59–77.

3. John Cage, *Silence* (Middletown: Wesleyan University Press, 1973), 51.

4. See chapter 2, note 12 for documentation of skepticism about the story and the technician's diagnosis of what was almost certainly tinnitus.

5. Michel Serres, *The Parasite* (Minneapolis: University of Minnesota Press, 2007), 53.

6. Wolfgang Iser, "Why Literature Matters," in Rüdiger Ahrens and Laurenz Volkmann, eds., *Why Literature Matters: Theories and Functions of Literature* (Heidelberg: Winter, 1996), 13–22.

7. See, for instance, Jan Mukařovský, *On Poetic Language*, ed. and trans. John Burbank and Peter Steiner (New Haven: Yale University Press, 1976).

8. Theodor W. Adorno, "Memorandum: Music in Radio," Columbia University archives, Paul F. Lazarsfeld papers (June 1938), 30–31, quoted by Richard Leppert, "Commentary," in *Theodor W. Adorno: Essays on Music* (Berkeley: University of California Press, 2002), 219.

9. Ibid.

10. Paolo Cherchi Usai, *The Death of Cinema: History, Cultural Memory, and the Digital Dark Age* (London: British Film Institute, 2001).

11. The same telos awaits more durable media as well, only over a longer time frame. Richard Kostelanetz, with a measure of either humor or pretension, states that his "two volumes of ostensibly blank books . . . could not be publicly exhibited, because pages so white cannot be fingered" ("Fictions in My History," in Kostelanetz, *The Old Fictions and the New* [Jefferson, NC: McFarland, 1987], 7–8).

12. Rosalind Krauss, "Two Moments from the Post-Medium Condition," *October* 116 (Spring 2006): 55–62.

13. See Rosalind Krauss, *A Voyage on the North Sea: Art in the Age of the Post-Medium Condition* (London: Thames & Hudson, 2000).

14. For the popularization of the phrase, see Lucy R. Lippard, *Six Years: The Dematerialization of the Art Object from 1966 to 1972* (New York: Praeger, 1973).

1. Kyle Gann lists a score of additional recordings: Gann, *No Such Thing as Silence: John Cage's 4'33"* (New Haven: Yale University Press, 2010), 215–217.

2. Franz Kafka, *Gesammelte schriften*, vol. 5 (New York: Schocken, 1946), 237. There may be an interlinguistic pun between *musiciens* and *la musique d'chiens* (the music of dogs).

3. Quoted in Denis de Rougemont, *Journal d'une époque* (Paris: Gallimard, 1968), 567; Marcel Duchamp, *Notes*, ed. Paul Matisse (Boston: G. K. Hall, 1983), Note 9.

4. Kafka, *Gesammelte Schriften*, 5: 237.

5. Duchamp, *Notes*, Note 12.

6. George Brecht, *Water Yam* (New York: Fluxus, 1963), n.p.

7. Alphonse Allais, *Album primo-avrilesque* (Paris: Ollendorff, 1897), 25.

8. Another version of the score had the sentence repeated on the other side (Branden Joseph, *Beyond the Dream Syndicate: Tony Conrad and the Arts after Cage* [New York: Zone Books, 2008], 156).

9. Joseph Roth, *The Radetzky March*, trans. Joachim Neugroschel (Woodstock: Overlook Press, 2002), 206.

10. Young explains: "I felt certain the butterfly made sounds, not only with the motion of its wings but also with the functioning of its body and that unless one was going to dictate how loud or soft the sounds had to be before they could be allowed into the realms of music that the butterfly piece was music" (La Monte Young, "Lecture 1960," in Mariellen R. Sanford, ed., *Happenings and Other Acts* [London: Routledge, 1995], 60).

11. For information on the concert programs of Corner and Lane, see Adrian Glew's invaluable "Amor Vacui," in *Voids: A Retrospective* (Zurich: JRP|Ringier, 2009), 350–361.

12. Cf. BBC News World Edition, "Silent Music Dispute," 23 September 2002, http://news.bbc.co.uk/2/hi/2276621.stm (accessed 13 June 2011).

13. "Le cinéma et la revolution," *Internationale Situationniste* 12 (September 1969): 104.

14. John Cage, "A Composer's Confession," in *John Cage: Writer: Previously Uncollected Texts*, ed. Richard Kostelanetz (New York: Limelight, 1993), 43.

15. Pierre Cabanne and Marcel Duchamp, *Entretiens avec Marcel Duchamp* (Paris: Belfond, 1967), 81.

16. Gann, *No Such Thing as Silence*, 133–134, quoting "The Flip Side: Spin It and Get Acquainted," *New York Post*, 16 January 1952.

17. Ibid.

18. The phrase is not conventionally grammatical. "Afrazarmo," a *hapax legomenon*, suggests the third-person plural of the Duchampian *atrasar* (to delay): *atrasamos* (we lag). A delay in tape hiss, as one would say *une retard en verre*.

19. Yoko Ono, *Grapefruit: A Book of Instructions + Drawings* (New York: Simon and Schuster, 1970), n.p.

20. The back cover comes "con la foto del primitivo grupo D/C [with a photo of the original D/C group]: Gancedo, Gutiérrez, Pazos y Vigo"; for more on the eponymous journal from La Plata, see Gwen Allen, *Artists' Magazines: An Alternative Space for Art* (Cambridge: MIT Press, 2011), 254. My thanks to Riccardo Boglione for information on the discs by Villa and Vigo.

21. Ross Russell, *The Sound* (New York: MacFadden, 1962), 54.

22. See "Show Business: Summer Diversions," *Time*, 17 August 1970.

23. See *High Performance* 3, no. 9 (Spring 1980): 21; and Stewart Home, *The Assault on Culture: Utopian Currents from Lettrism to Class War* (Oakland: AK Press, 1991), 71–72.

24. See Cleanth Brooks, *The Well Wrought Urn* (New York: Harcourt, Brace & World, 1964), chapter 11.

25. See Heinrich Böll, *Doktor Murkes gesammeltes Schweigen* (Cologne: Kiepenheuer & Witsch, 1958).

26. William Langley, "Thrill to the Sounds of Silence," *The Telegraph*, 12 November 2001 (http://www.telegraph.co.uk/culture/4726499/Thrill-to-the-sounds-of-silence.html), accessed 28 July 2012.

27. *Silent Music* is subtitled "A Duo," and the container of seeds reads: "Blow them in the air, and chase them"; for performance documentation of "les artistes soufflent vers le public des 'graines aériennes' [the performers blowing 'air seeds' toward the audience]," see Agostino di Scipio, "Heidegger, Hölderlin et John Cage," *Revue d'esthétique: de la composition: l'après Cage* 43 (July 2003): 35. Yoko Ono, "Music," in *Grapefruit*, n.p.

28. Yoko Ono, "Ono's Sales List/N.Y.C., 1965," in *Grapefruit*, n.p.

29. The term "granulation noise," according to a contemporaneous source "comes from the fact that the noise sounds like grains of sand being mixed with the signal" (*DB: The Sound Engineering Magazine* 19 [1985]).

30. Stephen Williams, "For Car Cassette Decks, Play Time Is Over," *New York Times*, 4 February 2001.

31. Friedrich Kittler, *Gramophone, Film, Typewriter* (Stanford: Stanford University Press, 1999), 46.

32. Georg Wilhelm Friedrich Hegel, *Phänomenologie des Geistes*, vol. 2 (Berlin: Verlag Dunder und Humboldt, 1832), 260.

33. James Breslin, *Mark Rothko: A Biography* (Chicago: University of Chicago Press, 1993), 306.

34. Robert Watts, in *Extended Play* (New York: Emily Harvey Gallery, 1988), n.p.

35. Susan Sontag, "The Aesthetics of Silence," *Aspen* 5 + 6 (Fall-Winter 1967): n.p.

36. Quoted in Olivier Zahm, "La beauté sera contemporaine," *Art Press* 144 (1990): 27.

37. Guillaume Apollinaire, "Merlin et la Vielle Femme," in Apollinaire, *Alcools*, ed. Garnet Rees (London: Athlone Press, 1975), 77.

38. Sontag, "The Aesthetics of Silence," n.p.

Index